Smithsonian Folkways Recordings

AMERICAN
MUSICAL
TRADITIONS

Smithsonian Folkways Recordings

AMERICAN MUSICAL TRADITIONS

Volume

4

European American Music

Jeff Todd Titon

Bob Carlin

SCHIRMER REFERENCE

GALE GROUP
★
THOMSON LEARNING

New York • Detroit • San Diego • San Francisco
Boston • New Haven, Conn. • Waterville, Maine
London • Munich

Copyright © 2002 by Schirmer Reference, an imprint of the Gale Group

Schirmer Reference
1633 Broadway
New York, NY 10019

Gale Group
27500 Drake Rd.
Farmington Hills, MI 48331

Library of Congress Cataloging-in-Publication Data

American musical traditions / [general editors] Jeff Todd Titon, Bob Carlin.
    P.   cm.
"Published in collaboration with The Smithsonian Folkways Archive."
Includes bibliographical references, discographies, videographies, and index.
Contents: v. 1. Native American music—v. 2. African American music—v. 3. British Isles music—v. 4.
    European American music—v. 5. Latino and Asian American Music.
ISBN 0-02-864624-X (set)
1. Folk music—United States—History and criticism—Juvenile literature. 2. Music—United States-History and criticism
    —Juvenile literature. 3. Ethnomusicology—Juvenile literature. [1. Folk music—History and criticism. 2. Music—History
    and criticism.]
I. Titon, Jeff Todd, 1943-   II. Carlin, Bob.

ML3551.A53 2001
781.62'00973-dc21

TABLE OF CONTENTS
VOLUME 4

TABLE OF CONTENTS
VOLUMES 1, 2, 3, AND 5

VOLUME 1: NATIVE AMERICAN MUSIC

VOLUME 2: AFRICAN AMERICAN MUSIC

VOLUME 3: BRITISH ISLES MUSIC

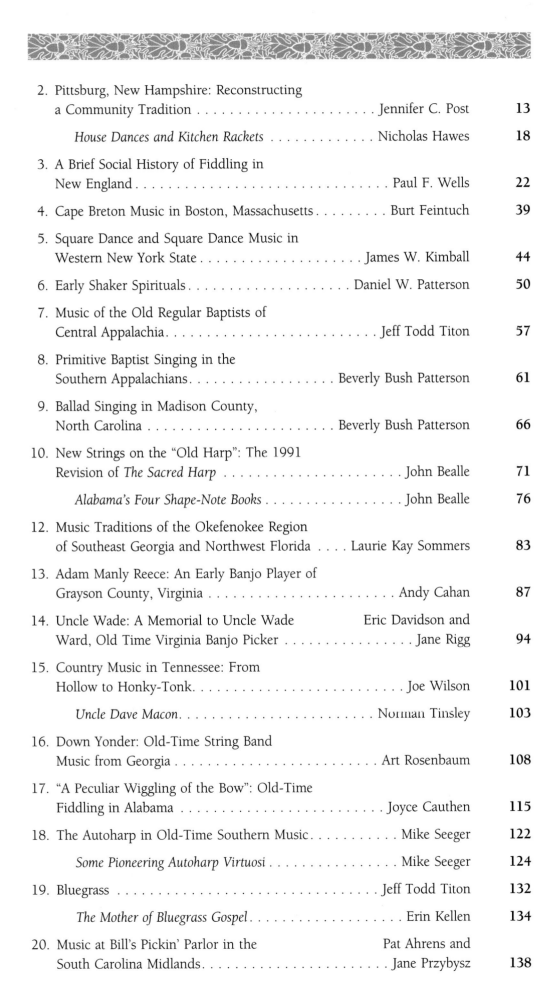

VOLUME 5: LATINO AMERICAN MUSIC AND ASIAN AMERICAN MUSIC

LATINO AMERICAN MUSIC

INTRODUCTION TO *AMERICAN MUSICAL TRADITIONS*

Jeff Todd Titon

This five-volume work presents an American musical mosaic. Folklorists and ethnomusicologists whose research centers on musical traditions in the United States wrote authoritative essays specifically for *American Musical Traditions*. We solicited additional materials from the Smithsonian Institution's Center for Folklife and Cultural Heritage, particularly from Smithsonian Folkways Recordings and the Smithsonian Folklife Festival. Keyed to musical examples and illustrations on both the Smithsonian Folkways website and the Brown University website (addresses below), *American Musical Traditions* presents a combination of words, sounds, and images so readers can hear, as well as read about, much of the music under discussion.

It goes without saying that at the start of the twenty-first century, every community in the United States has music. But this has been true for as long as the continent has been settled by humans; among the Native Americans, music (and dance) has always played an important role in ceremony and recreation.

My great-grandparents grew up in a world in which people who wanted to hear music had to learn to sing and play it themselves. Today televisions, videocassette recorders, radios, and compact disc players can be found in most American households, along with collections of recordings. All of these are products of the twentieth-century revolution in electromechanical musical reproduction, permitting anyone to hear music on demand without performing it.

In addition to the old methods of distributing music, a dizzying array of new digital formats and delivery methods, including mini-disc, CD-R, CD-RW, mp3, and DVD, along with the World Wide Web, are bringing music into the new century, while musical performance itself is being reconceived with the help of electronic equipment, sampling, and computers. Today, of course, music from all over the globe is available at the flip of a switch or movement of a computer mouse. But every community also has its live music makers. Music is taught and learned in the public schools, in music academies, and by private teachers. Community bands and orchestras, informal chamber music groups, singer-songwriters with guitars, basement or garage rock and country bands, singers of all stylistic persuasions—these music makers can be found in just about every community, large or small.

Outside the mainstream there is another kind of music, one that members of certain populations regard as their own. While contemporary popular music is set in the present and strives for novelty and sales, and while classical music looks to the future and strives for originality, this other music, which in this book we call "traditional," is almost always linked to the past and bounded in certain ways. The traditional music we have in mind usually arises in connection with ethnic or regional identity, and sometimes it is connected to an original homeland outside the United States. The groups that possess traditional music often

attach it to particular (named) people and places, with ties to an older generation of source musicians from whom it has been learned.

Traditional music has sometimes been called folk music, but in university circles today the word "folk" carries troublesome baggage (such as nationalism, purity, and noblesse oblige) and so the younger generation of scholars tends to avoid it. Today the word "traditional" often substitutes for "folk," but "tradition" can be a troublesome word as well. Scholars have shown that it is naive to consider traditions a set of ancient, sacred rules, like the American Constitution, that we must interpret reverentially. Traditions turn out to be far more flexible than we ever imagined. After all, traditions must adapt to the present moment or they will fail; and more than a few traditions turn out, on inspection, to be the invention of things we want to believe about the past but that have little or no basis in fact. For example, the contemporary sound of "Irish traditional music"—represented by popular Irish bands featuring uillean pipes, fiddles, wooden flutes, guitars, tin whistles, citterns, bouzoukis, and bodhrans, a sound that is marketed as "Celtic music" and is sometimes pictured with ancient mists and druidic artifacts on album covers—turns out to be only a few decades old. The periodic revival of Celtic culture seems to be a tradition itself, one that the poet William Butler Yeats invoked more than a hundred years ago in *The Celtic Twilight*.

Today it is easy to debunk invented traditions wherever an ancient pedigree is foolishly sought, and music seems particularly susceptible to this kind of search. Yet when the dust settles we see that all living traditions bend the past to the present in order to continue into the future. Regarded in the present as manifestations of the past, they are thought to carry some authority (or not carry it) by virtue of that association.

In the upper Midwest, for example, where Germans, Swedes, Finns, and Norwegians settled more than a hundred years ago, many communities have retained, and revived, and in so reviving further developed, musical traditions that are recogniz-ably their own. The same is true of other ethnic immigrant populations in different parts of the country. It is a mistake to think that traditions are rigid. Change, it seems, is built into most musical traditions. African Americans created music styles such as the blues, spirituals, jazz, and soul music, all featuring improvisation. Hip-hop, the most modern musical manifestation of this improvised cultural tradition, has its roots in the oral poetry of the African American "toast" (Jackson 1974) and in a lengthy tradition of vernacular dance. In African American musical traditions, innovation is the norm.

Geographical region, ethnic population, and musical style have guided most research into American vernacular musical traditions. This work reflects those boundaries. Volume 1 presents Native American music; Volume 2 offers African American music; Volume 3 concentrates on the music of the British Isles, including Ireland, in America. These are the three areas that have received the most attention from musical scholars. In the last thirty years or so, research has increasingly focused on the music of European and Asian immigrant ethnic groups. Volume 4 therefore presents music from European American immigrant communities, including those from France, Italy, Germany, Poland, Czechoslovakia, Hungary, Sweden, Norway, and Finland; and Volume 5 offers music from the Spanish-speaking communities as well as Asian American music. Readers who wish to learn more about how and where ethnic groups settled in the United States are referred to James Paul Allen and Eugene James Turner, *We the People: An Atlas of America's Ethnic Diversity,* and to the *Harvard Encyclopedia of American Ethnic Groups.*

Organizing these volumes according to ethnic groups must not leave the impression of a rigid, balkanized United States of tight-knit musical enclaves. Classical music is available to all. Few consider this Western art music to have ethnic boundaries. Popular music that comes from the media is also open to all. While many musical communities do take stewardship of music they identify as their own, their people also participate in the mainstream of America's popular

music styles that do not reflect the perspective of any single group. In addition, they may adopt practitioners who learn their traditional music but who did not grow up in their communities.

Although the Navajo, for example, continue to practice their traditional ceremonial and recreational music, they compose music in new modes reflecting influences from contemporary gospel music, Hollywood film music, acoustic guitar–based singer-songwriter music, and New Age music, among others. Yet the most popular music on the reservations is country music, and Navajos regularly form country and rock bands.

Nor should we think of traditional music as extending unchanged back through time. The accordion, a musical staple for several generations among Hispanic musicians on the Texas-Mexican border, was borrowed from German immigrants to that region. The guitar, regarded by some as the American folk instrument par excellence, gained its great popularity only in the twentieth century. And the five-string banjo, identified today with hillbillies and bluegrass musicians, derives from an African instrument that, along with the African American population, significantly changed the sound and style of vernacular dance music in the American South. Although this work emphasizes those styles of music that the various ethnic musical communities consider to be their own, we do not wish to claim that this is the only, or necessarily the principal, music with which the people in these communities are involved.

These volumes are not meant to cover each and every musical tradition. It would be impossible to do so; first because this work is not large enough, and second because the scholarship available is uneven in coverage. There are many more musical communities than scholars surveying the subject. We have selected representative communities and musical genres to give an idea of the range of traditional music in the United States. Some of this research is current, representing musical communities today; some is historical and represents musical communities in the past. The writing

includes two main perspectives: essays on communities and examples of their music, and interviews or profiles of particular musicians and musical groups. Although this is a large work, we do not claim to be comprehensive or definitive; thus we invite further research. Because each volume has an introductory essay describing its contents, in what follows I will discuss the origin and development of the project as a whole.

From the outset, this reference work was conceived to reflect recent research by folklorists and ethnomusicologists on the one hand, and the holdings of the Smithsonian Institution's Center for Folklife and Cultural Heritage on the other. Since the early 1970s, public-sector folklorists, ethnomusicologists, and their academic colleagues have surveyed ethnic and regional music-making in many communities across the United States. Often sponsored by arts councils, cultural organizations, and community initiatives, and in many cases underwritten by the Folk Arts Division of the National Endowment for the Arts, the American Folklife Center of the Library of Congress, and the Smithsonian's Center for Folklife and Cultural Heritage (formerly the Office of Folklife Programs), from about 1977 to 1995 folklorists could be found in nearly every one of the fifty states, surveying folklife and expressive culture (including music) and documenting and presenting the products of this research. Those products were unprecedented in number and quality. Fieldnotes, booklets, recordings, videos, festivals, tours, exhibits, and apprenticeships most often were targeted back into those communities rather than meant for archives or a central data bank.

Cutbacks and reorientation in public funding for the arts, however, coupled with the lack of formal, ongoing, institutional support, have redirected public-sector workers' efforts toward heritage and tourism. Thus, it seemed an appropriate moment to ask these fieldworkers and arts administrators to contribute essays to a project that would gather some of this work together. Accordingly, in 1995 I sent out a prospectus for this work along with invitations to all

the state folklorists and ethnomusicologists listed in the *Public Folklore Newsletter* as well as to numerous academic colleagues, inviting topics, entries, and proposals for additional contributors. It was a long process, but several people responded positively and the fruits of their labors are evident throughout these volumes, as their contributions make up a substantial proportion of this work. Obtaining them and guiding their direction was my main task. Co-editor Bob Carlin's primary job was to select materials from the Smithsonian Institution for these volumes.

Many contributors to this project also worked, at one time or another, for the Smithsonian Folklife Festival, formerly known as the Festival of American Folklife (FAF); and therefore we could draw upon that work for their contributions to this volume. The Smithsonian Folklife Festival is an ongoing, multicultural, international event, staged annually since 1967 in the nation's capital on the mall between the Lincoln Memorial and Washington Monument. It is the largest and by far the most expansive, longest-lasting folk festival in the United States. Typically it runs for two weeks during late June and early July and features a few hundred singers, musicians, dancers, storytellers, crafters, and other folk artists in an outdoor museum setting meant to celebrate the diverse folkways of the United States and other lands. The Festival presents these folk artists on stages, in tents, and in open-air locations where they perform and demonstrate for an audience of tourists amid a celebratory atmosphere. During the more than thirty years that the FAF has run, the staff has implemented a cultural policy that involves more than merely a demonstration and preservation theater. Theirs is a vision of a multicultural world living in harmony, celebrating mutuality while learning from different traditions.

From the outset, the festival planners understood the importance of documentation as well as presentation. Every event that took place on every stage was recorded by festival staff. Festival recordings and related materials are housed in the Ralph Rinzler Folklife Archives and Collections at the Center for Folklife and Cultural Heritage, Smithsonian Institution. Each year an elaborate program booklet is prepared for the public. It contains essays introducing many of the individuals and the communities featured at the festival. Written by the folklorists and ethnomusicologists who had researched the music, crafts, and other expressions of folklife for the annual presentations, these essays are both authoritative and accessible. Often they are the best short introductions to the musics of particular ethnic and regional communities; we have drawn liberally on them for this volume. The Smithsonian's other contribution derives from the materials in Smithsonian Folkways Recordings.

Folkways Recordings, begun in 1948 by Moses Asch, reflected the very broad tastes of its founder. From the Folkways catalog you could hear everything from the demonstration collection of world music recorded at the turn of the twentieth century for the Berlin Archiv to the music of Leadbelly, Woody Guthrie, and Pete Seeger, as well as the famous Harry Smith *Anthology of American Folk Music,* recently reissued by Smithsonian Folkways.

But Asch did not stop there. Modern poetry in the voices of the authors, bird songs, and even the sounds of factory work fell within the recorded output of this eclectic operation. Folkways was one of very few record companies in the 1940s and 1950s publishing folk music from American communities, including Native American and European immigrants, along with the British American and African American music that collectors had been emphasizing throughout the twentieth century. Many, but not all, of these albums came with copious (and only lightly edited) documentation by the field researchers and other experts, in the form of notes slipped into the double-channeled Folkways album cover. Folkways recordings cost a little more than most, but they provided more, too; and in many instances they provided the only recordings available representing various populations on the planet. During the folk revival of the late 1950s and early 1960s, Folkways was the first to

present the traditional music of Roscoe Holcomb, Wade Ward, Doc Watson, and others from the southern Appalachian Mountains. Much of their material is of enormous historical value and, for that reason, we have preserved the original text that accompanied their works.

In 1987, the Smithsonian's Folklife division acquired Folkways Recordings and hired Anthony Seeger to direct the operation. (In 2001 Seeger was replaced by Daniel Sheehy, formerly the Director of the Folk Arts Program, National Endowment for the Arts.) Smithsonian Folkways kept all of the back catalog in print (it can be ordered at any time from their website), and they have produced more than a hundred new albums; we have drawn liberally on those with American subjects for this work. Finally, we have gone outside of commissioned articles and Smithsonian materials to obtain other well-documented descriptions of musical communities where they were needed to fill in gaps. We present the whole as a spicy stew, a mosaic, and a mix that we think will appeal and stimulate the reader's appetite for more.

LINKS TO WEBSITES

On occasion, the essays in *American Musical Traditions* discuss recordings that are part of the vast Smithsonian Folkways library, particularly those essays that were originally Smithsonian materials. The relevant Folkways catalog number for the recordings appears in each essay's headnote, when available, or elsewhere in the essay. Readers may then visit the Internet's World Wide Web to listen to those recordings; in many cases, they are available for direct purchase online after they have been previewed. The Smithsonian recordings, in both Liquid Audio and RealAudio format, may be downloaded from the Smithsonian Folkways website, which is found at http://www.si.edu/ folkways. There, readers should click on the "Liquid Audio" link to go directly to the Smithsonian's catalog of recordings.

In addition, I am building my own site at Brown University to house links to record-

ings and other materials that are not part of the Folkways collections. As *American Musical Traditions* was going to press, the site was still under construction, but content is being added. It can be located at http://www. stg.brown.edu/MusicAtlas.

VOLUME 4: EUROPEAN AMERICAN MUSIC

This fourth volume of *American Musical Traditions* brings together research on various European immigrant groups and their music as it has been performed in the United States. Unlike the other volumes in this series, it is organized by immigrant culture, beginning with France and moving through other regions of Europe. Overview essays provide a general portrait of each musical tradition and identify areas where it has flourished in this country. Then, individual chapters focus on specific immigrant communities and their musical traditions, along with key performers.

GLOSSARY AND INDEX

Each volume of *American Musical Traditions* includes a glossary of terms used in that volume and an index that includes citations to all five volumes in the series. Throughout the essays and sidebars in each volume, certain terms appear in boldface, indicating that the term is fully defined in the glossary at the back of the book. The glossary also includes "See" and "See also" references to make locating the appropriate term easier. The index in each volume is comprehensive—that is, it includes citations to all five volumes of *AMT,* not just the individual volume. Numerals followed by a colon and then the page number are used to indicate in which volume a citation appears. In addition, page references in bold refer to a main essay or sidebar on that topic and page references in italics refer to photos; maps are clearly indicated. Index sub-topics are indented beneath the main topic. For example, an index citation for drums might look like this:

ACKNOWLEDGMENTS

We gratefully acknowledge the assistance of the Smithsonian Institution's Folklife division, the National Endowment for the Arts' Folk Arts Program, the Scholarly Technology Group of Brown University, and Schirmer Reference in making this project possible. We thank the many artists and musicians who cooperated with the researchers who wrote the entries, as well as the researchers themselves who are named in this book as contributors. Special thanks to the authors of the introductions to each volume: Burt Feintuch, David Evans, Thomas Vennum, Philip Nusbaum, and Tom Van Buren. Thanks to Art Rosenbaum for his wonderful cover designs. In addition, we would like to thank Richard Carlin for overseeing this project and keeping it on track during his tenure at Schirmer. Thank you to Charlotte Heth for her expert review of the Native American volume. Finally, we are grateful to those in the Smithsonian Institution who helped with this project. Anthony Seeger and the staff of Smithsonian Folkways made their archives available to us. Diana Parker, director of the Smithsonian Folklife Festival, and Richard Kurin, head of the Smithsonian's Office of Folklife and Cultural Heritage, helped us obtain additional information related to the musical communities represented down through the years at the Festival.

We would also like to thank our editors including Deborah Gillan Straub, Stephen Wasserstein, and Brad Morgan, as well as the members of Gale's production and design staff, including Wendy Blurton, Evi Seoud, Mary Beth Trimper, Randy Bassett, Barb Yarrow, Pam Reed, Christine O'Bryan, Tracey Rowens, Cindy Baldwin, Margaret Chamberlain, and others who provided able assistance.

BIBLIOGR\APHY

Allen, James Paul; and Turner, Eugene James. (1988). *We the People: An Atlas of America's Ethnic Diversity.* New York: Macmillan.

Jackson, Bruce, compiler. (1974). *"Get Your Ass in the Water and Swim Like Me!": Narrative Poetry from the Black Oral Tradition.* Cambridge: Harvard University Press.

Thernstrom, Stephan. (1980). *Harvard Encyclopedia of American Ethnic Groups.* Cambridge: Harvard University Press.

INTRODUCTION TO EUROPEAN AMERICAN MUSIC

Philip Nusbaum

Philip Nusbaum is a music professional who conducts research from his position at the Minnesota State Arts Board and also plays in bluegrass and country bands. For over three decades, he has hosted folk music programs on radio and has conducted extensive field recordings of many types of traditional music. His work has appeared on commercial recordings and on local and national public radio. His writing about traditional music has appeared in liner notes and in scholarly and popular articles.

In the United States, what has been considered interesting about folk music changed dramatically during the twentieth century. Towards the beginning of the century, folk song investigation was fueled by the research of literary scholars, the enthusiasm of ardent but amateur folklore collectors, and the philosophy of romantic nationalism. One early discovery was that song texts brought to the United States by Europeans were lost or changed by immigration, and investigators responded by describing the changes and also lamenting either the death of folk music or its corruption in the United States. When a folk song survived immigration, assimilation, and language change, it was handled as a cultural success.

However, the twentieth century witnessed the professionalization of the folklore field and the maturation of cultural sciences. As a result, in the latter part of the century, in addition to song texts, scholars became interested in music style, music industry technological developments, audience makeup and taste, and economics. As a result of the awareness of the complexity of experiencing folk music, folk music idioms tended to be viewed as constantly in flux as they responded to social and cultural change. Instead of seeking "pure" forms, as was commonplace a century earlier, late twentieth century scholars acknowledged the process of *creolization,* the combining of various ethnic and popular genres that occurs when folk musicians representing neighboring cultures come into contact with each other. Growing scholarly sentiment in the last few decades of the twentieth century no longer regarded creole expressions as bastardized ones, but as expected results of culture contact.

For example, in addition to the traditional **quadrilles** handed on through French Canadian oral tradition, French Canadian music in Rhode Island includes country songs and light **jazz**, clear indications of contact with the American mainstream. In some cases, as in **Cajun music**, players of the music express pride in the cultural blending

that led to their style. In other cases, players are unaware that their playing represents a creolization process. For example, Scandinavian American **fiddlers** in the upper Midwest frequently express surprise when told by players from Scandinavian countries how *American* upper Midwest Scandinavian playing seems.

The difference between approaches at the beginning and end of the twentieth century reflect changing ideologies. The earlier approach, reflecting the mixture of academic and amateur interests in folk music, embraced both the precision of literary analysis and nostalgic sentimentality about the "old days." The later view finds strength in the mingling of diverse cultures as reported by **ethnography**. Regardless of how one chooses to view folk music, there are plenty of examples of styles that retain particular traits over time and those that respond to cultural change with stylistic change.

Some traditions exhibit both tendencies, as when there are tunes current for many generations that are reorchestrated by succeeding waves of players. In Irish music, for example, the more that Irish traditional music has become a concert form played for diverse audiences, the higher the level of virtuosity that has become typical. The tendency to present tunes in medleys has been driven by the need to present dramatic interpretations for demanding audiences. Contact with players from other traditions led to a greater use of **harmonic** lines in Irish music. The **guitar**, not present at all a century ago, not only has become standard in the **instrument** lineup of an Irish band, but a specialized guitar tuning used to play Irish music, DADGAD (from bass strings to treble) has emerged.

The European musical traditions that came to America have been subject to several similar historical factors. First there was immigration itself, which placed European musical traditions in new contexts as each immigrant culture became a minority culture once on American shores. Whether or not it was the main reason for coming to America, most immigrants were interested in business opportunities. However, the immi-

grants found that the opportunities were most open to those who spoke English, the language used in most United States social life. Furthermore, particularly around World War I, speaking a European language raised suspicion about the speaker's patriotism. Add to that the fact that children of immigrants returned from public schools speaking English, and the use of the European languages faded.

An emphasis on social dance music is the second factor common to many European American traditions. European dance music traditions would also have faded were it not for the central place of social dancing in European American cultures, proceeding from the days of settlement. In many European immigrant traditions, social dancing provided the motivation for immigrants to get together to enjoy each other's company. Because social dancing was a setting for family and community socializing in the new world, European-based dance music traditions retained their vitality. While European-language singing exists in some of these traditions, danceability, and not the lyrics, was the chief appeal of the music. At the beginning of the twenty-first century, the "old-time" styles of Poles, Czechs, Germans, Slovenians, and Scandinavians represent American adaptations of European forms, and all are played in social dance settings.

The decline of European-language singing is the most obvious early change in European immigrant folk music, and the tendency towards **repertoire** based on traditional dance music is another. However, not all traditions continued to use folk dance music to accompany dancing. In some European American cultures, as members became more assimilated to American tastes, their social dance preference tended towards dance forms popular with most Americans. However, folk dance music was successfully marketed to European Americans through media such as radio, records, and, later, television.

Corresponding to the growth of listener taste for folk music distributed through the radio and records, these media gave folk musicians access to the greatest players in their idioms. Players listened repeatedly to record-

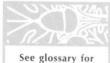

See glossary for definition of boldfaced terms

ings to improve their playing, and performance standards were raised. In some traditions, energetic or virtuosic performance standards evolved, and folk music became recognized as a legitimate medium for artistic expression. When virtuosic performance standards evolved, and listeners responded with a willingness to pay to experience a music style, European folk music forms originally intended to accompany social dances whose popularity slipped found a new venue in another popular American entertainment stage: the concert.

Such is the case for Jewish **klezmer** music, revived in the last three decades of the twentieth century. Klezmer bands play pieces composed for performance as well as selections from Yiddish theater and traditional dance music. Irish traditional music is a form with great concert appeal inside and outside of its original community, and the repertoire is based on traditional and composed dance music and songs. Another result of media dissemination of folk music was that some styles of traditional music gained fans in diverse audiences. The ascent of some folk styles has brought them into performance spaces where people from many backgrounds could appreciate them.

A fourth great change in European American folk music lies in the means of accessing the stylings. At the beginning of the twenty-first century, there exists a plethora of voluntary associations, each representing a given musical culture. While over a century ago there existed singing clubs and other grassroots musical organizations, nowadays it seems that every musical interest is represented by an organization, frequently in the form of a not-for-profit group. The organizations program types of musical occasions favored within the musical culture served, such as concerts, dances, and instrument lessons, and also provide opportunities for local players to perform. Organization-sponsored events are occasions for sociability. Many of the not-for-profit groups supporting folk music are actually folk dance groups, whose mission it is to preserve traditional dancing. Such is also the case with some French-based, Italian, Polish Górale,

Swedish, and Finnish traditions in the United States. Dancers join these groups because they are dedicated to preserving traditional dance, a different motivation than the kind of social dancing that one learns from growing up in a particular family or neighborhood.

Knowing that new members of their group might not come from the neighbors and families of current members but from the outside world, organizations representing musical cultures promote the music they favor to the general public. In order to spread the word about their activities among the general population, some organizations schedule events at public places such as shopping malls and invite the media to their events. They establish newsletters that both inform members about upcoming events of interest and promote the specific music styles they represent to the public.

The great number of folk music-related organizations that represent ethnic music idioms to the outside world reflects the fact that in the early twenty-first century, participants self-elect to participate in a tradition. In the United States, people have so many activities available to them that being part of a family or local network interested in a certain kind of folk music is not always a strong enough inducement to stimulate participation. Folk music voluntary associations see recruitment as a means of securing the future of their music and culture.

Folk music forms are symbolic. The more that members of a European group adopted English, the more those members of the group recognized artifacts from the old country (such as folk music) as symbols of their collective past. To ethnic group members, participating in their ethnic musical culture connects them psychologically with other members of their group, past and present. That folk styles symbolize specific cultures is most apparent in the least commercial forms, because sociability and celebrating heritage are important factors motivating folk music and folk dance performance in those cases. In this regard, one thinks of New England's French traditions, and New York/New Jersey Calabrians. Some European American

cultures have maintained schools for cultural training young people in folk music, for example, *tamburitza* music played by Americans of Serbian and Croatian descent, and Polish Górale tradition. Students in these schools are grouped in ensembles that play for ethnic calendar festivals and at ethnic ceremonial occasions. Folk dance classes are an even more prevalent means of presenting children their cultural heritage.

Not all members of musical cultures are members from birth of the culture represented by a given style. They might be brought in my marriage, because the adopted style represents the majority style in a locale, or because they are permitted to self-elect to participate. At the beginning of the twenty-first century in the United States, participation can be encouraged by public events that host a variety of traditions. Frequently, these events are presented by government-sponsored arts councils through the work of professional folklorists or other culture workers. Whatever the reason to affiliate oneself with a European American folk tradition, a participant in a

folk music culture frequently seeks out a particular style and participates in the musical culture representing it. Because accessing a given tradition takes effort, participants in musical cultures see themselves as fellow travelers. Having a common interest causes participants to view one another as available for friendship, and frequently, folk music organizations bring participants together for sociability.

The key to folk music survival has been adaptation. Most of the styles written about in this volume have undergone some kind of transformation during their existence in the United States. Language and repertoire changed to meet the demands of immigrants entering the American mainstream. The music frequently was used differently than previously, in many cases becoming a symbolic medium. Some forms have enjoyed popularity within a diverse population. By the end of the twentieth century, many were accessed differently than previously. Change and adaptation will probably continue to tell the story of European American folk music in America.

FRENCH TRADITIONS: THEIR HISTORY AND CONTINUITY IN NORTH AMERICA

Winnie Lambrecht

Winnie Lambrecht received a Ph.D. in anthropology from the University of California, Berkeley. She has written numerous articles on Franco-American culture and has consulted for, produced, or coproduced a number of documentary films, festivals, and exhibits, including the 1989 Festival of American Folk Life, focusing on French music. She has served as the director of the Folk Arts Program of Rhode Island since 1982. This essay originally appeared in the 1989 Smithsonian Festival of American Folklife program guide.

The people of Brittany, Normandy, Poitou, Quebec, and the French-speaking communities of New England, Louisiana, North Dakota, and Missouri share a common origin and linguistic affinity. Each of these communities has selectively preserved and modified this French cultural heritage in a specific historical and geographical setting despite pressures toward cultural homogenization and political attempts to restrict cultural continuity. From the Bretons of Basse-Bretagne to the Michif of North Dakota, Manitoba, and Saskatchewan, today's traditional music, verbal art, and material culture reflect the tensions between pressures toward conformity, with a singular national culture, and the rights of individuals and communities to assert their own cultural identities.

Francophone North America was mainly peopled by immigrants from the Atlantic coast of France and their descendants. The evolution of traditional French culture in the new continent was the result of historical forces specific to each area. Desires to maintain self-identity, to assert one's heritage, or to distinguish oneself from others altered the lifestyle of each group. Internal social and political transformations, external influences and pressures, and cultural elements borrowed from neighboring communities contributed to the traditions that took shape in the New World.

Cultural diversity is no less important within France. To the outside world, France might appear as a cultural unity, but in fact it is a country of considerable cultural diversity. One of the goals of the Revolution—national unification—was not welcome in those regions of France that were not only distant from the events in Paris but were also culturally and linguistically different. Ethnic minorities within France who spoke languages other than French were subject to the same kind of edicts as those that later forced French speakers in Acadia, Quebec, and Louisiana to adopt English, the language of the culture that came to dominate North

The survival of French traditions can be seen in the dress of this Cajun woman photographed in 1985 in Petit Davis, a small town in Louisiana on the False River. Her bonnet and clothing reflect the traditional styles still seen in Brittany in France.
Photo © Philip Gould/ CORBIS

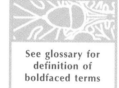

See glossary for definition of boldfaced terms

America politically and economically. This compelled conformity, and intolerance of cultural difference led minority communities in France to seek greater opportunity elsewhere, primarily in North America. Conditions in France prior to the Revolution prompted disenfranchised people, especially in the rural areas, to follow earlier mariners and explorers to North America. The French Revolution prompted new migrations among its dissenters (royalists, some of the Catholic clergy, and tenant peasants, the most notable of these counterrevolutionary groups being the *chouans*).

The complexities of these historical movements and their results can be illustrated by the case of French settlement in Missouri. French settlements in the Mississippi and Missouri river valleys were the result of early expeditions by fur traders coming from the north in search of additional bounty and explorers from the south in search of mines that had already been signaled by the Spanish explorer Hernando de Soto in the sixteenth century. These early French settlements started as forts or missions, and most had French populations too small to produce enough food for their own subsistence. They soon imported slaves from the French colonies in the Caribbean—Haiti, Martinique, and Guadeloupe. Indeed,

in many communities the African population outnumbered the French. Thus, many of the **oral traditions** in these communities reflect very strong African and Creole (Afro-Caribbean) influences.

The French in Missouri were cut off from regular contact with other French-speaking communities during the late eighteenth and early nineteenth centuries. English speakers started settling in the area in great numbers; political authority and mercantile activity became their domain, and the French found themselves a disenfranchised minority. As a result of these historical events, French musical traditions are scarce in Missouri and absent in neighboring Illinois. Instead, the Francophone community maintains its distinctiveness largely through its **foodways** and oral traditions. *Boudin noir* (blood sausage), beignets or *beign chauwage* (puff cakes), and *tart à bouillir* (a pie) are all part of the culinary tradition in present-day Missouri.

Today's varied mosaic of French-derived or -influenced oral traditions in North America results from various migrations: French who came to Quebec or Acadia, and others who settled in Louisiana; Acadians who returned to France and then migrated again to Louisiana; French Canadians who came down the Mississippi and settled in Illinois and Missouri; French *coureurs de bois* (woodsmen) who intermarried with Native Americans; slaves brought to French colonies to help meet agrarian needs; and *Québécois* (residents of the Canadian province of Quebec) who immigrated to New England. In some communities, a large number of active bearers of these traditions maintain them proudly; in others, French-derived traditions are scarce, and the numbers of active bearers are very small. In yet others, such as the Métis in North Dakota, French traditions have become part of a new cultural complex through ethnogenesis. Ethnogenesis is the conscious creation of a new cultural lifestyle by a group of people who, having lost their cultural identity through oppression or assimilation, feel the need to reassert a separate cultural community.

THE FRENCH IN THE NEW WORLD

From the early sixteenth century, French fishermen and mariners from Le Havre, Dieppe, Rouen, Honfleur, and other fishing ports explored the waters off the North American coast. Initially, these mariners carried their haul back to France; soon, however, they began to dry their catch on North American land and established depots in Newfoundland and the Acadian peninsula (the northern coast of Maine, the southern portion of the Gaspé peninsula, Nova Scotia, New Brunswick, and the Magdalen Islands). There they first came into contact with native inhabitants such as the Micmac, the Hurons, the Iroquois, and the Montagnais.

These early expeditions led to the beginning of New France and the establishment of French colonies on American soil. An active exchange sprang up between French fishermen and early settlers seeking furs from their Indian trading partners. By 1630 a number of trading posts were established, and French fishermen wintered in Acadian coves; about 1636 the first families arrived. They came mostly from the western parts of France, searching for economic gain and fleeing from political and religious persecution. These early immigrants brought with them the traditions, beliefs, and agricultural and maritime skills that had been passed on to them for generations. The demands of a new environment, the absence of familiar natural resources, and new economic and social challenges brought changes in the tool kit and habits of these settlers. The new circumstances called for both local inventiveness and borrowing from indigenous populations. Yet many of the French traditions survived, particularly in the verbal arts.

When the first census of the settlement of New France was taken in 1671, many families were headed by craftsmen whose skills were essential for the survival of small communities: toolmakers, gunsmiths, coopers, and weavers. Others listed themselves as farmers. Besides the 400 families counted, there were also coureurs de bois, fur traders who lived with Indians, and administrative officials. These founding families were seminal in shaping the nature of life in the New World; according to Truman Stacey in an article that appeared in the 1979 book *Franco-American Overview,* "three-fourths of all the Acadians living today, either in Louisiana or Canada, or Nova Scotia or Europe, are descended from the families listed in the census of 1671."

Early seventeenth-century French settlements in the New World attracted English resentment and reprisals. The English felt that these settlers and traders had intruded upon their lands, and a series of conflicts ensued. The fur traders, who had become the mainstay of French Canada, maintained contact with the Hurons, the Algonquins, and the Montagnais. These contacts provoked the anger of the Iroquois, who were trading with the British. Rivalries among European colonials and among Native American tribes resulted in a series of wars, culminating with the expulsion of the Acadians by the British, who had tactical and military superiority. On August 1, 1755, Governor Lawrence ordered all French to be removed from Acadia without their possessions.

Though many French settlers had already left Acadia after the area came under British rule in 1713, Governor Lawrence's order in 1755 forced the evacuation of hundreds of Acadians from the lands they had settled. Many French settlers were imprisoned, and many others were exiled. This period of imprisonment and deportation, known in French Canadian and French American history as *le Grand Dérangement,* continued until the Treaty of Paris in 1763. (Under the terms of the Treaty of Paris, which ended the French and Indian War, France lost most of its colonial possessions in North America, effectively destroying its plan to establish an empire on the continent.) Exiles were scattered, families torn apart and resettled in the British colonies along the Atlantic seaboard (Massachusetts, New York, Pennsylvania, South Carolina, and Maryland—the only place where they were welcomed, due in part to the Catholic presence in Baltimore). Some 60 percent of these exiles died before

A Cajun Mardi Gras celebration and dance held at St. Thomas More Church in Eunice, Louisiana, c. 1994. In the background, famous accordion player Marc Savoy can be seen accompanying the dancers.
Photo © Philip Gould/ CORBIS

reaching a safe haven. Rejected from most areas, they eventually found their way to French colonies in the West Indies, went to other parts of Canada, or settled in what would later become Louisiana, then under Spanish control. Throughout the 1760s, Acadians continued to come to Louisiana from temporary refuge in Canada, Nova Scotia, and the West Indies.

Other exiles asked to be sent back to France. They were resettled mostly in the seacoast towns of western France. With no way of supporting themselves and unwilling to settle under the quasi-feudal regime of the French monarchy, most of these families eventually migrated to Louisiana. Most of the Acadians arrived in Louisiana between 1765 and 1785 and settled along the banks of the Mississippi at Bayou Lafourche and west of the Atchafalaya Basin on Bayou Teche.

The beginning of a strong French presence in Louisiana dates from the late seventeenth century. French traders in search of

additional sources of furs had moved west to the Great Lakes and then south. Among these explorations, one of the most noteworthy was that of La Salle (full name: René-Robert Cavelier, Sieur [Lord] de La Salle), who led expeditions down the Mississippi into Louisiana in 1681. In his party were the first Europeans to come to that area and to reach the Gulf of Mexico from the north; they claimed the area for France in 1682 and named it in honor of King Louis XIV.

Small groups of settlers gradually came to Louisiana, but because few were attracted to the area, the early inhabitants brought black slaves from the French settlements in the Caribbean to till the land and raise crops. Officials in France also tried to attract other Europeans to the area. In the 1720s, German colonists first arrived in Louisiana, and many moved upriver, north of New Orleans to an area that came to be known as "the German Coast." Truman Stacey writes that "in the 1760s, the provisions generously of-

fered by the settlers of the German Coast saved the Acadian exiles. . . ."

The French settlers selectively appropriated cultural items from the various groups that contributed to the social fabric of life in Louisiana. Among these cultural practices were fishing techniques from the Anglo-Americans and cooking practices from African American slaves. Like earlier colonists, these settlers also came in contact with the indigenous populations of Louisiana such as the Houma, the Choctaw, the Coushatta, and the Tunica-Biloxi. The new residents borrowed certain agricultural practices, foodways, and other traditions from the indigenous populations. They learned how to weave palmetto, build dugout canoes, and use local flora for medicinal purposes. The Houma, in turn, incorporated elements of Acadian culture into their traditional lifestyle. They are said to be "among the most traditional speakers of the Acadian dialect in the state" (Gregory 1985, p. 106). Young Houma children today, particularly in Terrebonne Parish, are more likely to speak French than their Cajun contemporaries.

The Acadians, or Cajuns, as they came to be called, also incorporated cultural items from black Creoles from the Caribbean. Though Cajuns had few slaves, they were close to large plantations and absorbed the Afro-French Creole language. Contemporary Cajun foods such as gumbo and **Cajun music**—with its African American **blues** and Afro-Caribbean rhythmic influences—show direct influence from slaves and free people of color.

The movement of French-speaking immigrants out of French Canada did not stop in the eighteenth century. During the nineteenth century, French farmers in Quebec faced many difficulties: low productivity on farms, an inheritance system that led to the fragmentation of farms, and a burgeoning population. Many Québécois migrated to New England, where a thriving textile industry offered seasonal employment to immigrants.

Between 1830 and 1850, the textile industry in New England witnessed an extraordinary boom. The industry had first employed unmarried women and girls from the rural areas of northern New England. Newly arrived Irish immigrants also provided labor for the growing industry. Between 1860 and 1900, factory owners turned increasingly to the human resources of Quebec. In 1850 the permanent French Canadian population in New England was about 20,000; by the 1860s it had doubled. This growth in labor from Quebec was facilitated by the relative proximity of New England and the availability of cheap, rapid transportation by rail.

The alarming rate of emigration to New England led to a repatriation campaign by the Quebec government in 1875. Government offers of inexpensive farmland, fare reductions on railroad tickets, and visits to mills by French Canadian members of the clergy were all part of this effort to stem emigration. As a result, half of the French Canadians who emigrated to New England before 1900 subsequently returned to Quebec.

Though many French Canadians assimilated to their new homeland, a greater number maintained their language, traditions, and musical **repertoire**, as well as their family- and church-centered way of life. The immigrants had come mostly from isolated rural communities along the St. Lawrence and Richelieu rivers. These self-sufficient farming communities included the parish priest (often the most influential figure in the area), craftspeople, and merchants. The immigrants also maintained the ideal of *survivance*, or loyalty to the French Canadian inheritance and the duty of preserving its customs. The result has been a strong sense of ethnic identity and a commitment to preserving the use of the French language, despite the discrimination that French Canadians suffered in New England.

As the French moved west, fur traders and *coureurs de bois* intermarried with Native Americans. In spite of a desire on the part of French settlers to maintain their separateness, marriages between natives and the French were not limited to the western or more remote areas of colonization, and many such unions took place. It is estimated that 40 percent of French Canadians

today can claim some Indian ancestry (Dickason 1985, p. 19). Children of French colonists and Native Americans often became traders and cultural brokers, intermediaries between the two communities. Their isolation from the rest of New France caused them to adopt ways of life that differed from both their French and their Native American ancestors, and led to the formation of a distinctive culture known as Métis (literally "mixed"). Métis groups, each with its own history and traditions, are found in various areas of the Great Lakes and north and west of that region. The Michif people of the Turtle Mountain Reservation in north central North Dakota are among those who have retained a number of French-derived traditions.

Marriages between the French and the Native Americans they encountered and on whom they depended for survival and trade also produced other elements of culture that partook of both traditions. Michif, the language spoken today by the Métis of the Turtle Mountain Reservation, probably developed early during contact between the French and the Cree. The complex history of the Métis of the area, as well as that of the Cree and the Chippewa, reflects all of the tragedies that characterized the treaties and land claims between the United States government and Native Americans. It is made even more complicated by the fact that native tribes moved freely between what became two distinct countries separated by a boundary that was meaningless to the Cree, the Chippewa, and the Métis.

Michif has been considered alternatively as a distinct creole language and as a dialect of Cree. Whatever its classification, it is the language of people on a reservation that is legally Chippewa, whose speakers have moved away from both Cree and Chippewa languages in speech and song. Indeed, J. C. Crawford (1985, p. 233) writes that, in Michif, "the noun phrase is a French domain; verb structure is clearly and thoroughly Cree, and syntax is Cree with French and probably English influence. Minor word classes seem to split, some words being French and some Cree."

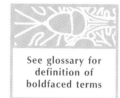

See glossary for definition of boldfaced terms

In Métis music and dance, too, there was an exchange between the French and the Native Americans: The native drum was discarded, and music was provided by "the **fiddle**, sometimes a genuine one but more frequently one made from a hollow piece of wood with catgut strings attached. The tunes were generally adaptations of old French folk songs while the dance itself was a lively number which in time became known as the Red River **jig**" (Dusenberry 1985, p. 121). To French speakers, the songs are recognizable as French, some referring to historical events that took place in the homeland of their French ancestors, such as the lyrics of the song "Napoléon Bonaparte":

> *En baissant les pavillons est mort Napoléon.*
> *Napoléon n'existerait plus.*
> *Nous parlerons de son histoire.*
> *"Je suis fort, fort bien entouré.*
> *Adieu, Français. Adieu, la France. C'est pour toujours.*
> *Tous les regrets j'ai dans ce monde c'est ma femme et mon cher enfant.*
> *Adieu, Français. Adieu, la France. C'est pour toujours."*

> *The flags are being lowered, Napoleon has died.*
> *He no longer lives.*
> *We will tell of his story.*
> *"I am surrounded from all sides.*
> *Adieu, Frenchmen. Adieu, France. Forever adieu.*
> *Of all I miss in this world, it is especially my wife and my dear child.*
> *Adieu, Frenchmen. Adieu, France. Forever adieu."*

(Turtle Mountain Music 1984)

MUSIC IN THE NEW WORLD

Mariners who came from France to exploit the fishing banks along the Acadian coasts accompanied their sailing and fishing efforts with **work songs**. The composition of fishing crews changed over the years, with seasonal crews recruited from the farmland in-

terior in addition to year-round mariners. There is nevertheless a certain unity in the musical repertoire these crews brought to the shores of the New World. Musical **instruments** also accompanied sailors on their journeys, as attested by Admiral Thévenard in 1776: "One of the concerns that good seamen know the importance of is the entertainment provided to crews during long journeys and periods without wind" (cited in *Chants de marins traditionnels des côtes de France* 1984). Horns and trumpets, **hurdygurdies**, and musettes (a French version of **bagpipes**) all found their way onto sailing and fishing vessels.

Even though the first settlers in the New World shared the same traditions, language, and religion, the priorities of their new life, the agricultural cycle, and the manner in which celebrations were observed moved their musical cultures in a direction different from that of the mariners. The small, self-sufficient farms of the colonists under the strong influence of the Roman Catholic church resulted in a culture distinct from that of France. According to Anne-Marie Desdouits (1986, p. 30), "The Church always directed and molded the acts and the thoughts of colonists, who, cut from their roots, had nothing in their new land to feed the beliefs and practices that had sustained them in their place of origin." Church leaders undoubtedly modified the nature of the dance and music traditions that survived or developed in Quebec and Acadia. Dance was viewed as frivolous if not sinful activity.

This state of affairs prevailed in France as well, where dance and music on Sundays and holy days were vociferously condemned, as an extract from a 1710 document from Plouaret indicates:

Nous avons condamné Gillette Kerguentel femme de Yves Le Sohier à 3 livres d'aumosne au profit de la fabrice de l'église de Plouaret pour avoir fait sonner et danser à jour de dimanche et Gilles Salic aussi à trois livres d'aumosne pour avoir fait sonné le méme jour, avec défense de les recevoir à la participation des sacrements jusques à y avoir satisfait.

We have condemned Gillette Kerguentel, wife of Yves Le Sohier, to a three pound contribution to the maintenance of the church of Plouaret because of her incitement to music and dance on a Sunday, and Gilles Salic also to a three pound charitable contribution for playing on that same day; it is forbidden to them to partake of the sacraments until they fulfill this obligation. (Bécam 1989, p. 9)

In France, the influence of the Catholic Church was lessened by the existence of other institutions and larger communities. There were, however, other reasons for the musics of the two continents to diverge. Musical traditions and repertoires transported from France were reshaped by contact with other cultures. Musical instrument making was not a priority in the colonies. Growing crops in a new environment, conflicts with some Native American groups and English settlers, and the lack of skilled artisans to provide adequate tools all reduced the opportunity for making musical instruments. Also, some of the instruments that were popular in France were not made for life in a colonial setting, such as the hurdy-gurdy (which seems to be making a comeback in Quebec, mostly with revivalist musicians).

Although the original French immigrants to the New World had brought with them few musical instruments, the Acadians were lovers of music and of dance. Where musical instruments were not available (or were forbidden, such as during Lent), dances were accompanied by voices, hand clapping, and foot stomping. The musical traditions of western France (homeland to most of the Acadians) included brass and reed instruments, as well as trumpets and the *vielle à roué* (hurdy-gurdy). Given the priorities of colonial life and limitations in instrument manufacture, the immigrants made do with new instruments borrowed from other peoples. Many of the tunes that the French immigrants brought with them were easily transposed to violins, which were more readily available. French settlers in Acadia

Zydeco fiddler Canray Fontenot, photographed in 1975. Cajun music combines French, African American, and Native American influences and is performed by descendants of all three groups. *Photograph courtesy the Smithsonian Institution.*

incorporated Scotch-Irish reels, jigs, and hornpipes into their musical repertoires, and danced **schottisches**, **mazurkas**, and **contredanses**.

Today these traditions continue and develop in Quebec and New England. New England communities such as Waltham, Massachusetts, have large populations of Acadian and Québécois descent with many formidable musicians, especially fiddlers and singers. In Quebec, couple dances other than the **waltz** are now less visible, but contredanses, **quadrilles**, **cotillions**, *rondes,* and *sets carrés* (**square dances**) are popular in many communities.

An unbroken community dance tradition thrives in places such as Ile d'Orléans and the Saguenay/Lac-St-Jean area. Other social events have sprung up recently, such as those held regularly in Montreal. *Veillées* (musical evenings) are as likely to take place in community halls as in private homes, and frequent daylong galas showcase the talents of regional musicians. During Christmas and on New Year's Day families and friends gather for song and celebration; for *La Fête de St-Jean-Baptiste* in June, people throughout the province gather for parades, bonfires, and concerts of traditional music in a celebration that today is more nationalistic than religious.

For French speakers in Quebec and, indeed, in every Canadian province, the question of language has long been inseparable from issues of identity and access to power and self-determination. A 1980 referendum to take steps toward provincial secession from Canada was rejected; still, many Québécois are adamant in demanding the right to use French in their daily lives without sacrificing political and economic equality with English speakers. In recent years increasing exposure to English-language media, economic pressures to assimilate to the Anglophone world that surrounds them, an influx of immigrants who want their children's second language to be English instead of French, and the steadily dropping birthrate among Québécois of French ancestry cause consternation among those who fear that their language and culture will disappear.

In Louisiana, toward the end of the nineteenth century, resettled Acadians adopted the **diatonic accordion** that had been imported by German immigrants and incorporated a number of fiddle tunes, **ballads**, square dances, and **hoedowns** from the increasing number of Anglo-Americans to the north. The repertoire of songs and instrumental music in Louisiana was further influenced by black musical traditions. Afro-French Creoles in Louisiana developed their

own musical style called **zydeco** by modifying Cajun tonality and adding **improvisation** and Afro-Caribbean rhythm patterns. This tradition is particularly strong today in the musical performances of people such as Canray Fontenot, "Bois Sec" Ardoin, and John Delafosse. The Lawtell Playboys, Nathan Williams and the Zydeco Cha Chas, and others play regularly in clubs in southern Louisiana.

The continuity, isolation, creolization, and, in some cases, end of musical traditions are indicators of the struggle for ethnic, economic, and cultural survival of French-speaking peoples and those with whom they came into contact over the last four centuries. Indeed, in Louisiana until quite recently, children were chastised for speaking French in public schools. Recognizing the persistence and importance of traditional culture and speech, the Committee for the Development of French in Louisiana (CODOFIL) was created in 1968. French, which until then had been an oral tradition, was offered in public schools, and Cajun children have since become literate in French.

As with other French-speaking communities in North America, an identifiably French musical repertoire was sustained in Louisiana, along with foodways and material culture that mark the state as a homeland to settlers of the French "diaspora." Today, revitalization of traditional music and recognition for continuing and transformed traditions comment aesthetically on the cultural wealth of French-speaking communities from Quebec and New England to North Dakota, Louisiana, and Missouri.

BIBLIOGRAPHY

Ancelet, Barry Jean. (1984). *The Makers of Cajun Music.* Austin: University of Texas Press.

Bécam, Didier. (1989). "Les sonneurs et la danse en Trégor aux 17è et 18è siècles." *Musique Bretonne* 89 (February):8–10.

Brault, Gerard J. (1986). *The French-Canadian Heritage in New England.* Hanover, NH: University Press of New England.

Carriere, Joseph Medard. (1937). *Tales from the French Folklore of Missouri.* Northwestern University Studies in the Humanities, Vol. 1. Chicago: Northwestern University Press.

Crawford, John C. (1985). "What Is Michif? Language in the Métis Tradition." In *The New Peoples: Being and Becoming Métis in North America,* ed. Jacqueline Peterson and Jennifer S. H. Brown. Lincoln: University of Nebraska Press.

"Dansez, Sarthois! Danses de caractère et pas d'été." (1984). *Cénomane* 15 (special issue).

Desdouits, Anne-Marie. (1986). "Le printemps dans la tradition France-Amérique." In *Le patrimoine folklorique des Franco-Américains,* ed. Claire Quintal. Quebec: Le Conseil de la Vie Française en Amérique.

Dickason, Olive Patricia. (1985). "From 'One Nation' in the Northeast to 'New Nation' in the Northwest: A Look at the Emergence of the Métis." In *The New Peoples: Being and Becoming Métis in North America,* ed. Jacqueline Peterson and Jennifer S. H. Brown. Lincoln: University of Nebraska Press.

Dusenberry, Verne. (1985). "Waiting for a Day That Never Comes: The Dispossessed Métis of Montana." In *The New Peoples: Being and Becoming Métis in North America,* ed. Jacqueline Peterson and Jennifer S. H. Brown. Lincoln: University of Nebraska Press.

Gagné, Marc, and Poulin, Monique. (1985). *Chantons la chanson.* Quebec: Les Presses de l'Université Laval.

Gregory, H. F. (1985). "'A Promise from the Sun': The Folklife Traditions of Louisiana Indians." In *Louisiana Folklife: A Guide to the State,* ed. Nicholas Spitzer. Baton Rouge: Louisiana Folklife Program.

Peterson, Jacqueline, and Brown, Jennifer S. H., ed. (1985). *The New Peoples: Being and Becoming Métis in North America.* Manitoba Studies in Native History, Vol. 1. Lincoln: University of Nebraska Press.

Rushton, William Faulkner. (1970). *The Cajuns: From Acadia to Louisiana.* New York: Farrar, Straus and Giroux.

Savoy, Ann. (1984). *Cajun Music: A Reflection of a People,* Vol. 1. Eunice, LA: Bluebird Press.

Saguin, Robert-Lionel. (1986). *La Danse traditionelle au Québec.* Quebec: Presses de l'Université du Québec.

Stacey, Truman. (1979). "Louisiana's French Heritage." In *Franco-American Overview,* Vol. 1, comp. Renaud S. Albert. Cambridge, MA: National Assessment and Dissemination Center for Bilingual/Bicultural Education.

Thomas, Rosemary Hyde. (1981). *It's Good to Tell You: French Folktales from Missouri.* Columbia: University of Missouri Press.

Voyer, Simonne. (1986). *La Danse traditionelle dans l'est du Canada: Quadrilles et cotillons.* Quebec: Les Presses de l'Université Laval.

RECORDINGS

Anthologie des chansons de mer, Vol. 1: Chants de marins traditionnels des côtes de France, 1984. Vol. 1. Le Chasse-Marée SCM 001.

Turtle Mountain Music. 1984. Folkways Records FES 4140.

FRENCH CANADIAN MUSIC IN RHODE ISLAND

Henry S. Hample

*Henry S. Hample is a doctoral candidate in **ethnomusicology** at Brown University. His writing has appeared in Maximum RocknRoll, Premiere, and VIBE magazines, and he is the founder of the New York–based jug band Washboard Jungle.*

A significant but relatively invisible minority in New England, French Canadian immigrants began crossing the border into the United States in the early nineteenth century and have held on to some of their cultural traditions for generations, even as interest in these traditions waned in Canada in the face of modernization. This trend is especially true in and around Woonsocket, Rhode Island, a mill town whose population was 70 percent Franco-American by 1920, the highest per-capita concentration of any city in the United States. (Anctil 1983, passim) In more recent years, French Canadian immigration has decreased while that of other minority groups has increased, and use of the French language in the area has declined dramatically. Nevertheless, the community continues to hold French Canadian **square dances** known as **quadrilles**. Though the dances are called mostly in English and the **repertoire** played by the quadrille bands includes many U.S. tunes, the quadrilles represent an unbroken local tradition that has survived against all odds.

HISTORY

The term "quadrille" originally referred to a French adaptation of the English **contra dance**, brought to Quebec in the eighteenth century. The quadrille consisted of five or more parts, each danced to a different tune, and like a contra dance, it was danced with men and women facing each other in two lines.

But the "quadrilles" danced today in Rhode Island are really quadrille-influenced square dances, always danced by four couples and never consisting of more than two parts. In any event, square dances were originally invented by the French, and they were imported to Quebec—as well as to other parts of North America—at about the same time as quadrilles.

Because of an agricultural crisis in Quebec, many Quebecois farmers sought work

in the mill towns of New England in the nineteenth century. The earliest French Canadian immigrants to Rhode Island appeared about 1820 (Bonier 1997, p. 95). By 1920, a large network of Francophone schools, churches, businesses, and fraternal organizations enabled Woonsocket's Franco-Americans to speak French virtually all the time.

One of the traditions the Quebecois immigrants brought with them was the *veillée,* or house party. Including live music, quadrilles, singing, and storytelling, the veillée typically took place on a Saturday night in a private home, where the carpet was rolled back and the furniture moved out of the way to make room for dancing.

French Canadian Music in Rhode Island

As veillées became less fashionable and Franco-Americans became more assimilated to mainstream culture, quadrilles moved into dance halls, with dance bands playing **jazz** tunes between quadrilles. Some bands later incorporated country-and-western songs in their repertoire.

Interest in quadrilles waned in the 1980s as the audience aged or passed away, but a revival in the 1990s led to renewed interest in the music form. Bands in the Woonsocket area now play several times a year at festivals, dinner dances, and other events.

MUSIC AND DANCE

Where the function of quadrille dancing was once primarily for young people to meet members of the opposite sex under socially approved conditions, today most quadrille dancers are in their sixties, seventies, and eighties, and the dances are primarily an affirmation of ethnic pride, as well as representing nostalgia for an era when French Canadian custom was followed more universally. The dances, of course, are also a form of entertainment, enabling elders to mingle with one another and often incorporating dinner, joke telling, raffles, and the like. Music at these affairs is absolutely essential: Quadrille music is sometimes played with no dancing, but it is unheard of to dance quadrilles without a live band present. The live music, then, adds a crucial element of authenticity to the event, in that it is far more effective than recordings at creating a gay atmosphere and conjuring up memories of old times.

Currently, there are two main quadrille bands in Rhode Island. Both bands are led by first-generation immigrants: fiddler Conrad Depot and singer/guitarist Marcel Carpentier. The bands perform **fiddle** tunes for the quadrille dances—usually two at a time—plus additional music, much of it French Canadian country and western, for couple dancing between quadrilles. A third band, led by third-generation Rhode Islander Colette Fournier, tends toward exclusively traditional music and sit-down

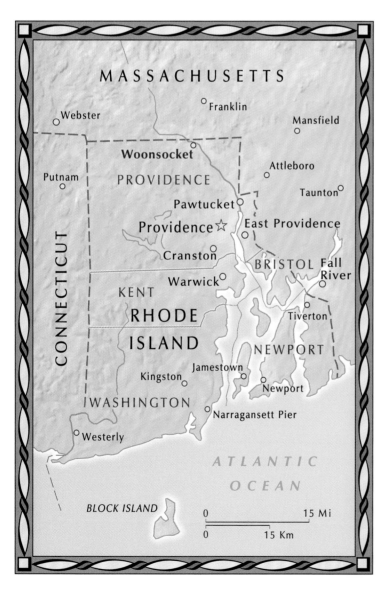

shows. There are two quadrille **callers**, George Menard and Jerry Poulin, both Rhode Island natives in their seventies.

The fiddle is the most important **instrument** in the quadrille band, playing the **melody** that the caller and dancers follow. Calling is mostly in English, with some French words and phrases; occasionally, these are made to rhyme with English phrases: "The other way/*De l'autre côté/Vous êtes trompé*/The other way." The accompaniment is provided by such instruments as acoustic **guitar**, electric keyboard, and bass fiddle. Virtually all fiddle tunes are in D **major** or G major and follow the standard thirty-two-bar AABB form, though sometimes the tunes are played slightly "crooked," with an extra beat or measure thrown in if the fiddler happens to have the tune in his or her head that way.

Couple dances, or "fancies," as they are usually called, are often danced to French Canadian country-and-western songs dating from the 1940s, 1950s, and 1960s, played on acoustic guitar and sung by one or more vocalists. Fancies are also danced to fiddle tunes, especially **waltzes**, as well as to light jazz if a saxophonist is present, or to recorded music.

Traditional **lyric songs** are sometimes sung, especially by Colette Fournier's band. Many of these are *chansons à repondre,* responsorial songs in which the audience repeats some of the lines sung by the leader.

Many songs are learned by **oral tradition**; others are learned from recordings, or from the two French-language radio programs in Woonsocket. There are several important collections of French Canadian traditional songs, such as those by Ernest Gagnon and Marius Barbeau, who helped preserve and popularize them.

Though the country-and-western songs were originally learned from electronic sources, many have more or less entered into oral tradition as "old favorites." Some of these songs were written by Quebecois songwriters, some were originally **Cajun music** from Louisiana, and some are French translations of American country-and-western songs.

Conrad Depot is considered to be the area's chief repository of quadrille tunes, though there are also a number of Franco-American fiddlers who choose to play a more generic New England repertoire with the Old Fiddlers' Club of Rhode Island. A number of Depot's more obscure tunes were collected in the early 1990s by Fournier, and these now constitute a miniature Rhode Island repertoire.

Some of the tunes played at quadrilles are well known as American fiddle tunes (for example, "Oh, Dem Golden Slippers," "Redwing") and are in the repertoire because they were once popular in Quebec. They are often regarded as French tunes, and many have French titles ("Les Souliers Dorés," "Les Ailes Rouges").

Those who frequent the quadrilles tend to judge live music by its liveliness and danceability. A song doesn't have to be in French or associated with Canada to fit in; one of Hank Williams's country-western songs or a Cajun **two-step** is more than welcome. Conversely, a moody song by the popular French chanteuse Edith Piaf may be out of place despite its being sung in French. A song's associations are, of course, important; some are traditionally associated with weddings, holidays, and other life events.

There are many Franco-Americans in Rhode Island who are not interested in traditional music, considering it lower class or old fashioned. Many who perform at or attend quadrilles are over the age of sixty and work at blue-collar jobs. Nevertheless, some regular dancers represent a higher income level, and younger people sometimes attend with their parents or grandparents. The city of Woonsocket has seen the erosion of much of its industrial economy; as a result, indigenous culture recently has been promoted as a tourist attraction, with the side effect of increasing long-dormant Franco-American pride.

DOCUMENTARY RECORDINGS AND FILMS

Unfortunately, none of the French Canadian bands in Rhode Island have released any

recordings. However, *Mademoiselle, voulez-vous danser?* (1999) is an excellent introduction to the fiddle style, as performed by musicians elsewhere in New England. Footage of Rhode Island quadrilles can be seen in *Side by Each* (2000), a video documentary created by Flickers Arts Collaborative, producers of the annual Jubilé Franco-Américain festival in Woonsocket.

BIBLIOGRAPHY

Anctil, Pierre. (1993). "The Franco-Americans of New England." In *French America: Mobility, Identity, and Minority Experience Across the Continent,* ed. Dean R. Louder and Eric Waddell. Baton Rouge: Louisiana State University Press.

Bonier, Mary Louise. (1997). *The Beginnings of the Franco-American Colony in Woonsocket, Rhode Island,* tr. Claire Quintal. Worcester, MA: Institut Français/ Assumption College.

Brault, Gerard J. (1986). *The French-Canadian Heritage in New England.* Hanover, NH: University Press of New England.

RECORDINGS

Mademoiselle, voulez-vous danser?: Franco-American Music in New England. 1999. Smithsonian Folkways 40116.

VIDEOS

Side by Each: Franco-American Cultural Life in Woonsocket, R.I. 2000. Produced and directed by George T. Marshall. Newport, RI: Flickers Arts Collaborative.

FRANCO-AMERICAN MUSIC AND DANCE TRADITIONS IN VERMONT AND NEW HAMPSHIRE

Jennifer C. Post

Jennifer C. Post is assistant professor of music and curator of the Helen Hartness Flanders Ballad Collection at Middlebury College. She has conducted fieldwork in both India and New England and has published articles on women and music in India and on traditional music in northern New England.

The movement of French Canadians from Quebec into Vermont and New Hampshire began as early as the seventeenth century, but the largest wave of immigrants arrived in the nineteenth century in response to the political climate in Quebec and declining availability and quality of farmland in the province. Many families who arrived to settle during the period benefited from better farming opportunities in these rural states, but others came specifically to work in local industry, especially the textile mills. The Vermont mills in Winooski and Burlington and the mills associated with the Amoskeag Manufacturing Company in Manchester, New Hampshire, attracted a large immigrant community beginning in the 1840s. After 1860, Vermont saw a decline in its French-speaking population as many families relocated to work in the mills in New Hampshire, Massachusetts, and Maine.

The settlement pattern of the French Canadian families was affected by linguistic, cultural, and economic factors. In Vermont and New Hampshire, French-speaking families settled in neighborhoods, sometimes in housing units made available by the textile industry. The "Little Canada" communities that emerged during this period provided opportunities for Franco-Americans to maintain a continuous relationship between social life and cultural expression in families and neighborhood groups.

Holding on to Francophone music and dance traditions contributed to their Franco-American identity as they established residential pockets in the towns and cities. Music and dance were enjoyed at events that took place regularly in small and extended family gatherings, as well as in neighborhoods and the lumber camps. Many of the musical traditions continued at least until the mid-1940s, when cultural and economic changes began to affect social life and local industry.

Social music and dance practices among Franco-American families in Vermont and New Hampshire demonstrate the impor-

tance of kinship and tradition, and reflect an interrelationship between French Canadian and Anglo-American cultural and social practices during the nineteenth and twentieth centuries. Their customs have traveled, grown, and changed for several generations in both rural and urban communities throughout the region.

SOCIAL EVENTS

House parties, called *veillées* or *soirées,* have been held in French-speaking families in Canada for generations. Like the kitchen dances of the English, Irish, and Scottish settlers, veillées contributed to the socialization process for members of local communities of Franco-Americans. They also helped maintain connections to the extended family, including those that remained in Canada or moved to other New England sites for employment. During holidays and on other social occasions, whenever people gathered, music and dance became an integral part of the celebration.

Willie Beaudoin of Burlington, Vermont, recalls the New Year's celebrations that were so important in his family:

> We would get geared up for New Year's Eve and New Year's Day because the family got together and [my brother] always brought his fiddle or I had my guitar and my family had a piano and we'd break out the **instruments** and the first thing you'd know . . . they'd all come, wish us happy New Year's, and we'd offer a little glass of cheers. And with the music, they really used to pack it in and now the house was chuck full of people and they used to sing, and it was a real joyful time of the year. It was a special day, really. (Beaudoin family interview, 1984)

Other members of the Beaudoin family remember parties that took place on weekends and at family celebrations:

> Whenever company would come from anywhere—Canada, Massachusetts—as soon as we knew they

were here, my father would say, we'll have everybody over. And before you know it, there was a houseful. We'd invite both sides—my side of the family, and of course his side of the family. We had people from Canada and people from Massachusetts, and we'd make music. (Beaudoin family interview, 1984)

Similarly, in New Hampshire, a mill worker interviewed in the late 1930s in Manchester remembered the veillées in that region:

> We had family reunions, mostly on Sunday, to amuse ourselves. They were real *veillées canadiennes,* and we certainly enjoyed ourselves. We sang without piano accompaniment, songs of Old Quebec, danced square and round dances and jigs, played games like *L'assiette tournante* [Spin the Platter] for forfeits, and played cards for the fun of it, mostly euchre, a game we learned here. (Lemay in Doty 1985, p. 28)

Singing traditions were also maintained in the lumber camps of northern New Hampshire and Vermont among French Canadian lumbermen *(les bûcherons).* Like their English-speaking counterparts, they would gather in the camp on Saturday nights to play games, share a wide variety of songs, and dance the *gigue.*

Today musical performances of Franco-American music continue in families and community gatherings in Vermont and New Hampshire. Annual and occasional celebrations of Franco-American heritage occur in Hardwick and Randolph, Vermont; Manchester, New Hampshire; and other locations. Franco-American music is also well integrated into other New England musical styles, providing a flavor heard in songs, their lyrics, and especially in dance tunes shared at **contra dances** and **square dances**, as well as fiddlers' contests and meetings, held in town halls, community gyms, and on outdoor festival grounds.

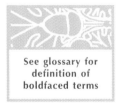

See glossary for definition of boldfaced terms

SONGS

Many of the songs (*chansons*) shared during family and community gatherings in northern New England were popular in Quebec households in the eighteenth and nineteenth centuries. Included are **ballads** and songs from France; those created in the homes, lumber camps, and on the waterways in Canada; and others expressing response to life in America. The maintenance of these singing traditions indicates significant interest in creating an ongoing cultural link to their homeland by holding onto their musical styles and language. Songs popular at social events such as "A St. Malo, beau port de mer," "En passant par la Lorraine," and "Ah! qui me passera le bois" reflect the influence of the French song tradition as well as Canadian history and geography on the local traditions.

Many of the songs performed in northern New England had been maintained by the voyageurs, the explorers and fur traders active throughout North America during the seventeenth and eighteenth centuries. They sang for amusement and to provide rhythmic accompaniment while they paddled their canoes on the Great Lakes and other waterways. The songs "A St. Malo, beau port de mer," "A la clair fontaine," "En roulant ma boule," and "Petit rocher de la haute montagne" were carried to the lumber camps and to farming communities in New England and continued to be sung in the 1940s and 1950s in Vermont. A version of "En roulant ma boule" was sung by the Roulant and LeCours families in Hardwick, Vermont in 1954.

En roulant ma Boule [excerpt]

En roulant ma boule en roulant,
En roulant ma boule.

Derrière chez-nous ya un étang
En roulant ma boule,
Trois beaux canards s'en vont baignant
Rouli, roulant, ma boule en roulant.
En roulant ma boule en roulant,
En roulant ma boule.
Trois beaux canards s'en vont baignant
En roulant ma boule,
Le fils du roi s'en va chassant

Rouli, roulant, ma boule en roulant
En roulant ma boule en roulant,
En roulant ma boule.

Le fils du roi s'en va chassant
En roulant ma boule
Avec son grand fusil d'argent
Rouli, roulant, ma boule en roulant
En roulant ma boule en roulant,
En roulant ma boule.

Avec son grand fusil d'argent,
En roulant ma boule
Visa le noir, tua le blanc
Rouli, roulant, ma boule en roulant
En roulant ma boule en roulant,
En roulant ma boule.

Visa le noir, tua le blanc
En roulant ma boule
Oh! Fils du roi tu es méchant
Rouli, roulant, ma boule en roulant
En roulant ma boule en roulant,
En roulant ma boule.

Oh! Fils du roi tu es méchant
En roulant ma boule
D'avoir tué mon canard blanc
Rouli, roulant, ma boule en roulant
En roulant ma boule en roulant,
En roulant ma boule.

D'avoir tué mon canard blanc
En roulant ma boule
Dessous son l'aile il perd son sang
Rouli, roulant, ma boule en roulant
En roulant ma boule en roulant,
En roulant ma boule.

The singing tradition also influenced the creation of new songs about New England. "Partant pour Manchester," for example, provides a narrative of one family's experience of traveling from Canada to Manchester, New Hampshire, to work in the mills. This song was remembered in 1940 by a Bennington, Vermont, woman who learned it from her grandmother. More recently, contemporary folk singer Donna Hébert, whose relatives moved to the north central New Hampshire towns of Ashland and Franklin to work in the mills, has written a

song called "The Shuttle" in which she narrates the experience of immigrant workers in the mills in Manchester. (See Smithsonian Folkways CD *Mademoiselle, voulez-vous danser?*)

The Shuttle [song text and music by Donna Hébert]

We left our home in St. Hubert to work the Amoskeag

In Manchester, New Hampshire, in 1883.

My parents and my brothers all work the same as I;

At the spinning and the weaving, we make the shuttles fly.

Six days a week we rise at four to work our sixteen hours.

Ma mère and me are spinners inside their tall brick towers;

Mon père, he's in the weaving room; mes frères, they sweep the floor.

We see them, but we cannot speak above the shuttle's roar.

You'll find all ages in the mill, 'tit enfants et grandpères;

Their wages are a pittance, not enough to pay their share.

All of us must labor here or else we do not eat;

Our home is in a tenement with no water and no heat.

On Sundays a great silence reigns, so sweet our ears do ring

And to our God together we may raise a voice to sing.

We rest so dear, so briefly, and visit where we may,

For Monday morn' will soon arrive when the shuttle rules our day.

My friend, she had an accident, three fingers she has lost;

Another boy was crushed to death, and who accounts the cost

Of health and youth spent quickly in thumping mills of brick and tin;

How do we keep our sanity in the shuttle's hellish din?

Oh, my friends and family in lovely St. Hubert,

Don't listen to recruiters when they ask to pay your fare.

Stay at home, don't listen to their blandishments and lies,

Or you'll end up, a slave like me to the shuttle that never dies.

At family and neighborhood gatherings, as well as in the lumber camps, ballads, popular songs, and children's songs were sung, usually without accompaniment. Group singing among Franco-American families and other community members dominated; *chansons à répondre*, sometimes called "answer songs," were sung antiphonally, with all members of the group joining in or repeating the **refrains**. Many songs were also sung in medley **form** (*potpourri*), with the first few lines of well-known songs such as "Do-do l'enfant do," "Alouette," "Sur le pont d'Avignon," and "Un Canadienne errant" performed as a single piece.

DANCES

Franco-American families brought their dance forms and styles to New England, although their performance practices reflect the influence of broader European traditions on social dance. Dances at family and community gatherings include **square**, **round**, and **longways** forms as well as **step dancing**.

Popular dances include the **quadrille**, **contredanse**, *rond*, square dance (*dance carrée*), and gigue. The quadrille, consistently a popular dance at Franco-American gatherings, is executed in parts; and dancers use square, circle, and longways formations. A form of the quadrille evolved to become the American square dance; this developed form among French Canadians is known as the dance carrée. While **callers** were used in the early years of dancing, the tradition of calling in French or English became popular in the nineteenth and early twentieth centuries with the influence of American square dancing. Longways dances, or **contra dances**, were also adopted from English traditions.

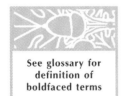

See glossary for definition of boldfaced terms

Sung circle dances were performed by adults at family or neighborhood veillées. In earlier years, round dances were often associated with children's games. In New England families, these dances were often performed by adults, sometimes relying on the singing of participants rather than instrumental accompaniment.

The gigue, or step dance, was originally a solo dance form for men, but it has been adopted for use by both women and men in New England. Step dance figures are used for competition, for entertainment, and often by Franco-American fiddlers, who, while seated, step to accompany their fiddling. Passed in families from parent or grandparent to child, the gigue was performed in the lumber camps and at family gatherings, and is performed today with great enthusiasm at social events, including local fiddlers' club meetings.

INSTRUMENTS

In Anglo- and Franco-American rural communities of northern New England, the instrumental ensemble that accompanied dances before the 1950s was comprised of locally available performers:

> For our round and square dances as well as jigs, the music was furnished by a fiddler who always played the same tune as long as you wanted him to—he knew no other—and by a fellow who played the accordion, but they never played together because their tunes were different. We didn't care about that and we danced and had *great* fun. (Lemay in Doty, p. 30)

Throughout northern New England, at local dances where European forms are shared, the **fiddle** has consistently provided the **melody** for dance ensembles. In Franco-American dance culture, the fiddle is also central, but the **button accordion** has played an important role as a melodic instrument for accompanying dances. The instrumental ensemble also includes a **guitar** and sometimes the **harmonica**, **Jew's harp**, **accordion**,

and spoons. The ensemble is generally supported by piano or another keyboard instrument. **Clogging**, or foot tapping while playing the fiddle, is also a popular form of rhythmic accompaniment for music and dance.

MUSICAL CHARACTERISTICS

Contact between Franco- and Anglo-Americans in various social settings has influenced Franco-American dance music in Canada and New England. It is not surprising, then, that the dance tunes are derived from English, Irish, and French melodies. Throughout the region, the Franco-American performance style is characterized as lively, fast-paced, and more strongly accented than other regional styles. The musical texture is further identified by the use of a wide variety of musical instruments (accordion, spoons, harmonica, Jew's harp) that distinguishes it from other New England dance music.

CONCLUSION

Since the mid–twentieth century, Franco-American traditions have changed with the intrusion of media and the dispersal of families from the region to other parts of the country. Singing traditions dependent on family and close-knit communities have not been sustained at the same level, although singing does continue in the family sphere. The dance traditions, though, still intermingle with traditions of other groups that have settled in the same region. Today, in northern New England, these forms of cultural expression remain in playing styles, tunes, and dance gestures. Song, dance, and dance music traditions, while still retaining many of their historic characteristics, exist as a unique combination of traditional and other regional customs.

BIBLIOGRAPHY

Beaudoin family. (1984). Interview by Fletcher Fischer. Videocassette. Vermont ETV.

Brault, Gerard J. (1986). *The French-Canadian Heritage in New England*. Hanover, NH: University Press of New England.

Doty, C. Steward, ed. (1985). *The First Franco-Americans: New England Life Histories from the Federal Writers' Project, 1938–1939*. Orono: University of Maine.

Hébert, Donna. Website. Available at http://www.dhebert.com/francotour2000.html. Includes lyrics to "The Shuttle."

Lane, Brigitte. (1990). *Franco-American Folk Traditions and Popular Culture in a Former Milltown: Aspects of Ethnic Urban Folklore and the Dynamics of Folklore Change in Lowell, Massachusetts*. New York: Garland Publishing.

Marcoux, Omer. (1980). *Fiddle Tunes of Omer Marcoux*. Transcribed by Sylvia Miskoe and Justine Paul. Bedford, NH: National Materials Development Center for French.

RECORDINGS

Brave Boys: New England Traditions in Folk Music. 1995. Notes by Sandy Paton. Recorded in the field by Sandy Paton, 1959–1977. New World Records 80239-2. CD.

Mademoiselle, voulez-vous danser? Franco-American Music from the New England Borderlands. 1999. Smithsonian Folkways SFW CD 40116. CD.

VIDEOS

Bonsoir mes amis/Good Night My Friends. 1990. Ben Guillemette and Lionel "Toots" Bouthot. 46 min. Portland, ME: Films by Huey.

New England Dances: Squares, Quadrilles, Step Dances. 1995. John M. Bishop. 29 min. Milton, MA: Media Generation. Distributed by Multicultural Media.

New England Fiddles. 1984. John M. Bishop. 48 min. Milton, MA: Media Generation. Distributed by Multicultural Media.

The Unbroken Circle: Vermont Music, Tradition and Change. 1985. Mark Greenberg. 59 min. Montpelier, VT: Multicultural Media.

MUSIC OF SOUTHERN MAINE
FRENCH CANADIAN COMMUNITIES

James Bau Graves

James Bau Graves is an ethnomusicologist with an abiding interest in the varieties of French music in North America. He is the artistic director of Portland Performing Arts in Portland, Maine.

Depending on who is doing the counting, between 16 and 40 percent of the population of the state of Maine is of French Canadian descent. The figures vary considerably because Euro-American ethnicity is not measured by census takers, generations of intermarriage have diluted the pool of individuals who self-identify with their Franco-American heritage, and "experts" engaged in data collection are usually compiling statistics in the service of some social or political cause. Regardless of the exact numbers, in the southern part of the state, Franco-Americans represent one of the largest (along with the Irish) ethnic populations.

French Canadians settled in the industrial mill towns of New England beginning about the middle of the nineteenth century. As recently as the 1950s, visitors to Lewiston or Biddeford, Maine, would have found themselves in a predominantly Francophone environment. This is no longer the case. Even in these French population centers,

English now prevails; young people no longer learn the language, and they enjoy few opportunities to experience traditional French culture outside the home. The music of southern Maine Franco-American communities combines elements received through their Quebecois heritage—a dance **repertoire** of **jigs**, **reels**, and **waltzes** usually performed on the **fiddle**, a body of folk songs and *chansons à répondre* or "answer songs"—with a variety of musical influences drawn from American popular culture, such as country and **bluegrass**. New England Franco-American communities form a substantial music culture, distinct from both Canadian and mainstream Northeastern music cultures, but closely linked to both.

HISTORY

The roots of French disenfranchisement stretch to the 1750s, when the dream of a French empire in the New World collapsed.

Already, following the signing of the Treaty of Utrecht in 1713, France had ceded Acadia, an area including Nova Scotia, New Brunswick, Prince Edward Island, and part of the contemporary state of Maine to England. In 1755, British troops forcibly expelled the majority of the French population from this vast region, expropriating homes and farms and transporting the Acadian population in dangerous, disease-ridden vessels to points south. *Le Grand Dérangement,* as the years of terror surrounding the removal came to be called, shattered the French presence in the Maritimes. Many of the refugees ultimately made their way to Louisiana, then a French colony, establishing the beginnings of "Cajun" culture in the bayou country west of New Orleans. Four decades later, Louisiana, too, was sold by the French.

Music of the Southern Maine and French Canadian Communities

Meanwhile, the British moved against the French stronghold at Quebec. In 1759, following a brief battle on the Plains of Abraham before the walls of Quebec City, French governance in Canada came to an end; English dominance was complete. But the Quebecois, then as today, refused to surrender their culture. Rather, they developed a cohesive identity in opposition to the British overlords, maintaining their language, traditions, and sense of themselves as a separate nationality. Roman Catholicism was central to the shaping of this identity, and among many Quebecois, the sustenance of French culture in America became a religiously sanctioned obligation. According to the ethos of *le survivance,* it was the sacred mission of the Quebecois to preserve Catholicism in America; the maintenance of the French language and customs became the means to that end. Surrounded by Anglophones, the French Canadians stuck to their farms, their churches, and their culture.

Beginning in the mid-1800s and increasing as the twentieth century dawned,

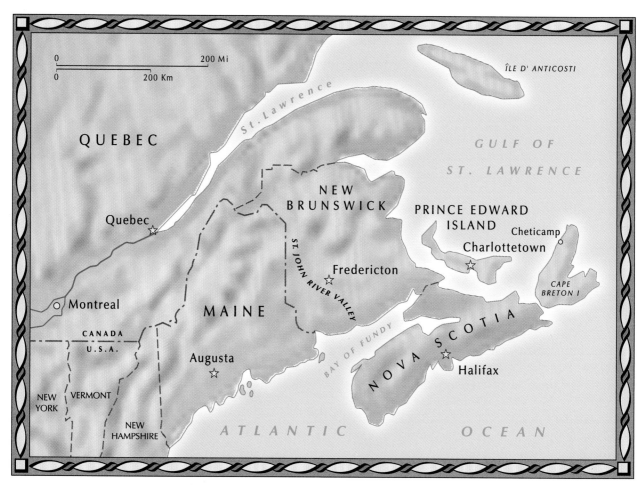

a great migration brought French Canadians to the new industrial centers of northern New England. Grinding poverty, large families dividing up ever smaller agricultural properties, and lack of economic opportunity drove over a million immigrants from their farms in Quebec to life in the textile sweatshops of Manchester and Nashua, New Hampshire; Lowell, Massachusetts; and Lewiston and Biddeford, Maine. In Canada, the great majority of the French population still lived on the land; in New England, they were urbanized from the start, working and living in close proximity to Irish, Italians, Eastern Europeans, and African Americans, as well as the Anglo-American factory owners.

Maine's new Franco-Americans came largely from Quebec, but subsequent immigration to southern Maine mill towns has also included many Acadians, descendants of the survivors of le Grand Dérangement who now reside mostly in northern Maine and New Brunswick, along the St. John River, and on Prince Edward Island.

In the United States, assimilation, rather than separation, was the goal of most immigrant communities. The dominant Anglo culture prohibited the use of French in schools and the workplace; students were taught "American" values, which excluded French language and culture. First-generation immigrants, and some of their children, still maintained strong ties to their families in Canada, but over the course of a century, Franco-Americans developed their own culture, with roots in Canada and continuous influences from Quebec, but with a separate aesthetic of its own. The segregation embodied by le survivance yielded to syntheses with mainstream American culture as generations of Franco-Americans grew up on **jazz** and country music as much as on traditional jigs and reels.

MUSIC

Maine Franco-Americans have their musical roots among the social and dance musics of

Quebec and the French Maritimes. This constitutes an amazingly rich musical heritage, which has itself been subjected to major Scottish and Irish incursions since 1680, when French immigration to North America virtually ceased. French Canadians brought with them the musical legacy of the Norman, Breton, and western French communities from which most of the American immigrants came, and they maintained this repertoire in an environment that remained comparatively isolated for the next two hundred years. Contemporary Quebecois is quite close to seventeenth-century continental French, having maintained linguistic structures that have long ago disappeared in the homeland.

Migration of French Canadians to Northern New England in the mid-1800s

Lucien Mathieu (fiddle), Nick Chamberlain (guitar), and Lgonie Roy (piano) playing at a home dance in the late 1940s.
Photograph courtesy Lucien Mathieu

DANCE TUNES

French Canadian dance music, as it was brought to Maine by immigrants, consists predominantly of reels, with some jigs and waltzes. Reels are the fast, **duple-meter**, sixteen-bar dance tunes that typify **Celtic music** on both sides of the Atlantic. Reels are played for most **quadrille** dancing, as well as for solo **step dancing** and a variety of social dance configurations.

Played less frequently for dancing, but still an important part of the repertoire, are jigs, which are the triple-time, 6/8, equivalent of reels. The gigue, a virtuosic solo step dance, may once have been performed to the tune of a gigue (jig), but most gigeurs today prefer to dance to reels. Waltzes, traditionally couple dances in 3/4 time, are also an important part of the dance repertoire. Also occasionally heard are hornpipes, syncopated tunes in 12/8, imports from the British Isles that have made their way into the French Canadian tune collection along with strathspeys, Scottish 9/8 tunes that are heard among musicians from Cape Breton Island, Nova Scotia, including a few French performers (mostly from Cheticamp, one of the only surviving French villages in Cape Breton).

This repertoire and the fiddle, its champion **instrument**, came to New England with the nineteenth- and early twentieth-century French Canadian immigrants. It arrived just in time for the onslaught of radio. The effect of the mass media on Franco-American musicians could not be overstated. In addition to social demands for assimilation to the American mainstream, musicians had to contend with a host of competing musical agendas from other ethnic groups, as well as the pervasive impact of commercial radio and recordings. Country music, in particular, resonated with Franco-American musicians, and soon the repertoire of jigs and reels expanded to include southern Appalachian breakdowns and fiddle show tunes. **Square dancing** with calls began to replace the traditional quadrilles.

Among the most pervasive influences on fiddling styles in Maine was the powerful radio presence of Don Messer, the Prince Edward Island fiddler and host who dominated Maritime music in the 1950s and 1960s, and whose repertoire is still a revered part of Downeast fiddling styles. ("Downeast" refers to coastal Maine and the maritime provinces of Canada.) Although Maine was on the outside edge of Messer's broadcast range, he was a favorite among many Franco-American homes. "We'd listen to Don Messer's show," recalls championship Maine fiddler Lucien

Mathieu. "We'd hear it for a few minutes, and then it would fade out."

SONGS

A similar assimilation affected Franco-American vocal music. The Quebecois song repertoire is enormous, including a wide variety of **ballads**, **chorus** songs, and many chansons à répondre, in which a soloist's lines, or final **phrases**, are repeated by whatever chorus is at hand. It has been suggested that this song **form** originated with the earliest voyageurs, explorers and fur trappers who used it to keep time for ten or twelve rowers in a single canoe, and who reputedly possessed songs with hundreds of verses, suitable for keeping a crew at work for hours. The wealth of this heritage, along with its conservatism in the face of foreign encroachment, is evident in the fact that contemporary musicologists have recorded over 20,000 French songs dating to the seventeenth century or earlier.

In the United States, as time passed, many of the old Quebecois **chansons** were forgotten, and much Franco-American musical culture became embedded in a handful of songs that were preserved in *La Bonne Chanson*, a 1937 publication that was widely distributed on both sides of the border. Organized by the Reverend Charles-Emile Gadbois, *La Bonne Chanson* popularized folk songs selected for their religious and patriotic inspirational value. Advanced by the Roman Catholic clergy as representative of the best of Quebecois musical culture, the book was actually a collection of bowdlerized versions of those songs that supported the church's position and teachings. Gone was the repertoire of risqué ballads, songs that pointed to the failings of priests, encouraged social mobility, or questioned authority. Simple and popular children's songs prevailed; songs that everybody knew. The energetic Father Gadbois organized dozens of festivals, concerts, and congresses, including one in Lewiston, Maine, in 1944, to advance his version of French Canadian heritage. His proselytizing yielded substantial fruits. As Franco-American memories lapsed, *La Bonne Chanson*, which was found in every church and many homes, became canonized as the major source for the music of the old country. Franco-Americans embraced and passed down this repertoire, often unaware of its actual source.

FRANCO-AMERICAN TRADITIONS TODAY

Traditional music of any form plays little part in the lives of most southern Maine Franco-Americans. Since the 1970s there has been a revival of the dance music tradition, due to the resurgence of country dancing (often among non–Franco-Americans) and the popularity of fiddle contests. At most New England fiddle contests today, competitors are required to demonstrate their abilities by playing a reel, a jig, and a waltz, thus sustaining the bulk of the traditional repertoire. The Maine French traditions have become inextricably bound with American country and bluegrass styles, and the most popular musicians—fiddlers Simon St. Pierre, Ben Guillemette, and Lucien Mathieu—have built their careers around these styles as much as through their mastery of the old repertoire. The music is played today for entertainment, at social functions and occasional weekend dances.

Beyond family settings, there are few opportunities for Franco-American singers to share their heritage with their community or the public. In recent years, folk festivals and public sector arts presenters have offered a new stage to the best Franco-American performers, and a handful of cultural activists who believe this legacy holds something of value are striving to revive traditional dance and music styles that have fallen into disuse.

DOCUMENTARY RECORDINGS AND FILMS

Regrettably, there are very few existing recordings that document the Franco-American musical traditions of southern Maine. A few suggestions are included in the Resources section, but they are difficult to find.

RESOURCES

RECORDINGS

Ben Guillemette. 1981. Rooster Records LP 107.

Fiddler from Maine. 1977. Simon St. Pierre. Revonah Records.

The Maine French Fiddlers: In Memere's Kitchen. 1997.

VIDEOS

Bonsoir mes amis/Good Night My Friends. 1990. Ben Guillemette and Lionel "Toots" Bouthot. 46 min. Portland, ME: Films by Huey.

CAJUN MUSIC

Barry Jean Ancelet

Barry Jean Ancelet is professor of French and folklore at the University of Louisiana at Lafayette. He is the author of numerous works on French Louisiana, including Cajun and Creole Music Makers *(University Press of Mississippi, 1999), and has contributed to several documentaries, among them* J'ai été au bal: The Cajun Music and Zydeco of Louisiana *(Brazos Films, 1989). Ancelet also produced volumes 1 and 2 of* Alan and John A. Lomax: The Classic Louisiana Recordings, 1934–1937 *for Rounder. In addition, he directs Lafayette's annual Cajun Music Festival and hosts the* Rendez-vous des Cadiens, *a weekly live radio show broadcast from the Liberty Theater in Eunice, Louisiana.*

In the seventeenth century, French settlers, primarily from the western provinces of Poitou, Vendée, and Brittany, came to what is now Nova Scotia to develop the colony then called *Acadie,* or Acadia. They and their descendants, who called themselves Acadians, prospered there despite the political turbulence caused by the ongoing conflict between the British and the French over colonial domination of North America.

In 1755 these French colonists were exiled from their homeland by the British, who had gained ultimate control of the colony in 1713. Many of the exiles eventually made their way to another French colony, Louisiana, hoping to reestablish their broken society there. By the time they began to arrive in 1765, Louisiana had been transferred to Spain, but these settlers, who were generally prosperous farmers, were welcomed. There they found themselves living among French Creoles (descendants of the first French settlers), Spanish Creoles,

African Creoles (descendants of the slaves brought to work on the plantations), and even a small pocket of German Creoles (mostly Alsatians). (The term "Creole" referred to those who were born in the colonies, as opposed to indigenous populations and immigrants from various parts of the Old World.) Later, especially after Louisiana became a state in 1812, Scottish, Irish, and other Anglo immigrants arrived, as well as Italians, Syrians, and Lebanese. Over the years, these cultural influences blended in a version of the melting pot to produce what is called Cajun culture today, with people whose last names might just as easily be delaHoussaye or duBoisblanc, Romero or Segura, Schexnayder or Hoffpauir, Johnson or McGee, even Boustany or Abboud, as well as Broussard, Arceneaux, or Guidry.

Today's Cajuns are found primarily in the prairies and along the bayous of southern Louisiana, bordered on the northeast by the Mississippi River, on the northwest by

the piney woods that stretch from central Avoyelles Parish to just north of Beaumont, Texas, and on the south by the Gulf of Mexico. *The Founding of New Acadia* (1987) and *From Acadian to Cajun* (1992) by Carl Brasseaux recount the history and evolution of the people called Cajuns. Edwards and Pitre's *Cajun Country* (1991) offers an overview of Cajun culture and **folklife**.

HISTORY

Cajun music is the child of the same parents that produced **jazz**, the **blues**, and rock and roll—that is, European and African influences meeting on the neutral territory of the American frontier—but this sibling sings in French. It is the result of the same blending process that produced all aspects of Cajun culture. From Native Americans, Cajun musicians learned wailing singing styles and new dance rhythms; from African Creoles, they learned the blues, percussion techniques, and improvisational singing; from Anglo-Americans, they learned new **fiddle** tunes to accompany Virginia **reels**, **square dances**, and **hoedowns**. The Spanish contributed a few tunes. Refugees and their slaves who arrived from Saint-Domingue (the colonial-era name for the island that is now split between Haiti and the Dominican

Republic) at the turn of the nineteenth century reinforced the new **rhythmic patterns** with a syncopated West Indian beat. Jewish German merchants began importing **diatonic accordions** (invented in Vienna in 1828) toward the end of the nineteenth century. The **guitar** arrived in Cajun country by way of African American blues musicians and Anglo-American country pickers.

The turn of the twentieth century was a formative period in the development of Louisiana French music. Some of its most influential musicians were the African Creoles, who brought a strong, rural blues element into Cajun music. Simultaneously, the French Cajuns influenced the development of the music of African Creoles, called **zydeco**, with lyrical themes and structured dance rhythms such as the **waltz**. Although fiddle music did not completely fade from the scene, the **accordion** rapidly became the mainstay of traditional dance bands. It was loud, durable, and relatively easy to play. Limited in the number of notes and keys it could produce, it simplified Cajun music; songs that could not be played on the accordion tended to fade from the active **repertoire**. Meanwhile, fiddlers were often relegated to playing a duet accompaniment or a simple percussive second line below the accordion's melodic lead.

By the mid-1930s, Cajuns were reluctantly, though inevitably, becoming Americanized. Their version of the French language was banned from schools throughout southern Louisiana as early as 1916 as the United States, caught in the nationalistic fervor that surrounded World War I, tried to homogenize its diverse ethnic and cultural elements. In southern Louisiana, speaking French was not only against the rules, it became increasingly unpopular as Cajuns attempted to escape the stigma attached to their culture and began imitating their Anglo-American neighbors, especially those from Texas, in earnest. These social and cultural changes were clearly reflected in the music recorded during the 1930s and 1940s. The slick programming on radio inadvertently forced the comparatively unpolished traditional sounds underground. The accor-

The Balfa Brothers' band was one of the first Cajun groups to perform at folk festivals around the world. Left to right: Wil and Dewey Balfa (fiddles), Nathan Abshire (accordion), Festival of American Folklife organizers Ethel Raim and Ralph Rinzler, and Rodney Balfa (guitar). *Photograph courtesy of the Smithsonian Institution*

dion faded from the scene, along with the popularity of the old-style music. As **western swing** and **bluegrass** sounds swept the country, **string bands** that imitated the music of Bob Wills and the Texas Playboys and copied Bill Monroe's "high, lonesome" sound sprouted across southern Louisiana. Freed from the limitations imposed by the accordion, stringbands readily absorbed various outside influences.

Dancers across southern Louisiana were also shocked in the mid-1930s to hear music that came not only from the bandstand but also from the opposite end of the dance hall through speakers powered by an automobile idling outside the building. The **electric guitar** was added to the standard instrumentation, and drums replaced the **triangle** as Cajuns continued to experiment with new sounds borrowed from their Anglo-American neighbors. As amplification made it unnecessary for fiddlers to bear down with the bow to be audible, many developed a lighter, lilting touch, moving away from the soulful styles of earlier days.

By the late 1940s, the music recorded by commercial producers signaled an unmistakable tendency toward Americanization. Yet an undercurrent of traditional music persisted. It resurfaced with the music of Iry Lejeune, who recorded, in 1948, "La

Valse du Pont d'Amour" in the emotionally intense, turn-of-the-century style and in French. The recording was an unexpected success, presaging a revival of the earlier style, and Iry Lejeune became a pivotal figure in Cajun music. Dance halls providing traditional Cajun music flourished, and musicians such as Lawrence Walker, Nathan Abshire, and Austin Pitre brought their accordions out of the closet and once again performed old-style Cajun music. Local recording companies began recording them. Cajun music made a comeback, though bearing the marks of Americanization.

As a result of the growth in popularity of rock and roll and country music in the late 1940s and 1950s, scholars and musicologists began to take an interest in Cajun music and sought to preserve it. Alan Lomax, a member of the Newport Folk Festival Foundation who had become interested in Louisiana French folk music during a field trip in 1934, encouraged the documentation and preservation of traditional Cajun music. He encouraged the Newport board to send fieldworkers Ralph Rinzler and Mike Seeger to southern Louisiana to identify a group of Cajun musicians to perform at the 1964 festival. Among those who were invited to the festival was Dewey Balfa, who was so moved by the overwhelming reception given the

Boozoo Chavis

Nick Spitzer is a folklorist widely known for his work on Creole cultures and cultural policy and as a public radio broadcaster. Artistic director and host of the "Folk Masters" concert series from 1990–1997 at Carnegie Hall and Wolf Trap, he also served as senior folklife specialist for the Smithsonian Institution and as the first Louisiana State Folklorist. In addition, Spitzer hosts American Routes, *the nationally broadcast weekly public radio music series. He is professor of cultural conservation and urban studies at the University of New Orleans. The following essay originally appeared in the program guide for the Folk Masters 1992 concert series, held April 1–May 8 at the Barns of Wolf Trap in Vienna, Virginia.*

Zydeco accordionist Boozo Chavis photographed in Lake Charles, LA, 1992.
Photograph by Jeff Tinsley, courtesy of the Smithsonian Institution.

For many Americans, the **accordion** is associated with the sounds of Lawrence Welk or music lessons of the worst type. Grateful Dead guitarist Jerry Garcia says he quickly abandoned the accordion his mother gave him for an **electric guitar** he found in a pawnshop window. Despite its clunky associations, the accordion has long been a versatile and culturally well-traveled **instrument**. In the last decade, the **squeezebox** has undergone a resurgence in national recognition if not outright popularity.

The **diatonic accordion** was invented in Berlin and Vienna in the 1820s and spread throughout Europe to America. It was introduced to French Louisiana in the 1880s, probably by German immigrants from the Midwest, and reinforced by Sears and Roebuck catalog sales. Similarly, in Texas, German contact with Mexicans seems to have brought the instrument into the music of the region. Throughout the country, the accordion became popular as a portable, inexpensive, loud, self-accompanying instrument. Sailors could take it to sea, as they had done with **concertinas** before it. The high cost of a parlor pump organ might not be worth it if an accordion could handle the **hymn** or Tin Pan Alley tune of the day.

In the hands of European immigrant communities across the Midwest—Polish, German, Russian, and Slovenian—the accordion brought the music of the old country to a new home. It was, in fact, from this multiethnic region that Lawrence Welk, of Russian-German background, arose to dominate national television in the 1950s and 1960s with the kind of assimilated, sanitized style that the next generation found so repugnant. But in communities isolated by rurality, language, and class, the accordion was still being played in a wide array of ethnic styles. Indeed, the instrument had suffused into so many different traditions, transforming them in the process, that one prominent folklorist was moved to call it a "Teutonic Plague."

In reality, the accordion has been a symbol of cultural resurgence for Louisiana Cajuns and Creoles since World War II, though it had been

old-time Cajun music there that he returned to Louisiana determined to bring home the message of acceptance. Working on a small scale at first with family and friends in his neighborhood around Mamou, Eunice, and Basile, he eventually obtained funding from the Newport Foundation and later the National Endowment for the Arts to organize

and present school programs and special concerts.

In 1974, Balfa and Rinzler convinced the Council for the Development of French in Louisiana (established in 1968) to host a special concert celebrating Cajun music and zydeco. The concert exceeded even the expectations of its enthusiastic organizers and

widely disfavored in the Depression era of the 1930s by Cajuns who wanted to play a more **fiddle**-based hillbilly style. Actually, anti-Cajun music partisans in Louisiana in the 1960s and 1970s continued to dismiss the instrument and the music as "nothing but chank-a-chank. . . ." All the while Louisiana black Creoles crowned their favorite accordion kings each Saturday night. Perhaps a final indication of the accordion's arrival, or new acceptance, was a conference sponsored by Texas Folklife Resources devoted to the squeezebox in the Lone Star State with an associated tour of Texas Accordion Kings.

Country **zydeco** music is played on the diatonic accordion. It is a "push-pull" instrument that produces a different note in each direction—like a **harmonica** with bellows and unlike the **chromatic-scale** piano accordion. Diatonic "button" accordions are usually not tuned to standard 440 (that is, tuned to produce an "A" that vibrates at 440 cycles per second) and have a lush set of overtones that compensate for their more limited scales.

Lousiana zydeco is a mix of Cajun tunes, African American **blues**, and Caribbean rhythms. Played on the accordion with a rhythm section of *frottoir* (**washboard**), **guitar**, and **bass**, zydeco includes fast, syncopated **two-steps**, **waltzes**, and blues. The music is performed wherever people gather to dance—at nightclubs, church halls, benefit dances, baseball games, and trail rides—from the Lafayette area in southern Louisiana to Texas, as well as in California cities with large migrant Creole communities. In the last several years, zydeco has become a "world music"—so worldly that some smart producers figured out that zydeco's appeal might sell a few more hamburgers or jeans as background music in TV commercials. The word "zydeco," in folk etymology, comes from the proverb *Les haricots sont pas salés,* meaning "no salt in the beans," referring to hard times when no salt-meat was available to flavor the beans. The term may also come from root

words for "I dance" and "I party" in several West African languages.

Urban zydeco musicians, following the lead of the late zydeco king Clifton Chenier, have largely left behind the more limited scales and choppy, acoustic sound of the diatonic button accordion. However, in the hands of a master like Wilson "Boozoo" Chavis, the possibilities of the small squeezebox become obvious. Chavis actually made commercial zydeco records before Chenier. In 1954 he had a big regional hit with "Papier dans ma soulier" ("Paper in My Shoe"). However, he abandoned a music career, feeling that the Louisiana record companies were crooked. For the next three decades he trained racehorses and raised a family.

In 1984 Boozoo went public with his music again in a startling appearance at the newly founded Southwest Louisiana Zydeco Festival. He's been in demand ever since, playing a blend of old-time zydeco and southern Louisiana blues. When Boozoo returned to playing music, he did so with another regional hit about his homeplace near Lake Charles called "Dog Hill." He has followed that with a variety of locally released dance records as well as bawdy songs like "Deacon John." At a recent Zydeco Festival held in a remote soybean field, as he strutted about the grounds in his ubiquitous Stetson cowboy hat getting praise from the men and kisses from the ladies, Boozoo said, "I play with all my heart and soul to give 'em what they want. I try to give them the tradition. All we old zydeco players might be dead and gone, but we always gonna have a young one gonna come up with it."

Editor's note: Wilson "Boozoo" Chavis died on May 12, 2001, in Austin, Texas, of complications following a heart attack. Since resuming his music career in the mid-1980s, he had become an inspiration to younger artists who helped launch the rebirth of zydeco.

Nick Spitzer

became an annual event celebrating the Cajun music and zydeco renaissance. Since then, Cajun music and zydeco have won airtime on local radio, and many other festivals and concerts have been developed. New generations of young musicians have produced an explosion of new recordings and styles, along with Grammy nominations and

tours throughout the United States and other countries. These young musicians do not simply imitate older traditions; instead, they actively create within the tradition, experimenting with new styles, instrumentation, and original composition. Purists who would resist these changes ignore the fact that Cajun music is a living tradition and a

hybrid; **improvisation** and innovation have always characterized it. The blending and cultural fusion at the heart of the development of Cajun culture continue to be essential to its music.

MUSIC

Cajun music is essentially dance music with lyrics, the result of a merger of the highly repetitive instrumental dance music tradition and the unaccompanied song tradition. The music is played traditionally for house dances (called *fais dodos,* from the French baby talk for *faire dormir,* or "to put to sleep," because babies often slept while their parents danced into the night), weekend public dances, special events such as weddings, and street dances at local festivals. The dancing is in couples. These events offer opportunities for courtship as well as more general socialization.

In the past, Cajun music supported numerous active dance styles, such as *cotilliennes* (**cotillions**), varsoviennes, **polkas**, **mazurkas**, **schottisches**, reels, and **jigs**, but now one finds mostly waltzes, **two-steps**, and **swing** dances. Cajun singing is characterized by high-pitched vocals without **vibrato**. In addition to carrying through the dance halls in the days before electrical amplification, this singing style became part of the aesthetic of Cajun music, influenced by the French *complainte* (a mournful ballad) and the African American blues singing styles. A mournful, emotionally intense sound is achieved by such techniques as holding **pitch** on a single syllable for several beats, often singing as high, or nearly as high, as one can. Cajun singers traditionally have sung solo, though the unaccompanied tradition has included group singing.

The culture continues to evolve and has produced an emerging **harmony** tradition, clearly influenced by the close harmony style of **old-time music**. Because Cajun music almost always serves as dance music, its rhythmic patterns are regular and hard-driving, most often in 3/4, 2/4, 4/4, or 6/8 time. In the early twentieth century, especially be-

See glossary for definition of boldfaced terms

tween 1928 and 1938, the style was looser, described by musicians as "jumpy."

Beginning with the revival that followed World War II, there was a shift in style toward a smoother, tighter sound, as developed by such innovators as Nathan Abshire, Iry Lejeune, Lawrence Walker, and Aldus Roger. Bandleaders are now admired for the steadiness and smoothness of the beat. Improvisation can lead to lines of unequal length, but only rarely. There can be considerable **syncopation** from African Creole influence, but it is always framed by the regular meters.

SONGS

Cajun song lyrics are generally about love lost, wayward husbands, unfaithful wives, broken families, abandonment, betrayal, and loneliness. Until the recent compositions by the current, culturally active generation of young musicians, there were no songs in the tradition that referred directly to the 1755 exile. Yet most songs are indirectly about its results. Certain themes seem to be resilient, including frustrated courtship, a forlorn lover's unrequited love (for example, "Jolie Blonde"), a prisoner's lament and request for salvation, a contrite unfaithful lover's appeal for reconciliation, or a spurned lover's rejection of reconciliation. These are not inconsistent with the themes of the older unaccompanied tradition. Such songs were often sung at wedding dances to remind the couple of what was possible if they were not careful. There are few happy songs in Cajun music; even lively sounding two-steps can be about a sinner's condemnation or a lover's frustration, such as "Attrape-moi mon chapeau" ("Get Me My Hat"), which describes a young man's hurried departure from his girlfriend's house because her father is furious about the courtship.

Cajun song lyrics must function within the framework of dance music. Consequently, they tend to be short, impressionistic, and intense so that they might capture the attention of the dancers, even if briefly. Until the era of commercial recordings, song lyrics were usually improvised around a

theme or idea attached to a song. Recordings created the notion of fixed texts, though many singers continue to improvise lyrics even to well-known songs. The ability to create spontaneous lyrics that are appropriate to the theme of the song is admired, though contemporary composers lament this practice, which alters or ignores their poetry.

TUNES

Tunes are typically preserved by the traditional process, that is, handing down from one generation to the next by observation and imitation, without formal instruction. With rare exception, Cajun musicians do not read music. Even those who may have learned to do so in a high school band program do not play Cajun music by sight. Early instrumental tunes came to Cajun country in the collective memory of the settlers. They were preserved during the difficult early years when **instruments** were not available, such as during early colonization in Acadia, during the exile and subsequent wandering, and during the reestablishment in Louisiana, by humming, called *musique de bouche,* or whistling.

When the Cajuns did begin to acquire instruments, they were not always the same instruments their ancestors had known. But the collective memory and cultural esthetics were strong, so a fiddle was sometimes pressed into service to sound like a biniou or a cabrette (types of bagpipes) common to western French instrumental tradition, producing distinctive bowing techniques and a self-accompanying drone that became an integral part of the Cajun fiddling style.

The tunes of Cajun music are the result of the blending of influences found in southern Louisiana. Some are French in origin, some are clearly borrowed from other traditions. The accordion arrived in Louisiana in the middle to late nineteenth century and immediately became popular, for a few simple reasons: It was durable, it was loud, and it was relatively easy to play, based on the **diatonic scale**. Percussion was improvised with *cuillers* (spoons), *petis fers* (triangles), and *frottoirs* (**washboards**). Guitars were added around the turn of the twentieth century as harmonic percussion accompaniment to the lead accordions and fiddles. Performers experimented with other instruments, including pianos, dobros, **banjos**, **mandolins**, horns, basses, and **trap** drums, in the period that accompanied the electrification and amplification of the music during the 1930s and 1940s.

There has been a considerable amount of original composition among dance band musicians, some influenced by contemporary trends such as western swing, country, and early rock and roll. Cajun music still produces a number of original songs each year. The ones that are felt to be culturally appropriate become part of the traditional repertoire performed by the many dance bands that are active in the region. Those that are not fade into disuse.

MUSIC AND SOCIETY

Cajun music is considered a vital expression of Cajun culture. Historical documents from as early as the exile refer to the Cajuns' love of music and dancing. Yet some singers and musicians remain on the artistic fringe of society; they are admired in the dance halls, though not always outside. Cajun music seems to have a cathartic effect on its fans. Cajuns typically love sad two-steps and sadder waltzes. Lots of Cajuns sing and play informally at private parties and **jam sessions**. Music is an integral part of Cajun life. Many Cajuns whistle, hum, and sing their music in the bathtub or the car, while working or playing.

Much of Cajun social life has been organized around music. Weekly neighborhood house dances were the principal occasion for socialization and courtship in the nineteenth and early twentieth centuries. The people who attended these by-invitation-only events were the same ones at the local butchery co-ops (called *boucheries*) or Mardi Gras celebrations. Children learned to dance at group figure dance parties called *danses rondes.* In the 1930s, public dance halls began to open. The dance halls attracted peo-

ple from different neighborhoods and consequently were sometimes the site of interregional conflicts. Socialization eventually began to occur on a broader level as improved transportation and consolidated school and church districts reinforced each other to widen and blur the lines of allegiance. Some of these became periodically popular as meccas for dancers and musicians.

Because the dance halls typically sold alcohol, children were generally excluded from hearing Cajun music. These children were understandably attracted to music they could hear on the radio, such as country and rock and roll. Cajun music was also featured at local festivals, weddings, and private parties, providing limited access to the younger generation. More recently, restaurants in southern Louisiana have begun featuring Cajun music in a setting where the whole family can attend. Cajun music is featured by local radio stations on a limited basis, usually on Saturdays and Sundays, and by one local television station in the early morning. Festivals have also been organized to celebrate the music itself. Many children have become interested in Cajun music again due to these efforts and those of musicians, such as Dewey Balfa, who began to organize presentations in the schools in the 1980s.

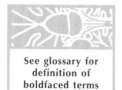

See glossary for definition of boldfaced terms

DOCUMENTARY RECORDINGS AND FILMS

There are literally hundreds of commercially available recordings of Cajun music, but a few good anthologies condense the historically important material quite well. Arhoolie's Old Timey label covers the early periods of Cajun music, as well as the major developments in Cajun music from its first recordings in 1928 through the 1950s, in the *Louisiana Cajun Music* series. *Cajun and Creole Music: The Lomax Recordings* features the field recordings of John and Alan Lomax as well as a twenty-eight-page booklet of transcriptions, translations, and notes to the songs. The two volumes of *Cajun French Music from the Southwest Prairies* contain the

recordings of then Newport Folk Festival fieldworker Ralph Rinzler between 1964 and 1967. *J'étais au bal: Music from French Louisiana*, recorded by Ron and Fay Stanford in the early 1970s, was issued with an accompanying booklet of information on the culture and the music and remains one of the best and tightest anthologies of Cajun music and zydeco ever compiled. *Cajun Music and Zydeco* and *More Cajun Music and Zydeco* present a broad collection of significant historical and contemporary recordings. The documentary film *J'ai été au bal* presents the history and development of both Cajun music and zydeco from their origins in unaccompanied tradition through the contemporary renaissance.

BIBLIOGRAPHY

Ancelet, Barry Jean. (1989). *Cajun Music: Origins and Development.* Lafayette: University of Southwestern Louisiana Center for Louisiana Studies.

Ancelet, Barry Jean, and Morgan, Elemore, Jr. (1999). *Cajun and Creole Music Makers.* Jackson: University Press of Mississippi. Originally published in 1984 as *The Makers of Cajun Music,* Austin: University of Texas Press.

Ancelet, Barry Jean; Edwards, Jay; and Pitre, Glen. (1991). *Cajun Country.* Folklife in the South Series. Jackson: University Press of Mississippi.

Brasseaux, Carl. (1987). *The Founding of New Acadia.* Baton Rouge: Louisiana State University Press.

———. (1992). *From Acadian to Cajun.* Jackson: University Press of Mississippi.

Broven, John. (1983). *South to Louisiana: The Music of the Cajun Bayous.* Gretna, LA: Pelican Press.

Gould, Philip. (1992). *Cajun Music and Zydeco.* Baton Rouge: Louisiana State University Press.

Savoy, Ann Allen. (1985). *Cajun Music: A Reflection of a People.* Eunice, LA: Bluebird Press.

Whitfield, Irene Thérèse. (1969). *Louisiana French Folk Songs.* New York: Dover.

RECORDINGS

Cajun and Creole Music: The Lomax Recordings. 1934. Swallow 8003-2.

Louisiana Cajun French Music from the Southwest Prairies. 1989. Recorded 1964–1967. Two volumes. Rounder 6001, 6002.

Cajun Music and Zydeco. 1992. Rounder 11572.

J'étais au bal: Music from French Louisiana. 1974. Swallow 6020.

Louisiana Cajun Music. 1971. Five volumes. Old Timey OT 108-111, 114.

More Cajun Music and Zydeco. 1995. Rounder 11573.

VIDEOS

J'ai été au bal: The Cajun Music and Zydeco of Louisiana. 1989. Chris Strachwitz and Les Blank. 84 min. Brazos Films.

TRADITIONAL MUSIC OF THE CALABRIAN (SOUTHERN ITALIAN) IMMIGRANT COMMUNITIES IN THE UNITED STATES

Rebecca S. Miller

*An ethnomusicologist and public-sector folklorist, Rebecca S. Miller has documented and presented the traditional arts of a number of immigrant and refugee communities throughout the United States since 1982. Her work has culminated in publications, recordings, festivals, and radio and video documentaries. Miller spent 1996–1997 doing dissertation research on traditional music and cultural representation in Carriacou, Grenada, on a Fulbright fellowship. She received her doctorate in music (**ethnomusicology**) from Brown University in 2000.*

The traditional music of Calabria, Italy, is actively preserved and performed by several communities of immigrant Calabrians in the United States. The largest Calabrian communities are located in Westerly, Rhode Island, and in Belleville, New Jersey, with additional populations in Brooklyn and Buffalo, New York.

Their native land, Calabria, is located in the southernmost portion of Italy (Sicily is just off Calabria's west coast). A rugged, mountainous region, Calabria has been historically isolated, a circumstance that has helped preserve a body of extraordinary music, vocal, and dance styles. The population of Calabria in general has suffered over the years from grinding poverty, yet Calabrian expressive culture is rich with diversity, nuance, and intensity. Formerly agricultural workers and laborers in Calabria, the immigrants in the Westerly, Rhode Island, community work at the local Guild guitar factory, for the defense industry plants in nearby Groton, Connecticut, and, like Calabrians elsewhere in the United States, as tradespeople, steelworkers, and small business owners, among other occupations.

The significant musical expressions of Calabrian immigrants include folk and traditional music and song rarely heard in the larger Italian American communities in the United States. Calabrian musical **repertoire** includes traditional dance music played on a number of **instruments**, unaccompanied choral singing, and a wide variety of song **genres**.

HISTORY

The Calabrian culture emanates from an impoverished region in southern Italy. Chronic unemployment and illiteracy, coupled with overall neglect on the part of the national government, have historically forced a high level of migration to the United States and Canada beginning in the middle to late nineteenth century. Since the early decades of

the twentieth century, the history of southern Italians in general, and Calabrians specifically, is marked by back-and-forth migration between Italy and the United States. Early Italian immigrants established communities in upstate New York, Brooklyn, New Jersey, and Rhode Island. The early years of the recording industry took advantage of this growing market along with the changing aesthetic tastes of the newly arrived Italians. Like many other immigrants in the early years of the twentieth century, the newly arrived Italian Americans largely ignored the folk cultural expressions of their native land. Instead, they listened to the steady stream of newly recorded popular Italian music, such as **mandolin** orchestras and Neapolitan (that is, originating in Naples) songs.

The years following World War II saw a surge of Italian immigration to the United States. The new arrivals from Calabria joined their extended families and friends in the already established Calabrian communities. Unlike earlier immigrants, some folk traditions were retained, including folk **foodways** and, to a certain extent, the Calabrian dialect.

In the 1960s and 1970s, another surge of Calabrian immigrants came to the United States, among them many of the traditional musicians who play Calabrian folk music today. These musicians found only the odd opportunity to perform folk music for family and friends on special occasions; outside of their community, they had virtually no visibility.

By the late 1970s, anthropologists such as Anna L. Chairetakis, along with folk arts presenting organizations, notably the Center for Traditional Music and Dance (formerly the Ethnic Folk Arts Center in New York City), began organizing concerts and later, beginning in 1983, regional tours of southern Italian musicians, singers, and dancers. These events included many of the Calabrian musicians from Westerly, Rhode Island, and Belleville, New Jersey, and occasionally featured visiting musicians and singers from various regions of Italy. These projects were possible thanks to a growing overall interest in and funding for the folk

Calabrian immigrant woman and daughter originally from Catanzaro, Italy, who immigrated to Minnesota in the 1920s, when this photo was taken. *Photograph © Minnesota Historical Society/CORBIS*

and traditional arts by state and federal arts councils, including the National Endowment for the Arts. The immigrant Calabrians have performed for Italian American audiences throughout the northeastern United States since then and have played for large, general audiences at such venues as the Smithsonian Festival of American Folklife in Washington, D.C.; ArtPark in Lewiston, New York; at universities; and in concerts presented by local and state arts councils, including the New York State Council on the Arts. Apart from community performances, this music can be heard today in concerts and at folk festivals—events typically sponsored by arts presenting organizations and Italian American cultural groups.

That Calabrian music has been presented to the general public in such major venues has brought enormous pride to the musicians. Many Italian Americans, like their counterparts in Italy, are often conflicted over traditional Italian music because it is associated with the lower class, one historically steeped in poverty. Typically, when Italian Americans become interested in their cultural heritage, they gravitate toward Italian classical music and opera or listen to Italian pop music. Thus, the recent public attention enjoyed by Calabrian folk musicians

(and other immigrant musicians from southern Italy) has served to reintroduce this folk music to diverse Italian American communities, foster appreciation for these folk artists and the rarely heard styles, and affirm the importance of traditional culture to its practitioners and audience.

MUSIC

Calabrian instrumental music is an oral tradition and is passed down from older to younger players through listening and imitation. The music is performed on a number of folk instruments, including the *fischiettu* (cane flute), *zampogna* (**bagpipes**), **tambourine**, *coupa coupa* (friction drum), and **Jew's harp**. Other instruments include the *organetto* (**button accordion**), which is the most modern of the instruments; the **concertina**; the *triccaballacche,* a percussion instrument of Neapolitan origin, consisting of three prongs with

The Calabria Region of Southern Italy

small metal **cymbals** attached to its two movable hammers; and the *chitarra battente,* a sixteenth-century precursor to the modern **guitar**, which is used for both harmonic and percussive accompaniment.

Among the practitioners of this music are Belleville, New Jersey, residents Giuseppe DeFranco, a master of the organetto and other instruments; his wife, Raffaela DeFranco, an outstanding singer, tambourine player, and dancer; and their son, Faust DeFranco, who plays the triccaballacche and other instruments. In Westerly, Rhode Island, Francesco DeCaro is one of the leading exponents of the chitarra battente; his sons, Angelo and Giuseppe, are accomplished organetto players. Also in Westerly, Antonio DeGiacomo is a masterful player of the tambourine and Salvatore Rizzuto is a virtuoso player of the fischiettu.

The music is typically played to accompany social dancing, including **tarantellas,**

polkas, **waltzes**, and other styles. The antiquity of many of the musical instruments is echoed in the form of some of the dances. As Alan Lomax points out, "The *tarantella* [is] . . . still performed as if the dancers had stepped straight out of some Roman or Etruscan mural" (Lomax 1984). Other genres of Calabrian folk music include music to accompany singing and "shepherd's music," which is played primarily on the cane flute and organetto. This music, according to Westerly musician Angelo DeCaro, was played in Calabria to keep boredom at bay while shepherds watched their livestock in the fields.

The Calabrian vocal repertoire includes Easter carols, *cantastorie* (**ballads**), lullabies, ritual songs, love songs, and serenades. Texts reflect a unified and cultivated folk poetry tradition. In general, the vocal style is distinguished from that of northern Italy by its long **phrases**, drawn out cadences, and an often mournful quality. Both men and women generally sing in a highly resonant and high-pitched style. To achieve this delivery, performers often cup their hand around their ear as they sing in order to heighten the resonance.

The *villanella* is a type of unaccompanied choral singing and is performed by four or five participants, both men and women, who stand in a circle or near-circle. Two leaders alternate loudly sung, solo phrases, and the other singers join in on subsequent phrases in a somewhat rough unison, culminating in ragged, descending cadences. A highly characteristic **harmony** in this type of singing is the **drone** and is provided by one of the leaders or a **chorus** member. Particularly important to the style is the *lu iettu,* or high drone part, which is sung by a female member of the ensemble (see *Calabria bella, dove t'hai lasciate* 1979). In Calabria, agricultural workers sang villanella to pass the time as they toiled in the olive, grape, and citrus orchards. In addition, performances of this music traditionally took place during holidays, particularly at Easter, and at social occasions. Old Mediterranean in style, this choral genre is rarely heard today apart from some regions

in Calabria. The villanella is sung in the United States by members of the Westerly, Rhode Island, Calabrian immigrant community, including Antonio DeGiacomo, Carmine Ferraro, Angelo and Bambina Luzzi, and Assunta Luzzi.

Within Calabrian immigrant communities in the United States, traditional music and song are sometimes heard along with more popular Italian music at *fèste,* or festivals, which are sponsored by Italian cultural and sports clubs, political clubs, and Italian American professional organizations. Practitioners of folk music often perform at life cycle events, such as holiday celebrations (Easter, in particular), weddings, christenings, and engagement and anniversary parties. Notes Calabrian vocalist and guitarist Carmine Ferraro, "Sometimes we [are] together and we sing together, and it gives you a picture, a memory, of being young, of being home." (Interview with author, 6 December 1987)

BIBLIOGRAPHY

Chairetakis, Anna L. (1984). "Notes on the Italian Music Tour." In *Musica Popolare* [program booklet]. New York: Center for Traditional Music and Dance.

———. (1986). "Southern Italian Folk Music in America and Its Connections with Italy." In program booklet for Scampagnata Festival, Artpark, Lewiston, NY.

Lomax, Alan. (1984). "Musica Popolare." In program booklet for Second Annual Concert Tour. New York: Center for Traditional Music and Dance.

Schlesinger, Michael. (1988). "Italian Music in New York." *New York Folklore* XIV(3–4):129–138.

RECORDINGS

Calabria bella, dove t'hai lasciate? 1979. Smithsonian Folkways LP FES-34042.

Carmine Ferraro: Calabrian Traditional Singer. 1990. One program in the documentary public radio series "Old Traditions—New Sounds," produced and written by Rebecca S. Miller. New York: World Music Institute. Available for listening at the World Music Archives, Wesleyan University, Middletown, CT.

Chesta e la voci ca canuscite. 1986. Global Village Music GVM 675 (LP) and C675 (audiocassette).

Rimpianto: Italian Music in America, 1915–1929. 1986. Global Village Music C602P. Audiocassette.

Southern Italy and the Islands. 1957. Volume 16 of Columbia World Library of Folk and Primitive Music LP series. Columbia Masterworks KL 5173.

ITALIAN FOLK MUSIC IN NEW YORK AND NEW JERSEY

Anna Chairetakis

Anna Chairetakis is an anthropologist who has researched and written about society and culture in southern Italy and among Italian immigrants in the United States. In 1979, she produced two albums of Italian folk music recorded in New York, New Jersey, and Rhode Island for Folkways: In Mezz'una Strada Trovai una Pianta di Rosa *(FES 34041) and* Calabria Bella, Dove T'hai Lasciate? *(FES 34042). The documentation that accompanies those albums serves as the basis for this essay.*

The poet John Keats once wrote that the most beautiful melodies are the melodies unheard. Keats's words have a special significance when one thinks of the seldom heard and barely known *musica popolare* of Italy. Italian folk music deserves the interest and appreciation of a larger audience—and not least of Italian Americans—as it has lived too long in the shadows of Italian classical opera and Neapolitan and commercial songs. Classical composers such as Corelli, Mozart, Meyerbeer, Tchaikovsky, Scarlatti, Verdi, and Vivaldi, among others, admired Italian folk music and made liberal use of its melodies in their operas and concertos.

Yet in the United States today, the music of the Italian working people is ignored or belittled by many members of the Italian community itself—not so much because of its association with poverty, but because of the insidious and pervasive form of class prejudice that the Italian peasant and worker, especially of the south, have for centuries experienced, and still encounter. However, a new and enlightened appraisal will reveal that Italian folk music can hold its own with the best European and American music of its genre. It is certainly the most genuine musical expression of the Italians who immigrated to these shores.

The presence of a grassroots popular music in the Italian American community is one of its better-kept secrets. When aired publicly, the genuine village traditions seem to touch upon sensitive chords. Possibly, the power of the simple folk song clashes with the modernizing spirit that many wish to emphasize. Perhaps, too, this music evokes double-edged memories of the past. Above all, Italian folk music is extremely varied, locally and regionally. It is a mosaic work patterned by the flux of history over 2,000 years, by a variegated geography that in some places welcomes and nurtures, in others isolates or protects, and in yet others is harsh and exacting; it is the creation of a

people who have endured, fought off, and here and there blossomed with the passage of an amazing parade of civilizations, kingdoms, and migrations.

The music and dance, as well as the dialect and custom, of each Italian locale bear the stamp of a unique history. Overarching local and regional patterns are marked stylistic distinctions between the chorus-singing, harmonizing north (musically part of East-Central Europe) and the solo-singing, lyrical south (belonging to the Mediterranean and the Orient). Along the shorelines, in the agricultural expanses of Sicily, Puglia, and Campania, in Umbria and Tuscany, were fostered the large, complex forms of old empires and modern civilizations, while the mountains and remote interior villages of both north and south harbored the archaic musical traditions of Old Europe. Thus, one might say that there is no "national" folk music, one that can with justice represent either the whole of Italy or any Italian American community—for these, too, are mosaics of town or village enclaves. It may be this very lack of a national style that has preserved the genuine flavor of local music where it is still be be found.

Most Italian American folk music performers in the New York/New Jersey came of age in an essentially preindustrial agrarian economy that did not undergo a transformation until the early 1960s or thereabouts. Many of them worked in the cities of northern Italy and Germany before coming to the United States, leaving their families for months or years at a time. They had been muleteers, shepherds, agricultural workers, vendors, farmers, and artisans; in America they are industrial workers and own cars, homes, and businesses.

Yet in working-class Italian neighborhoods the old social relationships and dependencies between households constitute an important backdrop of security. Despite the hardships of their previous life, Italian immigrants speak fondly of Italy, giving the impression that it was a great personal sacrifice for them to have left it. Many say they miss the intimacy, sociability, and pretelevision pastimes of village and neighbor-

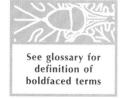

See glossary for definition of boldfaced terms

hood life—the storytelling, the gatherings, the festivities, the songs and dances. These are things some writers have been inclined to call "simple" pleasures, but they are not so simple; rather, they are more fully participatory, more effervescent, and more deeply rewarding than many amusements of contemporary life. At any rate, the relevance of contemporary American culture to everyone it embraces is questionable.

MUSIC FROM CALABRIA

Calabria is the toe of Italy, stretching out toward Sicily to the south. Its name derives from the Greek for "fine sea breeze." The Roman emperor Augustus called it Brutium after the great Roman family. At one time its shores were inhabited by ancient Greeks, who built the cities of Locri, Croton (home of Pythagoras), Rheghion, and Sybaris. The Romans wrested Magna Graecia from the Greeks and from Hannibal, let its cities wane, and converted the countryside into a livestock- and timber-producing dependency, provisioning Rome and the imperial armies. Subsequently, Calabria saw a sucession of masters—Byzantines, Swabians, the Normans, Angevins, Aragonese, and Bourbons—who built their castles and churches in the hills and along the coasts, introduced their languages and customs, and extracted what they could from their fiefdoms.

Long an exploited and neglected region, Calabria saw large-scale exportation of labor to the industrial north and abroad during the twentieth century. Former herdsmen and agricultural laborers say that at home they ate meat once a month at best, often only once or twice a year, when a family would kill its single pig. One woman tells of working a twelve-hour day in the olive groves and bean fields for a hundred lire (about twenty-five cents) and coming home to find nothing to eat but a few dried figs. Immigrant villagers do not miss these privations, but they seem to miss the sociability of traditional community life, which was given its continuity and spirit by local folkways and music—a life that is being choked and changed by mass entertainment. "I was

a muleteer," says Annunziato Chimenti, "but when they made the roads, my profession was finished, and I came to America. But there [in Italy] we loved each other; there was more affection. . . ." Even so, here and there in American cities, an extended family, a few friends, a pocket of immigrants from some small hamlet, have managed to make an interesting marriage between progress and a folk sociality.

Performers whose roots lie in the town of Acri and its satellite hamlets, Serricella, Cuta, and San Martino (in Cosenza province), now reside in communities in Brooklyn, New York, New Jersey, and Rhode Island that are close knit and in frequent touch with one another. Once the site of an inland outpost of Sybaris, Acri sits on the olive-drab, scrub- and chestnut-covered foothills of the Sila Greca and is surrounded by Balkan "islands"—villages settled in the sixteenth century by Albanians avoiding Turkish Moslem rule. The Piedmontese Waldensians (a Reformation Protestant sect) once had a stronghold in the vicinity, and the nineteenth-century proto-revolutionary Carbonarist brotherhood flourished in the province. The Capuchin monks, established in Acri for centuries, are portrayed in local fairy tales as wheedling lechers, though one of them, Beato Angelo, is revered as a saint. Local history has it that a century ago several hated landowners were burned in the public square by brigands, one of whom sopped up the dripping human fat with a piece of *pitta* bread. Residents of Acri can point out the iron spikes on an old communal building at the top of their town, which once impaled the heads of three of these bandits.

Those who come from the interior of Calabria speak of themselves as an abandoned people, betrayed by history. Rural folk say they are like the goats who have grown up wild in nature. Their answer has been to endure, to embrace life's pleasures, and to fight for bread and family with the stubborn individuality that has won the Calabrian the epithet of *capatuosto* (hard head), or, in the words of one adage, *cuore di ferro, braccia di acciaio*—"heart of iron, arm of steel."

Many of the underlying currents of traditional Calabrian life—which are essentially those of all of southern Italy—manifest themselves in the driving energy of **tarantellas** and **polkas**, in the irony and passionate directness of song lyrics, in the lingering melancholy of serenades, and in the prancing of the men and the demure circling of the women in dance. Calabrian women seem to be masters of rhyme and riddle; rhyme and counterrhyme spring forth for every occasion. At a Calabrian table, the hostess may lift her glass with these words:

> *Io ti dono questo fiore*
> *con affetto e con amore;*
> *e voi chi lo prendete*
> *che risposta mi darete?*

> I give you this flower
> with affection and with love.
> And you who take it,
> what reply will you give me?

And rising gracefully to the occasion, the knowing guest will reply:

> *L'amore è bello,*
> *il fiore è aggradito;*
> *io ti ringrazio*
> *con che mi hai favorito.*

> The love is fair
> the flower is pleasing;
> I thank you
> With that with which you have favored me [the wine].

The *villanella* is a type of three- to four-part song that was once a well-known contemporary of the madrigal. In Acri, it is a serenade delivered in **heterophonic chorus** by a mixed group of four or five singers who stand in a tight semicircle with their arms about each other. (In a mixed group, such proximity demands that the singers be related; an unrelated woman would stand slightly apart.) The **leader** throws his head back and delivers the first line, and the others sing the choral parts into one another's faces, producing the vibrating effect on the sound waves called beating. Normally, there are two alternating leaders in the Calabrian

chorus: One makes the primary statement (*ietta,* "throws out"), and the other "echoes" it (*revote,* "returns it"), repeating the line in part. **Songleaders** and chorus produce the **drone harmony** (*accuordo*). The high drone voice (*squillo* or *caiauto*) is usually sung by a woman. The songs can be reduced to an eight-line endecasyllabic poem (the **form** of the *strambotto*), which is how they were formerly transcribed by collectors. However, as Roberto De Simone points out, exclusive focus on the text has fostered the now questionable notion of a purely cultivated origin for these songs; it is of equal interest, for instance, to understand how the singers themselves divide up their roles, create repetition, and so on.

IN THE NEW WORLD

In homes and small clubs in Brooklyn, the Bronx, New Jersey, and elsewhere, there are people who prefer their own entertainment to television, dinner dances, or even the street festivals in which, in many cases, they have ceased to play a significant part.

- On Flatbush Avenue in Brooklyn, a farmer turned butcher serenades cuts of meat as he works in the freezer with long, eloquent **ballads** from his native Lucania.
- In Newark a factory worker treasures his **bagpipe**, though he has no oboist to accompany him, and few call for his services. So that the heat of his apartment will not crack and dry it, he makes the bag for his pipes out of a flowered material lined with rubber, instead of the usual goatskin.
- An ex-shepherd from central Sicily works in a Brooklyn factory. He still fashions and plays the Greek cane flute as his ancestors did. Calogero Cascio, a Sicilian himself, has located singers who are willing to perform the **work songs** that are Sicily's oldest

See glossary for definition of boldfaced terms

heritage in folksong—tuna fishermen's **shanties**, vendors' cries, threshing invocations, and Arabic-style shepherds' serenades.

In Brooklyn there is a large settlement of northern Italians from the Val di Non, a valley in the high Alpine slopes bordering the Tyrol. Once farmers, woodsmen, and artisans, they have gone into the construction trades and the professions in this country and remain a close-knit community through their Brooklyn social club, where they gather to eat, drink, play cards, and sing their mountain songs in the improvised four-part harmony that comes so easily to them. In keeping with the ancient democratic spirit of their villages, they deliberate carefully on all matters of group concern. At my first meeting with the group, Coro Trentino, I was told the members would not be able to sing for me without months, even years, of practice. Minutes later, a group of fifteen had gathered and were harmonizing effortlessly and superbly.

BIBLIOGRAPHY

Carpitella, Diego, ed. (1975). *L'etnomusicologia in Italia: Primo Convegno sugli studi etnomusicologici in Italia.* Palermo: Flaccovio.

Cirese, Eugenio. (1953–1957). *I canti popolari del Molise.* Two volumes. Rieti: Nobili.

Cocchiara, Giuseppe. (1954–1956). "Il Corpus di Musiche Popolari Siciliane di Alberto Favara." *Annali del Museo Pitrè* 5–7:54–62.

De Martino, Ernesto. (2000). *Morte e pianto rituale.* Turin: Bollati Boringhieri. Reprint of 1958 edition.

De Simone, Roberto. (1979). *Canti e tradizioni popolari in Campania.* Rome: De Santis.

Favara, Alberto. (1959). *Scritti sulla musica popolare siciliana.* Rome: De Santis.

Lomax, Alan. (1955–1956). "Nuova ipotesi sul canto folcloristico italiano." *Nuovi argomenti* 17–18:109–135.

GERMAN FOLK MUSIC AND THE OLD-TIME ORCHESTRA IN MINNESOTA

LaVern J. Rippley

The author of sixteen books and over 200 published articles, LaVern J. Rippley specializes in German immigration research. Among his works are a volume on the Bohemian-German roots of the Whoopee John Orchestra and others dealing with the old-time music of Minnesota and the upper Midwest. He is chairman of the German language department at St. Olaf College in Northfield, Minnesota.

When Minnesota became a state in 1858, Germans, most of whom came from Bohemia, had already settled in numerous Minnesota locations. This early tendency continued, so that by the 1990 census, 2 million of the 4.3 million Minnesotans counted reported German ancestry, making the Germans the largest ethnic group within the state.

In general, the Germans settled west of the Mississippi and Minnesota rivers. The most densely German counties in the state are Brown (New Ulm), Stearns (St. Cloud), Carver, Blue Earth (Mankato), Wabasha, Sibley, and Nicollet, followed closely by Waseca, Winona, Faribault, Jackson, Nobles, Freeborn, Renville, McLeod, and Houston—in other words, southern Minnesota. In the Twin Cities area, Ramsey (St. Paul) is somewhat more German than Hennepin (Minneapolis); the German presence also extends west to Wright, Morrison, and Stevens counties.

GERMAN FOLK MUSIC IN MINNESOTA

German American immigrants brought social dancing and music to Minnesota. Once settled, they established the types of German **brass bands** that played for entertainment after church on Sunday and for other special occasions. By the 1860s, there were reports of homegrown German American dance bands in Minnesota communities.

With the outbreak of World War I, a wave of anti-German sentiment swept the United States. In the state of Minnesota, the Commission of Public Safety fanned the anti-German hysteria by attacking the German-language schools, which outnumbered those in most other states and in Minnesota exceeded those conducted in other languages by 100 to one. As a result, many Minnesota Germans denied their origins, their culture, and their musical heritage.

These German American immigrant women in Minnesota, photographed around 1890, formed their own social club or "Turnverein" to maintain their culture.
Photograph © Minnesota Historical Society/CORBIS

See glossary for definition of boldfaced terms

For some reason, however, the musical style of German American dance music, without German lyrics, did not seem so "German" to local censors. Therefore, German-based dance music was able to escape the anti-German backlash of the World War I era.

In the years preceding World War I, the descendants of the frontier German American dance bands, for the most part headquartered in southern Minnesota, were enacting a musical synthesis. The new music, ironically called "old-time," wed brass **instruments** and the **concertina** and was performed for dancing. **Polkas**, **waltzes**, ländlers, and **schottisches** comprised the **repertoire** for old-time dancing. Today, despite the presence of mass-marketed forms of music such as rock and country, old-time music and dancing remain popular in the upper Midwest, particularly among older people. Not only ethnicity but also geographic location, religious background, and community traditions figure in shaping the clientele of old-time bands.

Since the early decades of the twentieth century, German old-time bands have flourished in southern Minnesota, northern Iowa, eastern South Dakota, and western Wisconsin. One might think of an old-time music region resembling an ellipse from about Yankton, South Dakota, to central Wisconsin.

Excluded from the ellipse is most of North Dakota, the northern one-third of both Minnesota and Wisconsin, the southern half of Iowa, and the southern quarter of Wisconsin. Eastern Wisconsin, like the western two-thirds of South Dakota, also stands outside the territory. For most musical groups performing within the ellipse, success has depended on following the style developed in New Ulm.

"OLD-TIME MUSIC" BY WHOOPEE JOHN AND OTHERS

All the old-time bands began activities on this side of the Atlantic without the use of a single note written on paper. In fact, until the 1930s, no players could even read music. They relied exclusively on musical ears, on the songs they had heard friends and family members sing and play, and on their abilities to reproduce tunes on **accordions**, with trumpets, clarinets, tubas, and saxophones, and later on concertinas, always with a drumbeat adequate to inspire dancing.

The life of concertinist and showman Whoopee John Wilfahrt, originally from New Ulm, serves as a microcosm of the development of old-time music. Whoopee's career began in the 1910s, when he played locally in a dance trio. Three decades later, at

the peak of his success, his ensemble some-times reached close to twenty players, and his group played over 300 dates per year, most of them dance jobs.

Whoopee credited his musical begin-nings entirely to his mother. On the back of the recording jacket for the album *Whoopee John the Great One* is the text of an interview he gave radio station WMNE in 1952. When he was eleven, he recalled, he had received an accordion for Christmas from his mother:

> We didn't have a radio or phono-graph, and I was too young to go to dances. The only music I could pick up was folk songs my mother used to sing around the house. So I made up music and played it on the ac-cordion until my father, tired of all that noise, told me to practice some-where else. I tried the kitchen pantry for a while but that didn't work, so I ended up practicing my accordion in the barn.

By the time he was fifteen, Whoopee was playing for Sunday-night house dances in Cottonwood and Siegel townships south of New Ulm. Soon it was time for a bigger box, a double-reed, twelve-bass instrument, and then a seventy-six-key concertina, pur-chased from a neighbor in 1911. Finally, Whoopee's father bought him a 102-key concertina for $150. In 1912, brother Eddie Wilfahrt started accompanying Whoopee on the clarinet, a neighbor boy came forward with a trumpet, and the band was on its way.

Other German-style bands followed in Whoopee John's footsteps. About 1933, John and Fezz Fritsche, the Six Fat Dutch-men, and the Schell's Brewery Deer Brand Band started. The Schell's band began as a civic entity to liven up "Sauerkraut Days." The band did not play for dances but rather performed on radio, for local events, and, on occasion, at the Minnesota State Fair. Fezz Fritsche, having taken over his father's band, gained popularity in the post–World War II

German Folk Music in Minnesota

era by recording for Victor. He had competition, however, from Babe Wagner, who recorded for Columbia, as well as the Schlottman band, the Eight Dutchboys, the Kalz band, Bill's Bohemian Band, the Jolly Dutchboys, and the Skinny Dutchmen (all trying to capitalize on the success of the "Dutchmen," the word being a corruption of the German *Deutsch,* or "German," and not an indication of any connection to the Netherlands). Today, Minnesota German bands do not typically record for major labels. However, many of them, including the Wendinger Brothers, a successful band from the New Ulm area, record privately and sell their recordings at performances.

The instrumentation of Whoopee's band set the standard for old-time German American dance bands that followed. In addition to the concertina, there was brass with the tuba and woodwinds such as the clarinet, along with a drummer who played a **trap** set. The accordion and the concertina gained popularity because they could provide the **melody**, along with chordal and bass accompaniment, and because they offered greater volume than the violin. Instrument builders such as Hohner in Germany and Lang and Arnold from the region adjacent to the Bohemian border in Germany (in the present-day Czech Republic) sent concertina salesmen to the United States, and their instruments soon dominated the German old-time music scene of Minnesota. However, when the Soviets occupied this area following World War II, cutting supplies of instruments and parts, German Americans such as Christy Hengel in New Ulm began constructing their own by hand, while Patek and Pearl Queen brands emanated from Chicago.

See glossary for definition of boldfaced terms

ROLE OF THE MEDIA IN POPULARIZING GERMAN FOLK MUSIC

The popularity of German folk and dance music owed much to radio and, to a lesser extent, television. Beginning in 1924, WCCO-AM in the Twin Cities sponsored Whoopee John every Saturday night from the German House, later renamed the American House, in St. Paul. WCCO offered especially important exposure, because its 50,000-watt, clear-channel signal beamed Whoopee's music to most Minnesota locations. WTCN-AM featured the band on Monday nights from the Marigold Ballroom in Minneapolis. These shows have long since been discontinued. In addition, the German (American) House fell to the wrecker's ball as part of state capitol remodeling. Because German old-time music was tied to social dancing, it responded to the forces influencing mainstream ballroom dance music, in particular, **big band** and **swing**. As the big band era faded, WCCO became less interested in broadcasts of dance music, including old-time music.

However, smaller outlets in the rural polka belt continued to provide media exposure to old-time music. In the early 1950s, WTCN-TV also broadcast the Whoopee John band. KNUJ-AM, which first aired May 22, 1949, became an important catalyst in connecting the old-time orchestra with its audience. KDHL-AM (Faribault), among other local outlets, continues to feature old-time broadcasts on a daily basis.

Local interests have recognized old-time music as a Minnesota phenomenon and have attempted to weave it into civic events. In 1953, after the city leaders of New Ulm resurfaced the city's main street, they offered a street dance for the public with music donated by different bands—twenty-one in all. Thus began the annual "Polka Day" in New Ulm, which lasted nineteen years. With each succeeding year, both the bands and the crowds increased, until the last Polka Day street party was held on July 26, 1971. To replace it, a private promoter started "Polka Days" at the Gibbon Ballroom, and the festival now attracts enough polka enthusiasts to support four stages and dance floors that operate concurrently about twelve hours each day, over a four- or five-day period.

GERMAN-LANGUAGE SINGING

The combination of acculturation to the American mainstream and the anti-German

sentiment of the World War I era caused a decline of singing melodies in German. In the early twenty-first century, an era with no appreciable anti-German sentiment, many German Americans appreciate German-language songs, even if they cannot understand the lyrics. Male **choruses** such as the New Ulm Concord Singers, a unit that fits the tradition of a German American Männerchor (men's choir) rather than an old-time band, feature German-language singing. Many contemporary melodies are broadcast on Sundays over radio stations KCHK-AM and FM of New Prague and KDHL-AM of Faribault.

CONCLUSION

In terms of participation in German folk music in Minnesota, old-time music has the greatest number of adherents. Although its audience is aging, the polka festival move-

ment has become more vital. Typical polka dancers remember the era of the ballrooms and use polka festivals to enact the type of social dance-based sociability that developed over the past few generations. The difference is that ballroom dances lasted an evening, whereas festivals occupy entire weekends.

BIBLIOGRAPHY

Rippley, LaVern J. (1992). *The Whoopee John Wilfahrt Dance Band: His Bohemian-German Roots.* Northfield, MN: St. Olaf College.

RECORDINGS

Erwin Suess and the Hoolerie Dutchmen. 1986. Eight volumes. North Star 132.

Whoopee John: The Great One. Available from Polka City, 7625 Bush Lake Rd., Edina, MN.

GERMAN AMERICAN SINGING SOCIETIES IN THE OHIO VALLEY

Alan Burdette

*Alan Burdette is an ethnomusicologist who works with American ethnic and regional musics. His research focuses on the relationship of performance to processes of community. He has spent several years doing fieldwork with the Germania Männechor Singing society in Evansville, Indiana. He is currently adjunct assistant professor in the Department of Folklore and **Ethnomusicology** at Indiana University.*

German Americans are the single largest national heritage group in the United States, and their presence has shaped American cultures at both local and national levels. One of the most pervasive musical institutions of the late nineteenth century was the German American singing society. Not only did singing societies organize musical performances, but they also served as a mediating institution for many German American families. In these social clubs immigrants had the fellowship of different generations of German Americans who could guide their development of a new cultural identity. Some of these organizations remain active today, and members continue to grapple with issues of identity and aesthetics.

Germans have been coming to America since the early seventeenth century, but immigration remained slight until 1815. It peaked when a half million Germans arrived during the 1880s alone. Over seven million Germans have settled in America since the beginning of the colonial period. They settled throughout the United States, but the upper Midwest and the Ohio River valley developed especially dense German American populations. The cities of Cincinnati, Ohio; Milwaukee, Wisconsin; Pittsburgh, Pennsylvania; New York; Indianapolis, Indiana; and Chicago, Illinois, all became centers of a rich German American culture.

It is important to remember that Germany did not exist as a nation until 1871 and that its boundaries have changed in the intervening years. Immigrants who came from German-speaking principalities of the former Holy Roman Empire came with some significant cultural differences separating them. A Prussian was not likely to understand the German spoken by someone from Bavaria, for example. Ironically, these Germans often used English to communicate with one another. In urban areas, ethnic social clubs such as the German American singing societies brought such diverse groups of Germans together.

In Germany, the attempts to unite these different cultures helped spawn the singing society movement. The Berlin Liedertafel ("song table") was formally organized in 1809 with the purpose of using poetry and music to help free Prussia from French political domination and reunite the German-speaking principalities.

During the same period, Hans Georg Nägeli, a schoolteacher, organized a men's choir to teach citizens about their national culture through music. He composed nationalistic songs for them to sing. A **repertoire** developed that celebrated camaraderie, the beauty and power of the German landscape, and the value of local folk cultures. Although these were idealized, romantic visions, they resonated with the desires of many Germans of the time. By 1840, when immigration to the United States had increased dramatically, organizations like these had become extremely popular in Germany. Immigrants began by simply forming similar singing societies in their new coun-

try, but the phenomenon soon outpaced that of Europe and became a movement with different motivations. Such groups were much less interested in nationalistic matters than they were in creating a strong sense of community. When transplanted to America, the repertoire of songs lost some of its nationalistic meanings and instead spoke to a longing for the "homeland" left behind.

A *gesangverein*, or singing society, is a private German American social club centered on choral singing. Traditionally, the choirs are all male, but women's choirs and mixed choral activity can also be a key part of these institutions. Thus, a club may be named the Liederkranz Männerchor (The Song-Wreath Men's Choir), but it could have both a men's choir and a women's choir who perform some songs together; it may also have a children's choir.

The first American gesangverein appeared in Philadelphia in 1835. Similar clubs soon followed. By 1915, at least a thousand such clubs had been founded across the

The Evansville, Indiana, Germania Männechor performs for the crowd at their 1997 Volksfest under the direction of John Schmitt.
Photograph by Alan Burdette

Members of the Evansville, Indiana Germania Männechor and their float for the 1909 German Day parade which an estimated 100,000 people attended. The float depicts the siren Lorelei and sailors who are under her enchantment.
Photograph courtesy Alan Burdette

United States, with most of them located in urban areas of the Midwest and Northeast. Texas and California also had areas of robust gesangverein activity. Few states did not have at least one singing society.

German Americans founded approximately seventy-five clubs along the Ohio River in cities such as Pittsburgh; Wheeling, West Virginia; Louisville, Henderson, and Covington, Kentucky; and Evansville, New Albany, Madison, Aurora, and Jeffersonville, Indiana. Cincinnati alone has had at least thirty-one such clubs in its history. Singing societies have ranged from small neighborhood-based ensembles to large, wealthy clubs active in national political lobbying.

In the mid–nineteenth and early twentieth centuries, gesangverein relied primarily on nearby clubs for support and competition. Just as today, they sang at each other's anniversary celebrations and attended each other's dances, plays, and festivals. At the same time, railroads made it possible for club members to travel to Chicago or New York for a national *sängerfest*, or singing festival. Today they are more likely to charter a bus, but the essential practice remains the same. The sängerfest is a gathering of several singing societies. The groups perform music for each other, then sing some selected pieces as a combined choir with several hundred singers.

The first such event was held among Cincinnati clubs in 1849. These gatherings eventually became the Nord-Amerikanischer Sängerbund (North American Singer's Union), which continues to organize sängerfests today. As of 2000, eighty-two clubs across the United States are active members of this organization. These clubs are divided into nine districts. A national sängerfest is held every three years, and district get-togethers are held in the years between. The national organization has caused some standardization in the repertoire, but it has also allowed clubs to share ideas. Especially today, when clubs are less common, the national organization relieves some of the isolation such groups might feel.

Most of these clubs had been founded before 1900, but the intense anti-German sentiments generated by U.S. involvement in World War I caused the demise of most of these organizations. Those that survived the war faced the mandates of Prohibition during the 1920s that cut off a significant part of their income and constrained their traditional social life. Sharing a beer with friends was an important public social gesture for many German Americans, and, like so many other Americans, they did not stop drinking alcohol because of Prohibition. However, it tended to make their social life less public.

The history of singing societies does not end with the post–World War I period. Those that did survive rebounded with renewed vigor, in part due to an influx of new immigrants escaping the disintegration of the German economy during the Great Depression of the 1930s and later the Nazi regime. The largest national sängerfest was held in 1938. One hundred and eighty-one singing societies came to Chicago with a total of almost 6,000 singers. Today the national festival still draws the participation of over sixty choirs. German Americans have also continued to found new singing societies, including the Männer-Gesang-Verein Harmonia of Kenosha, Wisconsin, founded in 1967, and the Cincinnati Kolping Sängerchor, in 1989.

Many clubs grew to a size that enabled them to construct a permanent facility for themselves. In large cities all over country one can find the present and former social halls built by gesangverein. Most of these buildings are substantial edifices and usually included rehearsal rooms, a ballroom with a stage, large kitchens, and a bar (*ratskeller*). Some even included restaurants, beer gardens, and, if they were associated with a *Turnverein* (a type of social club centered around physical health and athletics), a gymnasium or bowling alley.

These organizations typically have a large number of "social" or "passive" members who support club activities but do not sing in the choir. A group with thirty singers may have as many as 500 social members. These members help at fund-raising events, attend concerts, or simply support the club by paying their dues. Generally, the choir members are the decision-making body of such organizations, and key club officers must be singers.

Although gesangverein were part of a special movement from Germany, they were only one kind of German club popular in the United States in the late nineteenth century. Gesangverein were part of a large network of German clubs devoted to pursuits such as military drilling, marksmanship, intellectual and physical development, charitable causes, the promotion of German culture, veterans, and mutual aid. Of course, social clubs such as these were popular among Americans of all ethnic backgrounds as early as the Civil War and as late as the 1950s. Just like Elk Lodges, Oddfellows Halls, and Masonic Lodges of the nineteenth century, gesangverein provided a kind of social security and an organized social life for their members. Gesangverein also made it possible for thousands of German immigrants to fashion a new national identity. The clubs taught them English and American civics while providing spaces for them to continue to socialize according to their own aesthetics.

German American singing societies were sometimes organized along a particular German region such as Swabia or Austria. More often, though, they brought together people from a variety of Germanic cultures. Other clubs were distinguished according to class or occupational differences. The Cincinnati Bäckerverein, for example, was a singing society for German-born bakers. Rarely were these clubs divided according to religious lines. Catholics, Protestants, and Jews could be members together in the same clubs.

The music performed by singing societies draws on a varied repertoire of classical, folk, and popular song. The romantic and nationalistic origins of the phenomenon resulted in a penchant for folk songs or songs that symbolized German **folklife**. The gesangverein was such an important movement in the late nineteenth century that some composers wrote works with the singing societies specifically in mind. American popular song, especially the music of Stephen Foster, was also commonly performed by gesangverein from the 1880s to the 1950s. Works by classical German composers were part of the repertoire as well. The style of performance ranged from carefully rehearsed classical technique to a very informal approach to singing that was more about sociality than it was about any attempt to duplicate music conservatory standards.

Although a choir is the core element of singing societies, they often supported other kinds of musical activity. Members often formed dance bands, for example. They pro-

duced German operettas and plays in the years before World War I. In many communities, the network of singing societies and German social clubs was the nucleus around which a community symphony orchestra was formed.

German American singing societies today face several challenges. First, there is little new German immigration, and few of those who do immigrate are interested in gesangverein life. Second, few members today speak German. Third, American recreation and social life have changed considerably since 1900, and it is increasingly difficult to encourage young people to become involved. Germania Männerchor is one such club and s typical of singing societies across the United States. It shares a common institutional structure and repertoire, but also, like so many other clubs, it has developed its own community culture to which members direct their creative energies.

Germania Männerchor was founded in 1900 in Evansville, Indiana. At the time, Evansville was a mature industrial city on the Ohio River, and nearly 75 percent of its population was of German heritage. The core group of this organization is the *männerchor,* or men's choir, whose approximately thirty members rehearse three times a month and hold a business meeting once a month. The männerchor was the original impetus for the founding of the organization, and it remains the primary decision-making body of the club. A smaller *damenchor,* or women's choir, rehearses twice a month. The choirs regularly give seasonal concerts, and they annually participate in the regional or national Nord Amerikanischer Sängerbund Sängerfeste, at which they perform in a mass choir composed of other German singing clubs from around the United States. Membership also includes a women's auxiliary and nearly 500 male "social" members.

In 1913, when the organization built its present-day club hall, it was one of three German singing societies in Evansville. By the end of World War I, it was the only fully active club left. Members conducted their meetings in German until 1962, by which

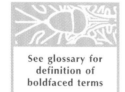

See glossary for definition of boldfaced terms

time it had become impractical to conduct business or attract members in a language that fewer and fewer members understood. One hundred years after its founding, the men's choir has just one German-born singer, and only a few of the other members speak German fluently. As a result, the German language is only occasionally heard spoken in the club. For the most part, the choirs do continue to sing in German, but the understanding and proper pronunciation of German song texts are challenges for many singers; by necessity, songs are learned by rote in rehearsals. Many members do have German immigrant ancestors, but today the they are far removed from them in cultural experience and knowledge.

Germania Männerchor has a vibrant social calendar filled with dances, dinners, concerts, bingos, and festivals. The organization has used elements of German and institutional history as cultural resources around which it has built a thriving local community. Not everything the group does is about German culture, but instead other components of the local community are celebrated. For example, some club members have brought back many first-place trophies from the citywide chili cook-off.

In the early twentieth century, when the Liederkranz Männerchor was still active in Evansville, the clubs were distinguished by the fact that the Liederkranz was the club for businessmen and Germania was the club for the working class. The demographics of the club today are difficult to generalize because members work in a broad range of occupations. The term "working class" is somewhat useful but not entirely accurate. In the past, the club was predominantly composed of men who worked in factories and in skilled trades, but many of those jobs are now gone. For example, at one time the club had a large number of brewery workers, but the city's sixteen breweries have long since closed. The iron-working and furniture-making trades once central to the Evansville economy have also gone to machines and to other countries. Among the current männerchor membership are men who work (or once worked, as many are retired) as teachers, salesmen, skilled

Evansville, Indiana's **Rhein Valley Brass play for dancers at Germania Männechor's 1993 Volksfest.**
Photograph by Alan Burdette

tradesmen (painters, plumbers, electricians, and carpenters), factory foremen, managers, and medical doctors, to name a few. None of the choir members are professional musicians, although a few have semiprofessional experience. Nearly half of the choir members are retired. Of these, most are under seventy. Of those who still work, most are in their thirties through their fifties. However, this does not necessarily indicate a decline in young members. Choir photographs from the past show that membership has always been "mature." As it is today, young men in the past were usually too busy getting started in their careers and had young children at home, making participation in club life difficult.

The Rhein Valley Brass, also based in Evansville, is a dance band composed of club members who play at club events and in the region. Founded in 1975, the group is a relatively recent addition to club life. Unlike other parts of the Midwest and northeast, the western Ohio River valley never developed a distinct regional **polka** band style. Although the Rhein Valley Brass does have its own particular style, with exuberantly quick tempos and syncopated drumming, the members have modeled themselves after German **brass bands**. It is also one of the few bands in the entire southern Indiana region, despite the large population of German Americans.

Germania Männerchor's social calendar is full most of the year, with everything from small biweekly dinner dances to a huge annual *Volksfest,* an event that evokes an old-fashioned Bavarian atmosphere with its emphasis on German food, beer, and nineteenth-century dance music. Other events include choir concerts, participation in sängerfests, appearances in civic parades, and a Christmas madrigal dinner called the Grandfest. Nearly all club events involve a meal followed by a dance with a live polka band. Each event defines the club's identity in slightly different ways. The Stiftungsfest (Founders' Day Festival) is more inward- and past-looking, whereas the Grandfest is more public and irreverent.

Originally growing out of Evansville's prewar German Day celebrations, the Germania Männerchor Volksfest has waxed and waned over the course of the club's history but today draws 15,000 guests over a three-day period. Three bands play simultaneously in different locations on the club grounds. Not only is this the primary fund-raising activity of the club, but it is an event in which club members invest a great deal of pride and energy. It is also the most public event of the club calendar and the venue through which most new members first come in contact with the club.

The Christmas Grandfest is unique to Germania Männerchor. For this event, members write an episodic play that builds on storylines from previous years. The plots frequently lampoon local politics and celebrate regional cultural emblems such as the popularity of fried-brain sandwiches in southwestern Indiana. Although the club once put on plays in German, this is a relatively recent practice that began as a fund-raiser but has become an important creative activity for some members.

While rehearsed choral performance learned from sheet music is the standard practice in gesangverein, informal singing around the bar, at dances, and during road trips has also been a feature of club life. For many members, this kind of activity epitomizes *Gemütlichkeit*: a strong feeling of comfortableness and conviviality. Gemütlichkeit is a concept through which members retain some connection with a German heritage with artistic materials that may not be German.

At its most basic, Gemütlichkeit simply requires that people come together to have a good time. It implies that the dance music includes polkas, that the singing is in German, and that a romantic vision of Germany permeates the costumes, food, and decoration at public events. Members of Germania Männerchor and many other gesangverein across the country know, however, that creating bonds of community is most important, and so they also leave some room for country music, for singing in English, and for their own participation in a multitude of American communities.

BIBLIOGRAPHY

Adams, Willi Paul. (1990). *The German-Americans: An Ethnic Experience,* tr. LaVern J. Rippley and Eberhard Reichmann. Indianapolis: Max Kade German-American Center, Indiana University–Purdue University at Indianapolis.

Bigham, Darrel E., and Petranek, Charles F. (1980). *Reflections on a Heritage: The German Americans in Southwestern Indiana.* Evansville, IN: Indiana State University (now University of Southern Indiana).

Burdette, Alan. (2000). "'Ein Prosit der Gemütlichkeit': The Traditionalization Process in a German American Singing Society." In *Land Without Nightingales: Music in the Making of German-America,* ed. Philip Bohlman and Otto Holzapfel. Madison: University of Wisconsin Press.

Greene, Victor. (1992). *A Passion for Polka: Old-Time Ethnic Music in America.* Berkeley: University of California Press.

Hinkle, Leroy Bommer. (1987). "The Meaning of Choral Experience to the Adult Membership of the German Singing Societies Comprising the United Singers Federation of Pennsylvania." Ph.D. diss. Pennsylvania State University, University Park.

Keil, Charles; Keil, Angeliki V.; and Blau, Dick. (1992) *Polka Happiness.* Philadelphia: Temple University Press.

Kirschbaum, Erik. (1986). *The Eradication of German Culture in the United States, 1917–1918.* Stuttgart: Hans-Dieter Heinz.

Snyder, Suzanne G. (1991). "The 'Maennerchor' Tradition in the United States: A Historical Analysis of Its Contributions to American Musical Culture." Ph.D. diss. University of Iowa, Ames.

DEEP POLKA: DANCE MUSIC FROM THE MIDWEST

Richard March

Richard March has been the Traditional and Ethnic Arts specialist for the Wisconsin Arts Board since 1983. He has a Ph.D. in folklore from Indiana University. Since 1986 he has been the producer and on-air host of "Down Home Dairyland," a weekly radio program of Midwestern folk music heard statewide on Wisconsin Public Radio, and has played a key role in several public television documentaries. He is also an organizer of the annual Rudy Burkhalter Memorial Accordion Jamboree and an active polka musician in the Madison, Wisconsin, area. The following essay is based on liner notes March wrote to accompany the 1998 Smithsonian Folkways recording Deep Polka: Dance Music of the Midwest *(SF CD 40088).*

The nineteenth-century European immigrants to the Midwest arrived with **polkas** ringing in their ears. The polka, a lively couple's dance in 2/4 time, had emerged from its folk roots to become a European popular dance craze in the 1840s. In elite Paris salons and humble village taverns, polka dancers flaunted their defiance of convention, eschewing the older staid dance forms such as the minuet and **quadrille** for this raucous and, for the times, scandalous new dance.

The nineteenth century was a period of revolution and social upheaval in Europe. The polka was symptomatic of the same historical currents that launched thousands of European villagers on their uncertain and perilous migration to the American Midwest. They became farmers, miners, lumberjacks, factory workers, and entrepreneurs in the new land, but they continued to enjoy the music and dance traditions of their old homelands, passing them on to the American-born generations.

Coinciding with the emergence of the polka was the booming popularity of **brass bands** both in Central Europe and in the United States. There was also the invention of a variety of **squeezeboxes—accordions** and **concertinas**. Innovative tinkerers in France, England, and Germany developed a new family of **instruments** based on the principles of the *sheng,* a Chinese **free-reed** instrument, but using the levers and springs of the Machine Age.

The squeezebox was the electronic keyboard of the nineteenth century. Like today's programmable keyboard, with its automated musical performance using electronic and digital technology, the squeezebox was a popular mechanical instrumental innovation for its time. A single accordion or concertina player could replace a small ensemble, producing melodies and **harmonies** on the right hand while the left hand provided rhythmic chords and bass notes. The prized possession in many an immigrant's pack was a button accordion or concertina, which

undoubtedly was used to play a lot of polkas.

The squeezebox and brass band earthquake had its epicenter in Central Europe. On its northern and southern fringes, some other instrumental traditions persisted or were developing in other directions. In Norway, at the time of the big wave of migration to America in the mid–nineteenth century, the **fiddle** remained the main folk instrument. In Midwestern Norwegian American communities, the fiddlers still dominate. They play a **repertoire** that blends old country polkas, **schottisches**, and *valsen,* or **waltzes**, with American sentimental tunes, **two-steps**, and **hoedowns**.

The nineteenth-century Croatians and Serbs from the Austro-Hungarian Empire were in the midst of an instrumental revolution. As part of a southern Slavic movement for cultural affirmation, a simple village lute, the **tamburitza**, was refined and standardized to enable orchestral play. At the beginning of the twentieth century, tamburitza **combos** that played polkas, waltzes, and *kolo* line dances (a category of folk line dances that are usually performed in an open circle) were formed in the Midwestern mining and industrial towns where these later immigrants settled.

Another later immigrant group was the Finns, who, like the southern Slavs, settled in the Midwest for the most part from the 1890s to World War I. Finnish villagers had warmly embraced the accordion by the time they migrated to the Lake Superior region. Finnish American accordionists such as the legendary Viola Turpeinen played a unique repertoire of polkas, waltzes, and schottisches that stylistically blends musical influences of Finland's neighbors and sometime rulers, Russia and Sweden.

Upon its arrival in the Midwest, the polka became a regional American folk tradition, much as the people who brought it over became American Midwesterners. At rural house parties with the rug rolled up or at corner taverns in industrial towns, a squeezebox or a horn was likely to keep the neighbors' feet stomping. A variety of distinct American polka styles evolved in different parts of the Midwest, shaped by the creativity of talented and influential musicians. The styles have ethnic names, for example, Polish, Slovenian, Bohemian (or Czech), and Dutchman (from *Deutsch,* or "German"). The ethnic name refers to the origin of the core repertoire and the ethnic heritage of many of the musicians, but the music often differs considerably from the old country tradition. In the Midwest, the music and dancing are shared among ethnic groups; most bands' repertoires and musical styles are ethnically mixed.

In the twentieth century, radio broadcasts and recordings transmitted the polka to wider audiences. Clear-channel WCCO-AM in Minneapolis/St. Paul broadcast Whoopee John's Dutchman music to six or more states, much like WSM-AM's Grand Ole Opry broadcasts out of Nashville, Tennessee, spread Southern traditional music far and wide. The 78-rpm discs of groups such as the Romy Gosz Orchestra and Lawrence Duchow's Red Ravens aided their efforts to become popular as regional touring dance bands.

Shortly after World War II, almost exactly a century since the original polka craze in Europe, polka music and dancing briefly entered American popular culture in a big way. Slovenian American accordionist Frankie Yankovic from Cleveland became the biggest star. His hits "Just Because" and "Blue Skirt Waltz" sold from coast to coast. His style melded Central European melodies with the rhythm of a chording **banjo** and walking bass borrowed from Dixieland **jazz**. ("Walking bass" is a style of bass line commonly used in jazz in which the bass player plays scales and partial scales emphasizing half-step intervals; the scales are timed to intersect occasionally with the tonic note of the chord being played.) His straightforward vocals were in English as well as the original Slovenian.

Yankovic's Slovenian-style synthesis attracted devotees nationwide, but Lil' Wally Jagiello established Chicago as the center of influence for the Polish American polka.

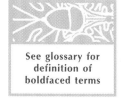

See glossary for definition of boldfaced terms

Little Wally Jagiello, "The Polka King," was among the most popular of all performers on the concertina. This 1999 photograph shows him performing in his retirement home in North Miami, Florida. *Photograph by Colin Braley, © Reuters Newmedia Inc./CORBIS*

Wally churned out record after record on his own Jay Jay label, converting many musicians to his "honky" Polish sound. ("Honky"-style polka stands in contrast to "dyno," the polka style launched by Eddie Blazonczyk in Chicago and dominant nationally since the mid-1960s. Honky more consistently uses the reed instruments, clarinet and saxophone, trading off leads with or playing contrapuntally to trumpets. Most players think the term originated as a reference to the reedy honking sound employed on the sax.) Through the 1950s, the polka made a serious run at becoming an established **genre** of American pop music. Then Elvis Presley hit and changed the program. By the 1960s, rock and roll had captured the popular music industry; polka retreated to its enclaves in a variety of urban and rural grassroots folk communities.

In these communities, during the last quarter century, polka musicians and dancers have organized institutions to perpetuate their passion. There is a network of polka dance halls, clubs, polka festivals, newsletters, mail-order recording outlets, accordion makers and dealers, and polka radio and television shows.

In the remainder of this essay, we discuss seven bands from Wisconsin who represent the four "core" polka styles—German,

Polish, Slovenian, and Czech—found in the Midwest. Also represented are three related dance music traditions that considerably overlap with the polka core—Finnish, Croatian, and Norwegian music.

KARL AND THE COUNTRY DUTCHMEN

Karl Hartwich was born in Moline, Illinois, in 1961. His father had relocated about 200 miles down the Mississippi River from his hometown near La Crosse, Wisconsin, in search of one of the good-paying factory jobs making agricultural implements in the Quad Cities area. But farming was in his blood, so the Hartwich family lived outside town in rural Orion, Illinois, where they raised hogs and field crops.

Despite their move to Illinois, the Hartwiches did not lose touch with their Wisconsin relatives. Karl remembers that at least twice a month they would make the trek upriver to attend dances at which his distant cousin Syl Liebl and the Jolly Swiss Boys were playing. Liebl, a Dutchman-style concertina player, is a natural musician, inventive, spontaneous, passionate, and original. Young Karl must have absorbed the style like a sponge.

Concertina player Karl Hartwich of Trempeleau, Wisconsin, playing with his band Karl & the Country Dutchmen at the Riverview Ballroom, Sauk City, Wisconsin, in 1998. He is playing a Chemintzer concertina made in Minnesota. Trumpet player Nic Dunkel of Black Earth, Wisconsin, is visible behind Karl.
Photograph by Bob Rashid, courtesy Rick March/Down Home Dairyland

In response to his pleas, Karl received a concertina as a Christmas present at the age of twelve. A few months later, he was sitting in with the Swiss Boys, and six months after that, at age thirteen, he had his own band, which he still leads to this day. Karl has turned out to be just as inventive and passionate a musician as his mentor. The concertina is always on his mind. Karl recalls driving the tractor on his family's farm, with dance tunes ringing in his head—the engine roaring, his left hand on the wheel, his right hand on the tool box beside the seat pressing out concertina fingerings on the vibrating metal.

As an adult, Karl has moved back up the river to Trempealeau, Wisconsin, a location more central to his band's regular gigs. Virtually every weekend he packs up the van and instrument trailer, and he and his sidemen converge on a dance hall or outdoor polka festival. Casual in his dress and personal style, Karl is nonetheless very serious about his music. He is recognized as the outstanding Dutchman concertinist of his generation. Paradoxically, his music is at once controlled and free. Karl has added more **syncopation**, chromatic runs (fill parts emphasizing half-step intervals played in the pauses between melodic lines), and improvisational flourishes to his play than his predecessors, but he uses only the old acoustic instruments and adheres to the basic Dutchman style.

Karl is one of the few full-time professional Dutchmen musicians. When not playing music, Karl loves living on the river. He is an avid fisherman. Between his band's dance gigs he catches Mississippi River catfish on treble hooks baited with chicken livers, then fillets and fries them to perfection.

THE NORSKEDALEN TRIO

Tilford "Tip" Bagstad was born on a western Wisconsin tobacco farm in the 1930s. The Norwegian farmers in the area southeast of La Crosse around Westby and Coon Valley have clung tenaciously to their old country traditions with the same intensity it takes to farm in this rugged, unglaciated coulee country.

Tip recently retired from raising beef cattle. For eighteen years he also had an off-the-farm job with the Wisconsin Department of Natural Resources supervising a trout habitat restoration crew. It was a job he could be enthusiastic about because he is also an avid trout fisherman. His wife, Elinor, a former elementary school teacher, is a skilled piano player, and both she and her

husband have been active community leaders. Tip frequently served on the boards of local organizations. Proud Norwegians, Tip and Elinor have been key players in the establishment of Norskedalen, a local community organization that operates a Norwegian cultural center and historical farmstead museum.

Although Tip had been a music enthusiast for a long time, it was only at the age of forty-eight that he took up the fiddle. There had been no shortage of older Norwegian fiddlers in his area from whom to hear and learn tunes. In 1982, Tip and Elinor joined forces with Beatrice Olson, a dairy farm wife and a fellow Norskedalen stalwart, to form the cultural center's house band, The Norskedalen Trio. The trio performs for community events such as Syttendemai (the annual Norwegian independence day festival in Westby), for Sons of Norway lodges, for weddings, and for visitors to the Norskedalen museum. They perform in Minnesota and Iowa as well as in Wisconsin, playing a repertoire of Norwegian and American old-time tunes.

THE HAPPY NOTES ORCHESTRA

When Norm Dombrowski was a teenager in the 1950s, he wasn't particularly inspired by the polka bands active in his hometown of Stevens Point, Wisconsin, a rural area of central Wisconsin populated by Polish American dairy and potato farmers. The Dutchman style of polka was the popular sound then at old-time dances. According to Norm, the bands he heard didn't sound too lively or spontaneous. Perched behind bandstands, the musicians seemed to have their noses stuck in their sheet music.

Then, in 1956, Chicago's "Lil' Wally" Jagiello performed for two nights at the Peplin Ballroom in Mosinee, just north of Stevens Point. Huge crowds turned out. At

Polka and Polka Dance Bands in the Midwest

that concert, Norm heard a modern Polish polka sound firmly grounded in the Polish folk music familiar to him from house parties and weddings. He was impressed because there was no sheet music and the band was very lively, reminiscent of rock and roll bands. Norm decided he wanted to play in this style, and, like his new hero, Lil' Wally, he was determined to become a singing drummer. By 1960 he was able to start the Happy Notes Orchestra with three friends, playing for dances locally and as far away as Minneapolis and Chicago.

Norm's musical talents seem to have been inherited by his children. By the 1980s, the Happy Notes had evolved into a family band as Norm's sons and daughters grew old enough to become competent musicians. Unlike many Polish polka bands, Norm did not adopt the modern streamlined style known as "dyno" or "push," choosing to remain closer to the "honky" style of music. Norm stresses Polish tunes and the singing of old Polish songs but also includes in the band's repertoire German, Czech, and Norwegian numbers to satisfy patrons of other ethnic backgrounds.

VATRA

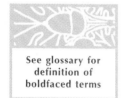

See glossary for definition of boldfaced terms

The name of this tamburitza **combo** means "fire" in Croatian. It is an appropriate name for the group of young musicians, considering their very skillful instrumental pyrotechnics. *Tamburitza* refers to a family of fretted stringed instruments ranging in size from smaller than a **mandolin** to larger than a string **bass**. Vatra's members—Chris Ulm, Boris Kuzmanovic, Ivo Gretic, Ryan Werner, and Dave Pozgaj—are all young Croatian American men from Milwaukee, born in the 1970s. They learned their music and singing during the 1980s in Milwaukee's junior tamburitza ensembles, which are community-based ethnic youth orchestras and dance groups.

The groups rehearsed at St. Augustine's Church, a Croatian parish surrounded by the hulking remains of the closed-down Allis-Chalmers tractor factory, a plant that pro-

vided a livelihood to so many local Croatian Americans in previous generations. On the tile floor of the church school gymnasium the boys who became Vatra met virtually every Sunday afternoon from the age of eight through their high school years to hone their playing and singing skills.

Learning the basics of the instrument by playing simple orchestral arrangements of Croatian folk songs, the boys soon became fluent in the idiom of the tamburitza. Then there came opportunities to play in a small combo—on stage accompanying other group members in dance choreographies, playing for parties and receptions, or just **jamming**. At picnics and church dinners they watched and sometimes were allowed to "sit in" with established regional tamburitza combos such as Zagreb, Sinovi, and Slanina.

In 1991, while they were still teenagers, Vatra started to take professional jobs. As they matured, Vatra eventually gained the reputation of being one of the best American tamburitza combos. They have played the Croatian ethnic "circuit" of lamb roasts and fraternal lodge halls from Pennsylvania to Los Angeles. Recently, Vatra also has begun to "cross over," playing for mainstream audiences in a "world music" bar in a trendy part of town and on the "Hotel Milwaukee" program on Wisconsin Public Radio.

THE STEVE MEISNER BAND

Steve Meisner was born in 1960 in Whitewater, a small Wisconsin town southeast of Milwaukee. At the time, Steve's father, Verne, was already an established musician, an accordion prodigy whose original band, Verne Meisner and the Polka Boys, was aptly named—the members were still in their early teens when they started taking professional gigs. That was the early 1950s, just in the wake of Frankie Yankovic's ascendancy. The Slovenian style of polka had become one of the most popular forms of music in Wisconsin. By the 1960s, the Verne Meisner Band was one of the best known polka groups in the region.

Polka dancers Don
McDermott (from
Madison, Wisconsin) and
Margaret Ferfenden
(from Lodi, Wisconsin)
at the Riverview
Ballroom, Sauk City,
Wisconsin, 1998.
*Photograph by Bob
Rashid, courtesy Rick
March/Down Home
Dairyland*

Steve received an ambivalent message from Verne when he first showed an early interest in music. Seven-year-old Steve's entreaties to his father to teach him to play were rebuffed at first. Then Verne thrust a momentous decision upon his young son: "If you begin to play, you have to promise that you'll never quit." Steve leaped at the challenge. Only a year later his father began to bring Steve along to play some jobs with the Meisner band, often placing the diminutive kid on a box so he could reach the microphone.

Steve started his own band while still in his teens and has continued the family tradition in the polka music business, playing regionally and nationally, producing his own CDs and videos, and organizing polka tours and cruises. Steve acknowledges his musical debt to the Slovenian-style musicians of the previous generation but has pushed the envelope of the **form** in hot arrangements and in original material that expresses a range of emotions.

THE OULU HOTSHOTS

County Trunk FF is a narrow country road running through Oulu Township in far northwestern Wisconsin. In jest, Bill Kangas

reckons that it stands for "Finn Freeway." On this hardscrabble cutover land thirty miles east of Duluth, named for the northernmost province of Finland, Finnish American farmers scratch out a living not far from the south shore of Lake Superior. The Oulu Hotshots, consisting of singer/drummer Bill Kangas and accordionists Glen and Leroy Lahti, grew up in this highly ethnic community. As children, they heard the music of local Finnish musicians Walter and Ailie Johnson. They also discovered old Finnish American recordings—78s with the music of songwriters such as Hiski Salomaa and 1950s LPs from accordionist Viola Turpeinen, a Finnish American cultural icon.

In the 1970s, the young Lahti brothers, accordion prodigies Glen and Leroy, began to perform for local events with the drumming provided by their elder brother Archie. When Archie shipped out on the Great Lakes iron ore boats in 1974, Bill Kangas joined the group as a singer and drummer. With Bill's strong Finnish and English language vocals, insistent drumming, and the energetic accordion playing of the two Lahti boys, the Oulu Hotshots became a sensation in the western Lake Superior area.

The Hotshots have played at all of the major Finnish American festivals across the

United States, from Massachusetts to California. They also have traveled to Finland, where their talents are appreciated. The Oulu Hotshots performed in Kaustinen, Finland, at the country's largest folk festival. But they did not ignore their hometown's Old World namesake—they played as well at the Garlic Festival in Oulu, Finand, right on the city square.

THE CLETE BELLIN ORCHESTRA

It is indicative of the unique cultural milieu of eastern Wisconsin that Cletus Bellin, proud member of the Walloon Belgian ethnic community of northeastern Wisconsin, is also the leader of one of the finest Czech-style polka bands in the Midwest. A proficient pianist and a very strong singer, Clete went to the trouble of learning the correct pronunciation of the Czech folk song lyrics from a friend in Pilsen, Wisconsin, not far from Clete's hometown of Forestville.

As a boy in the 1940s on a southern Door County, Wisconsin, farm, Clete was as likely to speak the Walloon Belgian dialect of French spoken in his highly culturally retentive community as the English he learned in school. Clete has had a lifelong interest in his Belgian culture, and, now in his fifties, he is one of the area's youngest remaining truly fluent speakers of Walloon.

In this corner of northeastern Wisconsin, the Walloon Belgians of southern Door County are neighbors to the Kewaunee County Czechs. In the cultural interchange that has developed, Czechs have adopted Belgian foods such as booyah (a soup), and the Walloons have accepted the Bohemian/Czech style of polka. Clete's career in music has included playing and singing in the eastern Wisconsin Bohemian bands of Marvin Brouchard, Gordy Reckelberg, and Jerry Voelker. For many years Clete worked as the radio station manager and on-air personality for WAUN-FM, a Kewaunee, Wisconsin, polka station. In addition to running the radio station, Clete was a polka **deejay** and news reporter and even hosted the station's shop or swap program.

In the 1980s, a local Czech heritage group sponsored U.S. tours by the musical performing groups Budvarka, Veselka, and Moravanka from the Czech Republic. Clete was so moved by their style of singing and play, a style from which the Wisconsin Bohemian bands had diverged, that he resolved to start his own band, performing as close as possible in their European manner. His group, the Clete Bellin Orchestra, is widely acclaimed and performs at polka festivals and Czech ethnic events throughout the country.

See glossary for definition of boldfaced terms

BIBLIOGRAPHY

Greene, Victor. (1992). *A Passion for Polka*. Berkeley: University of California Press.

Keil, Charles; Keil, Angeliki; and Blau, Dick. (1992). *Polka Happiness*. Philadelphia: Temple University Press.

Leary, James P. (1988). "Czech- and German-American 'Polka' Music." *Journal of American Folklore* 101(401):339–344.

Leary, James P., and March, Richard. (1991). "Dutchman Bands: Genre, Ethnicity, and Pluralism in the Upper Midwest." In *Creative Ethnicity: Symbols and Strategies of Contemporary Ethnic Life*, ed. Stephen Stern and John Allan Cicala. Logan: Utah State University Press.

———. (1996). *Down Home Dairyland: A Listener's Guide*. Madison: Wisconsin Arts Board, University of Wisconsin–Madison, and Wisconsin Folk Museum. Cassettes/book package of forty half-hour radio programs and companion essays.

Lornell, Kip. (1985). "The Early Career of Whoopee John Wilfahrt." *JEMF Quarterly* 21(75/76):51–53.

March, Richard (1985). "Slovenian Polka Music: Tradition and Transition." *JEMF Quarterly* 21(75/76):47–50.

———. (1989). "Slovenian- and Polish-American 'Polka' Music." *Journal of American Folklore* 102(403):81–84.

———. (1991). "Polkas in Wisconsin Music." In *The Illustrated History of Wisconsin Music*, ed. Michael G. Corenthal. Milwaukee: MGC Publishers.

Spottswood, Richard K. (1985). "Whoopee John Wilfahrt Discography: 1927–1941." *JEMF Quarterly* 21(75/76): 54–58.

RECORDINGS

Deep Polka: Dance Music of the Midwest. 1998. Smithsonian Folkways SF CD 40088.

Minnesota Polka: Dance Music from Four Traditions. 1990. James P. Leary. St. Paul: Minnesota Historical Society. Samples of Minnesota German, Czech, Slovenian, and Polish styles. Includes an essay placing Minnesota polka music in cultural and historical settings. Two LPs or audiocassettes.

MINNESOTA POLKA MUSIC

Philip Nusbaum

Philip Nusbaum is a music professional who conducts research from his position at the Minnesota State Arts Board and also plays in bluegrass and country bands. For over three decades, he has hosted folk music programs on radio and has conducted extensive field recordings of many types of traditional music. His work has appeared on commercial recordings and on local radio as well as on National Public Radio. His writing about traditional music has appeared in liner notes and in scholarly and popular articles.

In the nineteenth century, the **polka**, **waltz**, and **schottische** swept across Europe, largely supplanting the previously existing social dances. In Minnesota, European American social dance music featuring the polka, waltz, and schottische is frequently referred to as old-time (or old-tyme) music. Particularly in the settings for German, Czech, Slovenian, and Polish social dancing, this music is also known collectively as polka music. German, Czech, Slovenian, and Polish are style designations that knowledgeable polka musicians and dancers use as stylistic reference points.

THE MUSIC

Each polka style is named for a specific regional European ethnic group. Some bands are known for their European language vocals, although performances also feature vocals sung in English. When a group plays a piece with a European-language title and lyrics, members of the ethnic group referenced by the title or lyrics draw connections between themselves and their ethnic groups. However, affiliation with a given style of polka music is not limited to members of the group that gives the style its name. For example, if you live in a German American city such as New Ulm, Minnesota, and enjoy playing or dancing to polka music, you are most likely to prefer German-style music regardless of your ethnic background.

In each Minnesota European American culture, polka dances started as community or family affairs. After the early years of settlement, some musicians formed bands frequently based on **accordion** and **concertina** playing with stable memberships. The most popular of these bands evolved from duets or trios into professional dance bands. Mirroring **swing**-era developments, successful bands added band **instruments**. In the 1940s, for some playing situations, the Minnesota German bandleader Whoopee John assembled a band of close to twenty pieces.

However, twenty-first-century music industry economics has eroded the size of polka bands. Trios are now commonly seen at dance situations, where the concertina or accordion plays with a drummer and bassist. Bands playing any polka music style consider themselves fortunate to play in five- or six-piece configurations. Generally, the bands feature a concertina or accordion with a horn section for playing leads, united with a drummer playing a **trap** set and a **bass** player. In Minnesota German and Czech styles, the bass instrument is usually a tuba, and in the other styles it might be an electric bass, or the bass notes of an electronic keyboard.

The instruments used, particularly the concertina and accordion, have great symbolic values within the polka community. In the 1960s, the electronic accordion was popular because its ability to effect different types of sounds, available by flipping the instrument's buttons, was considered to be modern. In contrast, the limited types of sound quality variations available to concertina and button accordion players make these instruments seem old fashioned. However, towards the end of the twentieth century and into the twenty-first, the "sweet" tone and old-country association made the old-fashioned instruments desirable.

POLKA EVENTS

For the past century, polka music and dancing have helped Minnesotans celebrate occasions such as weddings, birthdays, and retirements. However, although polka fans today tend to think of their music and dance as old fashioned, they use modern means of accessing polka-related experiences. Many join polka organizations, such as the Polka Lovers Club of America (P.O.L.K.A.), in order to meet others who enjoy polka dance-oriented socializing. Recent decades have seen the development of polka festivals. Usually held over weekend, festivals often feature contracted polka dance bands that alternate playing so that there is live music performed for about twelve hours on multiple stages, indoors and outdoors. Polka events also attract listeners who discuss the playing of onstage musicians against a virtuosic standard.

Fans and musicians are willing to travel great distances for polka events. Once there, they make new friends and visit with old ones. Frequently, the area between attendees' motor homes parked closely together becomes a separate setting for socializing away from the festival ballrooms and outdoor stages.

THE FUTURE

The age of the typical polka enthusiast continues to rise. Many polka community members are asking themselves where the next generation of enthusiasts will come from. There is no compelling response to this question. However, other ethnic dance music-based idioms—such as Irish music, **bluegrass** music, and the **blues**—have survived despite the near disappearance of original social dance contexts for musical performance. Each of these forms has evolved into a virtuosic concert music style. Perhaps that could be the future of polka.

BIBLIOGRAPHY

Leary, James P. (1988). "Brass Bands and the Bohemian Hall." *Folklife of the Upper Midwest* 4:2 (May).

Leary, James P., and March, Richard. (1990). "Dutchman Bands: Genre, Ethnicity, and Pluralism in the Upper Midwest." In *Creative Ethnicity: Symbols and Strategies of Contemporary Ethnic Life,* ed. Stephen Stern and John Allan Cicala. Logan: Utah State University Press.

March, Richard. (1988). "Music of Midwest Polka Bands Comes in Four Ethnic Flavors." *Folklife of the Upper Midwest* 4:2 (May).

Nusbaum, Philip. (1988). "Polka Music and Polka Culture: The Case of Polka Days, Gibbon, Minnesota, 1987." *Folklife of the Upper Midwest* 4:2 (May).

RECORDINGS

Minnesota Polka: Dance Music from Four Traditions. 1990. James P. Leary. St. Paul: Minnesota Historical Society. Samples of Minnesota German, Czech, Slovenian, and Polish styles. Includes an essay placing Minnesota polka music in cultural and historical settings. Two LPs or audiocassettes.

MUSIC OF THE POLISH GÓRALE COMMUNITY IN CHICAGO

Timothy J. Cooley

Timothy J. Cooley teaches **ethnomusicology** *at the University of California, Santa Barbara. He first encountered immigrants from the Polish Tatra Mountains while employed by the Illinois Arts Council as a public-sector ethnomusicologist. His experiences with Polish Górale in Chicago motivated him to research the traditions in Poland and to write a dissertation on the musicians and music culture of the Tatras (Brown University, 1999). His publications include* Shadows in the Field: New Perspectives for Fieldwork in Ethnomusicology, *coedited with Gregory F. Barz (Oxford University Press, 1997), and the essay "Folk Festival as Modern Ritual in the Polish Tatra Mountains" in a 1999 issue of the journal* World of Music.

Górale means "mountaineer" and is used here to refer to immigrants from Podhale, the Tatra Mountain region of southern Poland. Górale are a distinct cultural and ethnic group in Poland, and many actively retain this distinction in the United States, more so than other Polish regional groups. Chicago boasts the largest concentration of Górale (and Poles in general) in America, leading some to quip that Chicago is the largest Górale village. Though spread around the city and its suburbs, the community is centered in the southwestern central part of Chicago along South Archer Avenue. Other historically important Górale immigrant communities are in Detroit, Michigan; Toronto, Ontario, Canada; and Passaic, New Jersey. Górale in Chicago actively cultivate a distinct music culture featuring unaccompanied **polyphonic** singing as well as singing and dancing accompanied by small ensembles of violins.

HISTORY

The Tatra region (Podhale) lies on the southern edge of Poland bordering Slovakia. The Tatras are the tallest peaks of the Carpathian range that extends southward to the Balkans. Over the centuries, migrants carried lifeways along the Carpathian chain, resulting in similarities among Carpathian cultures.

Large numbers of Górale moved to the United States between 1880 and the first decade of the twentieth century. A second wave of immigration came in the 1920s between the two world wars when Poland enjoyed a brief period of independence. In 1929, Górale organized the Zwiaøek Podhalan w Pólnocnej Ameryce (Podhale Alliance of North America), with branches wherever a critical mass of Górale could be found. The first branch was in Chicago. A steady exchange of immigrants between Poland and the United States keeps the Chicago community informed of developments in Pod-

hale, including musical developments. Several papers are published simultaneously in Chicago and Poland, including one, Tygodnik Podhalan´ski (Podhale Weekly), directed specifically toward Górale.

THE CHICAGO GÓRALE COMMUNITY

Together with their unique dance, costume, and dialect, music is a symbol of identity for the Górale community in Chicago as it is in Poland. The music sound itself is believed to reflect the mountainous geography of Górale's homeland—harsh and angular. Music of all mountain peoples is thought by some Górale to be similar in spirit. For many, Górale music is a link with the motherland, where they hope to return. Ability to sing, play an **instrument**, and dance in the Górale manner is considered a mark of pride in one's heritage. The structure of the music

and dance, which emphasizes the individual (the lead violinist, singer, or dancer) who has ultimate control over the music or dance, reflects the value given by the community to individual independence and achievement, especially for men.

Górale institutions in Chicago mirror those in Poland. For example, the culturally influential Związek Podhalan (Podhale Alliance) began in Poland (1904) and established two active branches in Chicago (1928, and reformulated as the Podhale Alliance of North America in 1929). The Chicago branch provides an important venue for events involving music in the Górale community.

Górale music is intimate, with no provision for large group singing or dancing, or for large instrumental ensembles. To allow more individuals to participate, non-Górale group dances such as **polkas** and **waltzes** are played in addition to Górale music at large gatherings. Instrumentalists are usually men and boys, but gender restrictions are

The Górale Homeland in the Tatra Mountain Region of Southern Poland

Górale musicians serenading a bride on her wedding day outside her family home in Chicago, Illinois, 1991.
Photographer: Timothy J. Cooley

changing, especially among young people in Chicago, where increasing numbers of girls and young women play violin. Women have greater parity in Górale singing traditions and may initiate songs. Most music making is practiced by young people (teens to thirties), but great respect is given to seniors who offer a song or dance.

MUSIC

In Chicago, Górale music culture serves recreational, ceremonial, and demonstration functions. Although not everyone participates in music making, musical proficiency is common among Górale, especially those who grew up in Poland before immigrating. When gathered together informally, Górale often break into spontaneous performances, usually of group singing. Ceremonial uses of music include important Roman Catholic feast days and life cycle rituals, especially weddings and funerals. Demonstration performances are staged shows at festivals, civic parades, or other functions that are often for non-Górale audiences. One excellent example of demonstration performances is an annual festival each November at the Dom Podhalański (Polish Górale Home) on Archer Avenue in Chicago. Although some Górale believe one cannot play the music

properly without experiencing life in the Tatras, several student ensembles in Chicago teach children how to play, sing, and dance in the Górale style.

Although Górale musicians play and sing popular Polish, American, and pan-European songs and dances (waltzes, polkas, **csárdáses**, etc.), music unique to Górale makes up the core **repertoire** of the Chicago community. The related categories of vocal and instrumental music typically have short **descending melodic phrases**. The scales in these melodic phrases often include a raised fourth **scale** degree above the home **pitch** or the **tonic**, a sound that is considered dissonant and avoided in most Western music systems. Tunes are not conceived of as fixed but rather as melodic ideas that are varied in performance. The same is true for song texts and dance steps.

Vocal music includes two basic related **genres**: *pasterski* ("pastoral") and *wierchowa* ("mountain peak song/tune"). The two styles share many characteristics. Both usually contain two lines of text (A and B lines) with corresponding music. The second line of music and text is repeated (ABB). The lead singer begins alone, and the accompanying singers join in after the A or first B line, harmonizing at the interval of a third or fifth below. Men and women sing in the same octave. Al-

Dancing the *zbójnicki* (robber's dance) at Chicago's *Dom Podhalanski* (Highlander's home).
Photographer: Timothy J. Cooley

though the border between them is blurred, pasterskis are usually rhythmically free, and wierchowas are typically in **duple time**.

All instrumental music is based on song, although texts are not fixed and may be sung to different tunes, and new texts may be improvised. A typical ensemble consists of a lead violin responsible for the highly ornamented melodies and one or more accompanying violins, together with a three-stringed cello-like instrument called a *basy*. Instrumental music is in duple meter clearly marked by the second violins and basy, which are bowed vigorously on the beat. Occasionally several types of wooden flutes and **bagpipes** specific to Podhale are played. Instrumental music can be for listening or for dancing. Music for listening includes instrumental versions of pasterskis and wierchowas, as well as *Sabałowas* (named after legendary mountain guide, storyteller, and musician Jan Krzeptowski-Sabała, 1810–1894) and *staroświeckis* ("of the Old World"). Wierchowas, Sabałowas, and staroświeckis typically have five-bar phrases in 2/4 meter.

Music for dancing called *po góralsku* ("in the Górale manner") follows a loosely organized **cycle** of dance/music genres. Po góralsku is danced primarily by one male/female couple, although the female dancer is first introduced to the dance area by a second

male, then with a special dance by a small group of women for each subsequent dance. The first male dancer controls the sequence of dance/music genres within the parameters of traditional practice. He calls for each dance by singing a line of a song; the band then picks up the **melody** and plays while he and his partner dance. The cycle begins with an *ozwodna* ("slowly"), a five-bar phrase genre similar to wierchowa. This is followed by a sequence of tunes/dances that may include additional ozwodnas, as well as *drobnas* ("small") and/or *krzesanys* ("striking").

Drobnas and krzesanys are closely related tune types combining virtuosic violin playing with elaborate and athletic dancing by men. They often have four-bar phrases, but many have unusual phrase structures. Each dance cycle ends with one or two tunes, both called *zielona* ("green"), while the dance couple touches for the first time with a specific turning step. A separate dance genre called *zbójnicki* ("robber's dance") is for a group of men and features specific songs and tunes. The best collection of instrumental music for listening and dancing is Mierczyński (1930/1973).

Improvisation is a valued skill in all aspects of Górale music culture, including the ability to improvise topical song texts to fit a situation. Singers also draw from a large

storehouse of texts preserved in oral tradition. The poetry has two rhymed lines per **verse**, each line typically has twelve syllables, and the second line is repeated when sung (ABB). Alternatively, the poetry can be conceived of as having four lines of six syllables each. The poetry is often loosely organized around themes of love, sex, courtship, and marriage; of place, especially the Tatra Mountains; about legendary robbers; and even on the theme of Górale music itself. Much of the repertoire of Chicago Górale is shared by Górale in Poland, and probably because this style of music is so strongly associated with the Tatra Mountains, there is no widespread movement to compose new texts about life in Chicago.

The most comprehensive collection of traditional texts from Poland is Sadownik (1971). The largest compilation of texts with English translations accompanies the CD recordings *Fire in the Mountains*, volumes 1 and 2 (1997). The two volumes comprise a nearly complete reissue of the earliest commercial recordings of Górale music from 1927 to the 1950s. Out of forty-five combined tracks, all but four were recorded in Chicago. The extensive notes connect Górale music with the formation of Górale cultural organizations in the United States. All songs are transcribed in Górale dialect and translated into English. Recently recorded in Chicago, *Polish Highlanders: Na & Żwo Gęśle—Music from the Southern Tatra Mountains* features traditional Górale music on side 1 and Górale versions of waltzes, polkas, and other styles on side 2.

BIBLIOGRAPHY

Mierczyński, Stanisław. (1930/1973). *Muzyka Podhala.* Kraków: Polskie Wydawnictwo Muzyczne.

Sadowik, Jan, ed. (1971). *Pieśni Podhala: Antologia.* Kraków: Polskie Wydawnictwo Muzyczne.

Wrazen, Louise. (1991). "Traditional Music Performance Among Górale in Canada." *Ethnomusicology* 35(2):173–193.

RECORDINGS

Fire in the Mountains: Polish Mountain Fiddle Music—Vol. 1: The Karol Stoch Band and *Vol. 2: The Great Highland Bands.* 1997. Yazoo CD 7012 and 7013.

Polish Highlanders: Na & Żwo Gęśle: Music from the Southern Tatra Mountains. 1991. Modal Music 911. Audiocassette.

CZECH MUSIC IN WISCONSIN

James P. Leary

James P. Leary is a professor of folklore and Scandinavian studies and the director of the folklore program at the University of Wisconsin. Born and raised in northern Wisconsin, he has done fieldwork in the Upper Midwest since the early 1970s, contributing to the production of numerous documentary sound recordings, public radio programs, and films. Leary is also the author of Midwestern Folk Humor, Minnesota Polka, Yodeling in Dairyland: A History of Swiss Music in Wisconsin, *and* Wisconsin Folklore *and coauthor (with Richard March) of* Down Home Dairyland.

Czech immigrants initially settled rural Wisconsin in the 1850s, clustering in distinct regions, each with its particular topography and ethnic mix. In hilly, unglaciated west central Wisconsin, fanning from the lower Wisconsin River valley northward, Czechs clustered around such communities as Muscoda, Wauzeka, Prairie du Chien, Hillsboro, and Yuba, alongside Yankees, Upland Southerners, African Americans, Irish, Norwegians, and Germans. In eastern Wisconsin's Kewaunee and Manitowoc counties, fertile flatlands hugging Lake Michigan's shores, the Czechs of Pilsen, Stangelville, Tisch Mills, Francis Creek, Mishicot, and Two Creeks mingled with French, Walloon Belgians, and Germans. The late nineteenth and early twentieth centuries brought a second influx of land-seeking, former peasant Czech Americans—Pennsylvania miners, Chicago factory hands, Cedar Rapids slaughterhouse laborers, and Nebraska sandhill farmers—to logged off or "cutover" acreage in such northern Wisconsin communities as Haugen, Moquah, and Phillips. Their fellow settlers included kindred Slavs—Slovaks, Poles, and Croatians—as well as Scandinavians and Germans.

Primarily Catholics, but also Hussite Lutherans and Freethinkers, Wisconsin's Czechs were widely dubbed "Bohemians" by themselves and their neighbors. Most hailed from Cechy, the westernmost sector of present-day Czech Republic, which, in the nineteenth century, was politically dominated and partially settled by Germans who called the place Böhmen, or Bohemia. Because Wisconsin is America's most German state, with more than half of its current population claiming German ancestry, the persistent Bohemian tag is hardly surprising. Small wonder, too, that, for several generations, Wisconsin's Czechs, as in Europe, relied on German rather than English as a second language, and that they were far more likely to modify their Central European customs slowly than to succumb

quickly to the so-called American ways of Anglo-Protestants.

Seasonal and life-cycle observances, churches, taverns, and fraternal halls linked Czech immigrants and sustain their contemporary descendants, often contributing to a flurry of festivals emergent since the rise of ethnic American consciousness in the 1970s. In Haugen, one example among many, weddings, funerals, the springtime blessing of seeds, and late-summer harvest celebrations have revolved around Holy Trinity Catholic Church.

The typically Wisconsin combination tavern, store, dance hall, and service station established by the Sokup family served locals into the early 1970s, while the venerable ZCBJ Hall—affiliated with the Západni Cesko-Bratská Jednota (Western Fraternal Life Association)—still offers a well-used stage and dance floor. The community launched Haugen Days in the late 1970s, featuring Czech food and music. Indeed,

Czech Music in Wisconsin

polka music is especially popular in Haugen and throughout Czech Wisconsin.

Although "polka music" has become a generic term encompassing polkas, **waltzes**, **ländlers**, **schottisches**, **mazurkas**, and other dances, the polka itself is a couple dance in 2/4 time that originated in the Bohemian villages of northwestern Czechoslovakia, near the Polish border. By the late 1830s, the village polka had entered the genteel parlors and courtly ballrooms of Prague, and by 1845, Bohemian military bands and dancing masters had carried polkas to Vienna and Paris. Soon they were the fashion in London and urban America. The polka's rise coincided with the development of the **accordion**, the standardization of wind **instruments** prominently used in military bands, the mass movement of European peasants to urban centers and North America, and the transformation of feudal monarchies into modern nation-states. Czech immigrants to Wisconsin, consequently,

Guitarist Adam May, concertinist Frank Hatina, and fiddler Mike Balaty in a Czech hall, Phillips, Wisconsin, ca. 1920.

Photograph courtesy of Toni Rohrig, author's collection

brought accordions, **fiddles**, an array of brass and reed instruments, marches and couple dances, and an evolving **repertoire** of songs, both starkly realistic and sentimental, regarding peasant life, European wars, experiences in their adopted country, and fond hopes for their abandoned homeland.

In 1868, Martin Rott, Sr., an immigrant, established a Bohemian **brass band** in Yuba that consisted of his own bass horn or tuba, a baritone horn, a cornet, two clarinets, and

a violin. Performing solemn marches for funeral processions, the Yuba Bohemian Band, active until the early 1950s, specialized in rollicking dance tunes for weekend gatherings, weddings, Fourth of July galas, and a two-day pre-Lenten festivity, *Maso Pust.* Its sound persists today in the playing of the She and He Haugh Band at Yuba's summer *Ceský; Den* (Czech Day).

As a second-generation Czech American born in 1875 on a Prairie du Chien area

The Yuba Bohemian Band, recorded for the Archive of American Folksong at the Library of Congress by Helene Stratman-Thomas (extreme right) and Aubrey Snyder (top row center), 1946.

Photograph courtesy of the State Historical Society of Wisconsin, WHi (S75)53

farm, Albert Wachuta learned to play the accordion and picked up songs "mostly from my mother, but some from other people too because in [those] days there was a lot of Bohemian singing" (Leary 1987, p. 48). One Wachuta favorite was the fatalistic account of a soldier in the Austro-Hungarian army from his mother's home village, Bechene, but made over in Wisconsin as "Vojak od Prairie du Chien" ("Soldier from Prairie du Chien"). Another, "Koline, Koline," was the bittersweet invocation of a city on a beautiful plain where wars raged.

The overlapping combination of informal singing, domestic **squeezebox** playing, and organized brass bands distinguished most of Czech Wisconsin. For every respected accordionist or concertinist (Albert Wachuta, Yuba's Joe Yansky, Haugen's Wencel Mancl, and Phillips's Frank Hatina), there was an equally esteemed brass band (Martin Rott's Yuba Bohemian Band, the Sokup and the Subrt bands of Haugen, and the Peroutka Orchestra of Phillips). In the more populous Czech communities of Manitowoc and Kewaunee counties, however, brass bands dominated, with the Pilsen Band (affectionately known as the "Pilsen Pissers" because of their fondness for *piwo,* or beer) setting the standard in the late nineteenth and early twentieth centuries. Yet whatever their in-

strumentation, Wisconsin Czech bands favored stately tempos, rich arrangements augmenting main melodies with introductory and transitional flourishes, and a love of **vibrato**, slight **dissonances**, **improvisation**, and feeling.

Grounded in Old World traditions, Wisconsin Czech musicians were nonetheless open to change. As early as 1870, Charles Mon Pleasure, a Franco-American fiddler, recruited Czechs to play **quadrilles** for high-tone balls:

> At that time we used the old-fashioned post horns and bugles, so we had the first violin, second violin, double bass, post horn, clarinet, and bugle. They were all Bohemians but myself. . . . The first ball that we played was for old George F. Switzer, a big old fat Dutchman, a darned good fellow too. . . . I had the only quadrille band in Prairie du Chien. Jim Williams, a Negro, had a band across the Mississippi at South McGregor [Iowa]. (Mon Pleasure 1910; quoted in Leary 1997, p. 37)

In the early twentieth century, African Americans, recently arrived from the South, brought the **syncopations** and slurs of **ragtime**, **jazz**, and **blues**, influencing Czech musicians such as Romy Gosz (1911–1966).

Trumpeter Romy Gosz and bandmates pose amidst a country wedding celebration, mid-1950s.
Photo courtesy of Jim Eisenman, author's collection

Born in Rockwood, north of Manitowoc, Roman Louis Gosz took over his father's band in 1928. Between 1931 and his death, Gosz recorded roughly 170 tunes for eleven labels—including Columbia, Decca, King, Mercury, and Okeh—that established a "Bohemian" polka instrumentation and sound scarcely diminished in eastern Wisconsin.

The overall Gosz style favored a slow **tempo** and heavy feel, anchored by stolid tuba and **trap** drums. A piano or **piano accordion** contributed rhythm and **fills**. Gosz's penetrating trumpet, often in **chorus** with a second trumpet and saxophones, introduced the **melody**, with clarinets frequently answering a phrase or chiming in with a countermelody. Parts were loosely arranged and distinguished by slurs, **slides**, and surges that fused old country Czech feeling with hot jazz intonation.

To the dismay of high school band teachers—who favored round notes and square rhythms while valuing external (i.e., classical) rather than local traditions—Romy Gosz inspired scores of young musicians, and his legacy remains formidable decades after his death. Like Kentucky's Bill Monroe, whose pioneering Blue Grass Boys provided both a standard and a training ground for subsequent **bluegrass** generations, and Muddy Waters, who inflamed legions of urban performers with his amplified makeover of Mississippi Delta blues, Romy Gosz and his band won regional disciples to carry his nineteenth- and twentieth-century Czech American synthesis into a new millennium.

BIBLIOGRAPHY

Barden, Thomas. (1982). "The Yuba Masopust Festival." *Midwestern Journal of Language and Folklore* 8(1):48–51.

Greene, Victor. (1992). *A Passion for Polkas: Old Time Ethnic Music in America.* Berkeley: University of California Press.

Janda, Robert. (1976). "Entertainment Tonight: An Account of Bands in Manitowoc County Since 1900." *Occupational Monograph* 28. Manitowoc, WI: Manitowoc County Historical Society.

Leary, James P. (1987). *The Wisconsin Patchwork: A Commentary on Recordings from the Helene Stratman Thomas Collection of Wisconsin Folk Music.* Madison: University of Wisconsin Department of Continuing Education in the Arts.

———. (1997). "Czech Polka Music in Wisconsin." In *Musics of Multicultural America,* ed. Kip Lornell and Anne Rasmussen, pp. 25–47. New York: Schirmer Books.

Leary, James P., and March, Richard. (1996). *Down Home Dairyland: A Listener's Guide.* Madison: Wisconsin

Arts Board, University of Wisconsin–Madison, and Wisconsin Folk Museum. Cassettes/book package of forty half-hour radio programs and companion essays, including "The Manitowoc Bohemian Sound" and "Czech and Slovak Music in Wisconsin."

RECORDINGS

Deep Polka: Dance Music from the Midwest. 1998. Smithsonian Folkways CD 40088. Includes performances by Croatian, Czech, Finnish, German, Norwegian, Polish, and Slovenian polka bands from Wisconsin.

Polkaland Records has reissued the bulk of the recordings made by Romy Gosz and many other northeastern Wisconsin polka bands from the 1930s through the 1970s. Contact Greg Leider, Polkaland Records, 109 North Milwaukee Street, Fredonia, WI 53021.

SOUTH SLAVIC AMERICAN MUSIC TRADITIONS

Richard March

Please see Chapter 10 in this volume for biographical information on Richard March. The following essay originally appeared in the 1981 Smithsonian Festival of American Folklife program guide.

In one of the important migrations in human history, South Slavs joined millions of southern and eastern Europeans in a risky journey across the Atlantic to North America. Leaving behind overpopulated villages or barren mountain pastures, they sought a new life in the smoky industrial cities and stark mining towns of the United States. This migration began in the last decades of the nineteenth century and has never really ceased. Although the rate of immigration has fluctuated widely, depending on conditions in the homeland and the varying needs of America's industries, South Slavs continue to come, often from the same villages as the earlier immigrants and often to the same cities and towns in the United States.

Like other ethnic or immigrant communities, South Slavs (Slovenes, Croats, Serbs, and Macedonians, as well as Bulgarians) cherish, nurture, and thoroughly enjoy the musical traditions of their homeland. If you should happen to be in any city with a South Slavic communiy, on almost any weekend of the year, you will more than likely find a variety of ongoing musical events. Something is sure to be going on at one of the churches or lodge halls.

At a Slovenian or Croatian Catholic church, there might be a performance by a **button accordion** group, a choir, or a *tamburitza* ensemble, while at a Serbian or Macedonian Orthodox church musicians play an **accordion** or clarinet backed by rhythm **instruments** for dancing. In addition, there are fraternal lodge halls and taverns that feature similar kinds of music; here one can listen to a song, join in a *kolo* or *oro* line dance, or grab a partner to enjoy a **polka** or **waltz**. Throughout the summer, there is sure to be a lamb roast at a church or lodge picnic grove. The strains of a tamburitza **combo** playing sad love songs is a feast for the ears.

For the South Slavs, music and musical events are a focus for community activity and social life. Actually, this ethnic music may take on many meanings: To a musician, it is a medium of self-expression, a role of posi-

tive status in the community, a pleasant pastime, or a total obsession. To a member of the audience, the music may be the most important aspect of a community event replete with food and drink, good company, an opportunity to speak in the mother tongue, and the celebration of a traditional fête.

One of the more persistent clichés about ethnic folk music is that it is slowly but surely dying out. Only a casual visit to a South Slavic community is needed to gain the opposite impression: that the music is flourishing, gaining new practitioners and fans. Veteran musicians whose bands in the 1930s recorded 78-rpm records still perform and receive the starry-eyed adulation of teenage musicians. Young musicians study tapes of the old-timers' songs, memorizing the lyrics when they no longer understand the original language. One young tamburitza player, when I asked if he could speak Serbo-Croatian, replied, "No, but I can sing it."

As members of veteran ensembles drop out, owing to health or personal reasons, their places are often filled by players young enough to be their sons or daughters. In many cases, they are in fact sons or daughters of musicians. It almost seems that musical talent is a dominant genetic trait. There are family combos entirely composed of parents and children or siblings. There are ensembles of young musicians in which every member is the child of an ethnic musician. Even the children of "mixed" marriages, that is, of a South Slav to an individual of some other ethnic group, seem to gravitate more to the South Slavic traditions than to those of their other parent. Thus, it is not uncommon to find South Slavic musicians with Irish or Polish last names, children who grew up absorbed in the South Slavic community through ties in the maternal line.

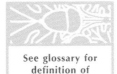

See glossary for definition of boldfaced terms

Although the music is certainly not dying out, it definitely is evolving. A sure sign that something *is* dying out appears when the tradition ceases to respond to changing stimuli in its cultural environment. South Slavic musicians play the music of their own nationality and whatever other music is pleasing to them. American popular songs, country-and-western numbers, and **big band jazz** tunes have entered the **repertoires** of South Slavic bands, but not in a willy-nilly fashion. Only certain melodies from other **genres** are appealing and meet the aesthetic criteria of the musical traditions. These find a lasting place in the repertoire, sometimes even becoming translated into a Slavic language. This filtering process assures that South Slavic American music will remain distinct from other American music while sharing some musical traits and repertoire with other traditions.

BIBLIOGRAPHY

Clissold, Stephen. (1966). *A Short History of Yugoslavia.* Cambridge: Cambridge University Press.

Colakovic, Branko Mita. (1973). *Yugoslav Migrations to America.* San Francisco: R & E Research Associates.

Govorchin, Gerald G. (1961). *Americans from Yugoslavia.* Gainesville: University of Florida Press.

RECORDINGS

The Balkan Records Singles. 1999–2001. The Gary Serenaders, Balkan Recording Orchestra, Dave Zupkovich, Marty Kapugi, and The Popovich Brothers. Four volumes. Balkan Records BAL CD501, 502, 503, 504. CDs.

Button Box Melodies, Volume II. 1998. Richie Yurkovich and Jeff Walker. CD. Available from IAMG, N10060 Fisher Ave., Willard, WI 54493, telephone (715) 267-3275, or by e-mailing iamg@mail.tds.net.

Button Box Polkas. 1982. Johnny Pecon and Lou Trebar. Delta International DI-7022-LPS.

Daleko je Selo Moje. 2001. Jerry Grcevich. CD. For information write to 210 Old Jack's Run Rd., North Huntingdon, PA 15642, e-mail zvijezda@netzero.net, or visit the web at http://www.tamburaweb.com/grce2.htm.

Dave Zupkovich Memorial Album. 1963. Balkan Records BLP 5011.

Grkmania. 1991. Joe Grkman. CD. For information write to P.O. Box 584, Library, PA 15129, call (412) 653-0419, e-mail grkmaniainfo@anthill.com, or visit the web at http://grkmania.anthill.com/.

Macedonian Horos. Joe Tricoff and His Orchestra. Available from Jay Tee Record Company, 714 Ardmore Dr., Dearborn Heights, MI 41827.

More Royal Tamburitzans. 1989. Request Records SRLP 8108.

Orchestra Balkan. 1979. Balkan Festival Productions.

Prav Luštno Je Pozim. 1981. Violet Ruparcich. Greyko Records GLPS 1015.

The Royal Tamburitzans. 1974. Request Records SRLP 8194.

The Royal Tamburitzans Are Here Again. 1979. Request Records SRLP 8125.

Sing with "Teddy" and the Popovich Brothers. 1979. Seven volumes. B. Pressner BP 3011, 3017, 3035, 3051, 3134, 3261, 3355.

Slovenian Carousel. 1995. Nancy Hlad. CD. For information write to P.O. Box 43313, Cleveland, OH 44143, call (216) 731-3617, e-mail nancy@polkas.com, or visit the web at http://www.polkas.com/nancyhlad/index.html.

Srpske Melodije. For information write to 22436 O'Connor, St. Clair Shores, MI 48080.

Sviraj Cijelu Noc. 1998. Peter Kosovec & Company. CD. For information write to 36355 Gregory Dr., Sterling Heights, MI 48312, or call (810) 979-2612.

Twenty-Six Instrumental Button Box Classics. 1999. Walter Ostanek and Friends. CD. For information write to WRS, P.O. Box 91906, Cleveland, OH 44101.

Vrijeme za Spek. 1998. Slanina. CD. For information call (630) 887-8420 or e-mail Slanina2@aol.com

Yankovic Classics. 1996. Grant Kozera and Eric Noltkamper. For information write to 12815 West Allerton Ave., New Berlin, WI 52151, call (262) 529-2552, or visit the web at http://www.polka-store.com/gkozera/.

DON LIPOVAC: BUTTON BOX ACCORDION

Jennie A. Chinn and Carl R. Magnuson

This essay originally appeared in Kansas Folk Art Apprenticeship Program: Selected Portraits, *by Jennie A. Chinn and Carl R. Magnuson, published in 1989 by the Kansas State Historical Society.*

Don Lipovac is one of the most respected musicians among the Slavic communities in Kansas City, Kansas. His influence on the development of traditional music in the area has been profound. Because of his involvement, the musical styles of several regions, particularly Slovenia and Croatia, have come together to create a "Kansas City" style of South Slavic music.

Don was born in the area of the Slovenian parish in Kansas City in 1935. His introduction to his Slovenian musical heritage began at an early age. When Don was three years old, his grandfather bought him a **button accordion**. His mother would sing folk songs from the old country, and Don would pick them out on the accordion by ear. It became obvious that even as a child Don possessed an extraordinary talent.

It was just like a miracle to me that I would be able to do this [pick out a song by ear]. I just didn't understand it. The priest of the parish, when he came to bless the house—I guess I was about five years old and I was playing—he wrote it up in the eastern Kansas *Register*.

In order to encourage Don, his parents provided him with music lessons. At the age of seven, he began his studies. The lessons required him to switch to the **piano accordion**. "When I started my first music lessons, for six months, on Minnesota Avenue," Don remembers, "I had a buddy and we would put our accordions on a red wagon and pull them." After six months, Don's uncle, who also played the accordion, recommended that Don begin lessons with Alfred Vacca from Kansas City, Missouri. As Don recalls now, that was a very fortunate move since Vacca was the best teacher in the area. Until he reached the age of seventeen, Don continued to study with Vacca.

During this period Don all but forgot about the button accordion and concentrated

his efforts on the piano accordion. As time went on, however, Don developed a stronger interest in traditional music. He bought himself a larger, more complicated button accordion and began to renew his skills.

> The Slovenians think the button accordion is more authentic. When you see one of the old-timers, if you play a piano accordion for them, they weren't as happy about the sound—they have different sounds.

Throughout his adult career, Don has maintained his interest in both the button and piano accordion.

In 1952, Don appeared on the *The Ted Mack Amateur Hour*. He auditioned in Kansas City and was accepted for the Kansas City show that was held in Municipal Auditorium. For winning the local competition, he received a trip to New York. After high school, Don continued his studies at the Kansas City Conservatory, now part of the University of Missouri, Kansas City. There he earned degrees in music theory and music education. From 1956 through 1958 he competed in accordion contests by playing classical music. In 1958, Don won the national accordion competition. The same year he appeared on *The Lawrence Welk Show* playing Slovenian polkas. These events brought Don to the attention of local booking agents, who scheduled him in clubs throughout the city.

Although he was studying classical music during his school years, he continued to play traditional Slovenian music at home and in the community. His mother would sing and he would play throughout the parish. Some of the families would invite Don to play at their house parties or at a wedding. Don remembers playing **polkas** and **waltzes** at functions when he was only ten or eleven years old.

While appearing on *The Ted Mack Amateur Hour*, Don came to the attention of a local tamburitzan orchestra. The group, called the Blue Danube Tamburitzans, was just beginning. All of the members had been students of a fine Croatian traditional musician by the name of Nick Rodina. As Don

Kansas City accordion master Don Lipovac.
Photograph courtesy Kansas State Historical Society

now explains it, the **tamburitza**, without amplification, was not very effective for large crowds such as weddings. The group wanted to increase its sound by adding an accordion.

Don was invited to a rehearsal. He had not really been exposed to this type of music, although the Croatian and Slovenian parishes are geographically very close.

> I was in a trance right away because the sounds were beautiful, the **instruments** were real folk instruments, pear-shaped instruments, and they had this look to them and it just struck me right away.

Don joined the orchestra. Although the other band members were good musicians, Don had far more formal training and because of this was able to pick up the music faster. He contributed to the group by becoming a teacher of sorts.

It was during this period in the 1950s that the traditions of the local Croatian and Slovenian communities began to come together.

> That was the neat thing about Kansas City. The Croatians—at least from 1950 on—were influenced by Slovenian music. We were playing a lot of Slovenian music. . . . I think that is unique to Kansas City, because you'd go to a wedding

The Radost Orchestra. Left to right: Paul Milanovich, Dan Vranesevich, Dave Vranescevich, and Joe Cindric.
Photograph by Paul Milanovich, courtesy of the Smithsonian Institution

and most people would dance to polkas and waltzes all night and they are Slovenian-type dances. Whereas you go to a Croatian club in Pittsburgh, Pennsylvania . . . and they don't even want to hear it. . . . There was a little resistance when I first came in. . . . The accordion was sort of like a necessity because of the public demand at weddings. . . . This is my own opinion.

These thoughts are echoed by members of the Croatian community. They credit Don with this mixing of traditions. Don was playing Slovenian music as he played at Croatian functions. The community accepted Don and became accustomed to the music. Don admits he may have had some impact. However, he also sensed that the Croatian community in Kansas City did not have the same attachment to the purely Croatian music that Croatian Americans in the eastern part of the

Tamburitza Orchestra Slanina
Photograph by Nick Spitzer, courtesy of the Smithsonian Institution

Croatian Tamburitza

Please see sidebar accompanying Chapter 5 in this volume for biographical information on Nick Spitzer. The following essay combines material that originally appeared in the program guide for the Folk Masters 1993 concert series, held March 5–April 10 at the Barns of Wolf Trap in Vienna, Virginia, and the program guide for the Folk Masters 1994 concert series, held March 11–April 16 at the Barns of Wolf Trap.

Tamburitza as played by Serbs and Croats has its roots in Turkish string playing, well leavened by song traditions of several Eastern European cultures including those of Hungarians, Slovenians, and Greeks. Large numbers of Serbs and Croats have historically sought a better life in the United States. Many found employment in rapidly growing industrial towns and cities of the East and Midwest. Tamburitza music is one of the strongest symbols of Serbs, Croats, and related Slavic peoples in cities such as Pittsburgh, Chicago, and Milwaukee.

Tamburitza (also *tamburica*) is a generic term for a family of fretted **instruments** that include the *prima, brač, čelo, bugarija,* and *berde,* ranging in size from smaller than a mandolin to larger than a string bass. The instruments are played in a driving rhythmic fashion and often accompany line and round dances, including *kolos* and *drmeš.* At the same time, the soul of tamburitza music lies in its emotional vocals devoted to love lost, love regained, the good life, drinking, and the recovery of a peaceful, pastoral homeland. After four generations in the United States, tamburitza has developed its own flavor with influence from pop, country, and bluegrass, as well as the blending of songs and dances from many regions and peoples within the former Yugoslavia.

Radost in Serbo-Croatian means "happy." The Radost Orchestra translates as the "Happy Boys Orchestra," according to group leader, vocalist, and *beglaite* player Paul Milanovich of Beaver, Pennsylvania, just outside Pittsburgh. The instrument, also called a *bugarija,* is likened by Milanovich to a rhythm guitar, and it is used in a complex, often contrapuntal rhythm arrangement with the other stringed instruments. The other Radost members are Dan Jovanovich on guitar and vocals, Joe Cindrich on *brač,* Dan Vranesevic on *čelo,* and his twin brother, David Vranesevic, on *berde,* a stand up, fretted bass.

The Radost Orchestra, in addition to its Serbian and Croatian background, traces its immediate repertoire to southeastern European music from Romanian, Slovakian, Italian, and Macedonian sources. Several of the band members work in liquor distribution by day and on weekends, playing tamburitza by night at wedding receptions, ethnic festivals, church fairs, and other community gatherings.

Currently there are more Serbs than Croats in the band, but unlike some groups, Radost's members disdain the potential for conflict between themselves and their often mixed audiences. When asked if they play mainly for Serbs or for Croats, the answer is a slightly taciturn "Yes!" from Paul Milanovich, who is appalled by the situation in the former Yugoslavia. He adds, "We play for anybody who wants to listen. . . . We play the music that brings people together. Our only policy is . . . if you don't like what we play, be it Serbian or Croatian or something else, leave!" Given the group's joyous vocals and engaging string playing, that seems unlikely.

Tamburitza Orchestra Slanina was formed in 1986 by five men of Croatian descent from three cities who were alumni from four different bands. Slanina, meaning "bacon" in Croatian, is something of a supergroup devoted to exploring new musical experiences while adhering to traditional style. In this effort, they have consciously returned to experiment within the Old World progressions, harmonies, and techniques.

Nick Spitzer

United States did. "Our crowd could polka," remarks Don. "They just wanted to polka. . . . Our generation was the first generation that left the Old World divisions behind."

Although Don continued to play the accordion, he also picked up a musical knowledge of the tamburitza. He was recommended over and over again as a teacher as well. Not only did he know the traditional music, but he could read music and explain the theory of it. This made him a valuable member of both communities.

Don continued to play with the Blue Danube Tamburitzans for several years until a key member of the group went into military service. At that time, the Kolo Club was

formed in the Croatian parish. This club for young people helped preserve the dances and music from the old country. What was left of the Blue Danube Tamburitzans became the group's core musicians.

By the 1960s the Kolo Club began to break up. The members, who were Don's age, were getting married and taking on other work. Don, however, stayed with his music full time. He explains, "With me it's a passion. . . . Art is not practical as far as making a lot of money, but it is a beautiful thing. . . . Without music my life would be empty." During this period Don married his wife, Joanne. She also came from a Slovenian family that was proud of its musical heritage. Today, she shares Don's passion for the music.

Don and a few of his friends tried to revive the Kolo Club in the 1960s. The results of this effort became the St. John's Tamburitzans. In 1966, Don offered a class in the tamburitza at St. John's School, a private Croatian institution. The first class had over forty students. The class was met with great enthusiasm and continues today. Don continues to direct the group, which has produced six record albums to date. Both Don and Joanne have devoted a great deal of time to the St. John's Tamburitzans in the last twenty-two years. "It is strictly for love," explains Don. "The folk songs are beautiful, the customs are beautiful; it's a thing of beauty if you see it in the right light."

Don has had a major impact on the traditional culture of both the Slovenian and Croatian communities in Kansas City. He estimates that he has taught traditional music to over 400 students and has written and arranged between 500 and 600 pieces of music. He has dreams of forming an adult orchestra. He estimates that there are at least sixty good tamburitza players in the city. He also is interested in keeping alive the button accordion traditions of his youth.

Don is quite accomplished in the button accordion today. At one point he had to ask himself, "Why did I ever quit?"

I had to relearn it—it wasn't easy, because I had forgotten a lot of the finger patterns and I had to go over it again. . . . I knew all this music— the first time it was a miracle to be able to feel your way through without thinking. When you are a little kid, you don't even know what's happening.

Nearly four years ago Don started a button accordion group. All of the members are adults of Slovenian or Croatian heritage, and most have been playing traditional music for a good part of their lives.

For three years Don worked with the group almost every Wednesday night. For this he received no pay. Rather, he did it for the love of the music. In 1988, the group applied for and was granted funding under the Kansas Folk Arts Apprenticeship Program. The money the group received went directly to pay Don for his services. The group works very hard and has accomplished a great deal over the years. One concert a year is played for the Slovenian parish, which offers the group a weekly practice space in the basement of Holy Family Church. The members of the group share Don's devotion to their South Slavic heritage and participate simply to keep the music alive.

See glossary for definition of boldfaced terms

HUNGARIAN FOLK MUSIC IN THE UNITED STATES

László Kürti

László Kürti is a member of the political science faculty at Hungary's University of Miskolc and the author of articles on music, dance, and symbolism. Making use of recordings he collected during the 1970s and early 1980s, he produced and annotated three albums of Hungarian music for Folkways Records, including Transylvanian Wedding Music *(FE 4015, released in 1983) and* Hungarian Folk Music from the Kis-Küküllo Region of Central Transylvania, Romania *(FE 4035, released in 1985). The following essay is derived from the notes Kürti wrote to accompany the 1983 album* Hungarian Folk Music in the United States *(FE 4020).*

It is difficult to discuss Hungarian "folk music" without understanding what this term means. One of the most burning problems with it is the idea of "folk," a category that is not clearly understood in the study of Hungarian immigrants. The diversity of cultural patterns and Hungarian immigrants' cultural values are still largely unknown in North America. Questions such as how immigrant communities were formed, what were the social institutions fostering the values of the immigrants, what roles these institutions played, and just how cultural systems have changed under various historical and socioeconomic conditions are yet to be answered by social scientists.

When I began to study Hungarians in the United States, it became clear to me that no community can be separated from its historical setting and the social forces that have shaped institutions and formal representations of ideas of the community. Every immigrant community, whether a large multireligious metropolitan community in New York or a removed mining settlement in western Pennsylvania, possesses certain elements and patterns that can provide a key to understanding its culture, **folklore**, and musical systems. For that reason, it is a highly questionable enterprise to develop and use an overarching category such as "folk music." This is so especially because "folk" may mean diverse and sometimes opposing values from community to community. Yet it is also clear that there are certain values and cultural patterns that identify distant Hungarian settlements as "Hungarian" and separate them from other Eastern European settlements.

Despite the fact that widespread Hungarian settlements share some common characteristics, it is important to note that every Hungarian community in North America is unique for one reason or another. The Buckeye community in Cleveland, Ohio, for example, has been known as a real old-timers' place and, as S. Erdély informs us (1964, 1979), the **repertoire** of the singers

there reflects a great deal of diversity. The Franklin, New Jersey, settlement was known for its excellent **brass bands**, founded by István Bendes (see Makár 1969). The Árpádon-Albany Hungarian community in Louisiana, studied by L. Dégh (1980), has a grape harvest festival, though the people were originally strawberry farmers. New York City always has been a center, providing first-class musicians and gypsy ensembles on the East Coast, and so on. The list of examples of Hungarian communities is endless.

There are some songs that outlive the community or a generation of immigrants. Many of these popular songs are the so-called old-timers' tunes, yet they are not part of the authentic "old-style" peasant music that was analyzed by Zoltán Kodály (1971). Nevertheless, they were brought from Europe and are passed from one generation to the next and from one ensemble to another The musical repertoire of the immigrants is in a constant state of flux. Because there have been many different immigration periods (1880–1914, 1918–1930s, 1945–1950, and 1956–1957), and many newcomers have filled positions in immigrant organizations, there have been new songs and tunes introduced into the repertoire. The dissemination of records of Hungarian music since the 1910s also has contributed to this diversity.

The newcomers, especially the 1956 generation (referred to as the "fifty-sixers"), had an incredible impact on the already established immigrant machinery. In some cases, they were caught by this machinery and went along with it. Most of the time, however—and this can be seen by the many new institutions and ideology that have emerged—they did not. For this very reason, it is highly questionable to say, as Erdély asserted, that "the Gypsy ensembles are among the few instrumental groups that retain their traditional compositions and performance practices." There are no two Hungarian bands that would play even the same melodies alike. It is obvious that bands such as that of Iván Dezsõ of the 1930s and New York's Gypsy Joe of the 1980s are unique in their compositions, repertoire, structure,

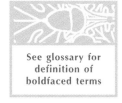

See glossary for definition of boldfaced terms

functions, and so on. Yet they are both Hungarian: serving Hungarian functions, playing Hungarian music, and maintaining a special national character.

Early twentieth-century immigrants transplanted musical institutions such as the *dalárda* (singing society) and the *fúvószenekar* (**brass band**), for they themselves were the product of a society that produced and maintained such institutions. There is no reason to believe that this is not the situation in the case of diverse song styles and dance melodies that belong to later immigrant generations and groups.

When the fifty-sixers arrived in the United States, there was a culture shock both for them and for the old-timers. Many musicians who were born in the United States or came earlier in the twentieth century agree that the new songs and different musical ideas brought by the newcomers were "strange" and foreign to their ears. For the fifty-sixers, the tunes of the old-timers were often outmoded, unheard of, or even meaningless. The song repertoire reflecting the mood of the 1920s Hungarian society is quite different from the songs produced by Hungarian miners in West Virginia. Similarly, the technique of violin playing among older musicians reflects a style fashionable or taught at one point in Hungarian tradition.

SOME PERFORMERS AND TRADITIONS
VOCALISTS

There is a strong tradition of Hungarian vocal music; many of the tunes are based on popular songs that were learned in the homeland and maintained in the United States. Mátyás Galló (1895–1980) is typical of the first generations of immigrants who came to America before World War I. Galló was born in a small, poverty-stricken settlement known as Nagygejöc, in Ung County, a northeast region of the Austro-Hungarian monarchy. She arrived in the United States in 1913 with her first husband and worked in cigar factories and mills in New Jersey. In 1916, the family moved to Cleveland, Ohio.

A Hungarian American miner and his wife pose for a photograph on the porch of their home in Calumet County, Pennsylvania. Coal mining was one of the occupations that Hungarian immigrants pursued in the United States. Often, they worked in terrible conditions.
Photograph by Ben Shahn taken in 1935 for the Farm Security Administration, photograph from the Collections of the Library of Congress.

Galló spent the rest of her life on the city's East Side, the Hungarian Buckeye community (also referred to as the Hungarian Debrecen City). There she held memberships in several Hungarian clubs. She spent her last two years in a nursing home in Akron, Ohio, run by the Hungarian Reformed Church. The majority of her songs reflect the general repertoire of her generation. Many were popular songs of the 1910s through the 1920s, including one about a World War I–era soldier and his burning desire to return home.

Vintondale, Pennsylvania, is a small mining settlement in the bituminous coal region of western Pennsylvania. Hungarians arrived here in large numbers around 1905–1907. By the 1920s, the Hungarian community was a well-organized immigrant society, with its own church, school, and social club. The prosperity, however, did not last long. The decline of the mining industry and the closing of the mines in Vintondale contributed to the fall of this community, a situation that was mirrored in Hungarian settlements in Virginia, Kentucky, and West Virginia.

Ilana Horváth Farkas (1894–1981) was a talented singer from Vintondale. She was born in Lévárt, in the former Gönör County of Hungary (annexed to Czechoslovakia af-

ter the Treaty of Trianon in 1919). At the age of eighteen, she was forced into marriage by her family and subsequently followed her husband to the United States. They settled in Vintondale immediately after their arrival in 1912. In 1924, a disastrous mine collapse took her husband's life, and soon after she married Miklós Farkas. Farkas was an able man who operated a *burdoshás* (boarding-house) and hotel for Hungarian miners. The hotel was a social and cultural institution for Hungarians. In fact, as Ilana later recounted, she learned many of her songs from the miners living in the *burdoshás*.

In an interview with me, Ilana sang a traditional Hungarian folk song. In a practice that is common among folk singers, however, she changed the name of the town—originally in Hungary—to Vintondale. Singers often change a place name mentioned in a song according to the place they live, came from, or to which they have a strong memory attached. This also personalizes the song, and often the singers will believe that the story told in the song actually "happened" in the town in which they live.

Many Hungarian immigrants worked in the mines. One was Gustáv Fülöp (1888–1978), who was born in Gergelyi (present-day Gergelyiuogornya), a village in Szabolcs County in northeastern Hungary.

Fülöp came to the United States in 1907 with many of his friends from the village. He worked at various jobs in New Jersey, Ohio, and Pennsylvania. In 1911, he returned to Hungary and was subsequently drafted into the army. While he was there, his family arranged for him to be married to the daughter of a well-to-do family in Mezóvari (present-day Vari). Fülöp did not like army service. After a few months, he deserted, along with several of his comrades, and returned to the United States. From that time on, until his retirement in 1953, he worked in the West Virginia coal mines. In 1922, he was able to bring his family to America. The Fülöp family lived in several small mine-patch towns, including Logan, Holden, and Sharples; these place names occur in many of Fülöp's stories and songs.

Fülöp's nickname was "Big Gus," because he stood six foot, four inches tall. Although originally from a peasant family, Fülöp's ideas about life and work had been changed fundamentally by his five decades of backbreaking work in the mines. In an interview with me, he recalled vividly the lifestyle of the miners, the strikes, and the mine accidents in West Virginia. He did not sing many songs about the fields, the shepherds, and the colorful Hungarian countryside seen through the eyes of the peasantry. His songs instead featured the *májnás legény* ("miner lad"). He had a huge repertoire of stories, **ballads**, songs, and religious tunes. One ballad, telling the story of a cowboy and his love affair with a well-bred baroness, was particularly interesting, because he sang it almost word for word as it was sung in Hungary at the turn of the twentieth century, when it had its first period of popularity.

Singer Kálmán Horosz (born 1908) represents a more recent generation of Hungarian immigrant, bringing with him newer and different types of songs. He was born in the former capital of Ung County, Ungvár (present-day Uzgood in the Ukraine). He

Hungarian Folk Musicians in the United States

came to the United States in 1937 and, after working in various factories, settled in Passaic, New Jersey, in 1940.

His song repertoire gave a good reflection of the struggling immigrants who came to this country during the 1920s and 1930s. The song "Lányok, lányok" is very popular among Hungarians, reflecting as it does nostalgia for the girls of the old country and their peasant way of dressing:

> Lányok, lányok ti nyújorki lányok
> Mért nincs néktek berakoitt szoknyátok,
> Ha nincs néktek berakoitt szoknyátok,
> Nem is vagytok ti nyújorki lányok,
> Tisztelem a régi szeretömet.

Lassies, lassies of New York,
How come you've no pleated skirts?
If you've no pleated skirts,
You're not from New York.
I'll greet my old lover instead.

In other communities, the name of the local town may be substituted for New York, a practice that was common in the homeland as well.

Also in Horosz's repertoire were humorous pieces such as "Ilyen ember kell nekünk" ("We need just such a fine man"), a series of nonsensical couplets, such as

> Száraz tónak nedves partiján, döglött
>   béka kuruttyol,
> Arra megy egy süket ember, meghallja
>   hogy lubickol.

In the water of a dry lakebed a dead
   frog is croaking,
A deaf man walks there and hears its
   splashing.

According to Horosz, songs such as this were sung by scouts, youth clubs, children, and sports teams on the occasion of trips or social gatherings.

Horosz also sang a group of songs that expressed a strong sense of Hungarian nationalism and pride, while at the same time lamenting the fact that the Hungarian people often suffered under foreign rule. These songs are known as irredenta Hungarene, and

were so strongly nationalistic that they were banned after the communist takeover of Hungary in 1947. Nonetheless, with some minor changes, such as replacing nationalist fervor with religious or socialist ideals, the songs have survived. One example, "Magyraok vagyunk mi," was originally an early nineteenth-century workers' song used at demonstrations, strikes, and marches. It has outlived this specific use to more generally express Hungarian pride.

BAND MUSIC

There is a strong tradition of both amateur and semiprofessional Hungarian American dance bands. One of the first was an ensemble led by Iván Dezsō in New York City during the 1930s. Little is known about Dezsō's life and career. He was born in the 1890s in Hungary and arrived in the United States sometime around 1910. He was not a professional musician; he worked in factories and, according to some of his contemporaries, in coal mines in Pennsylvania. He taught himself violin and by the early 1930s was playing at balls, dinner dances, and gatherings in New York's Hungarian community.

Dezsö was also a member of the Hungarian Theater, also known as the Sárossy Theatre, a group of amateurs and professionals active between 1936 and the 1960s. His biggest role was in the 1950 folk play Jancai Rigó, the Devil's Violinist, in which he played the lead part of the famous turn-of-the-century Hungarian gypsy violinist. His last role was the lead in Cigányprimás ("The Gypsy Violinist"), an operetta by Imre Kálmán staged in the spring of 1958. Dezsō probably died soon after, because the fall season opened without him.

Dezsō's band included a fairly typical lineup of **instruments**. The primás (first violinist) was Paul Zity (formerly Pál Szittyai), an Akron-born Hungarian. The **bass** player was Árpád Sziláygi and the second violinist Sziláygi's brother, Vilmos. The Sziláygi brothers were from the famous gypsy music dynasty that settled in Detroit in the early 1900s. On the piano was László Semsey, the only musician in the band who had a musical

education, training on piano and *cimbalom*. He was a pupil of László Kun, a former teacher of the cimabalom at the Hungarian Academy of Music, until 1922, when he came to the United States. It is interesting to note the presence of the piano in this "gypsy" orchestra, a feature that was accepted fairly early in Hungarian American musical ensembles.

Iván Dezső recorded at least thirty 78-rpm records. However, not all are in a Hungarian musical style. Much of his repertoire was drawn from popular Hungarian music of the 1930s, although the songs have since fallen out of popularity. The band recorded everything from slow listening songs to medium and uptempo **csárdás**. Playing a medley of slow-medium-fast **tempo** pieces is common in folk practice in Central Europe, and was a typical arrangement for this band.

Another very successful bandleader of the 1930s and 1940s was Jenö Bartal. He was born in Budapest in the late 1890s and came to the United States in 1921. Bartal had received training as a classical cellist, so it was natural for him to try to form his own dance band after coming to America. Unsuccessful in forming his own band, he turned to managing other orchestras and musicians.

By 1935, Bartal was musical director of his own orchestra, playing at several New York hotels. In the late 1930s and 1940s there was no other orchestra as famous as Bartal's "Singing Strings" dance band. But there was an obvious problem: Bartal's orchestra did not satisfy the needs of the Hungarian community. He was playing at upper-class places, such as the Hotel Lexington, that were unaffordable for most of the Hungarians, save the upper classes, who identified not with their fellow countrymen but with the upper social strata of American society. Bartal released several recordings on his own. Most of these, however, are not traditional music but various popular social dance tunes from the 1930s and 1940s.

Bartal's great reputation was based on several factors. His band featured excellent musicians, such as Sándor Aranyosi, a young gypsy *primás* who had a vast knowledge of

various musical styles besides Hungarian music, and Árpád Babos, a gypsy cimbalom player who arrived in the United States about 1910. Bartal was also a great entertainer, playing solo cello pieces between sets of the band.

However, Bartal's main emphasis was entertaining an exclusive set of fans. Through records, high-class restaurants and hotels, elite parties, and radio, Bartal was able to find an unusual audience for a Hungarian band. In 1939, his "Singing Strings" was selected as the best dance band of the year by the graduating class of New York University.

Bartal did record some traditional csárdás that gave the band some "ethnic allure" for its upper-class audience. In these recordings, it is interesting to note that both piano and cimbalom play the accompaniment and solo roles, a practice originated by Hungarian American bands.

Contemporary bands continue to carry on the tradition of appealing to both traditional Hungarian audiences and more modern ones. Their appearances are often limited to special occasions, such as picnics, harvest balls, and national holidays.

In the Hazelwood section of Pittsburgh, Pennsylvania, a large Hungarian enclave, there is an annual *szureti bál* ("harvest ball") organized by the Hungarian Reformed Church that is typical of this type of event held in Hungarian communities around the country. It starts out with dinner accompanied by a considerable consumption of alcohol. Around nine o'clock, the floor is cleared for dancing. During dinnertime, the band may play or just start to set up. Fruit is hung from the ceiling; once dancing starts, the dancers try to pull down a piece. If they are caught, they are fined by the judges, or are put in specially built jails until someone pays their bail. It is usually not difficult to find someone to pay the bail, which helps increase the money raised at these events. Harvest balls are held from September until the end of November. Usually several hundred people attend, and the income raised can be considerable.

See glossary for definition of boldfaced terms

At one Hazelwood ball, the band playing was led by Mickey Schwartz and included five pieces (drums, **accordion**, sax, violin, and electric piano). The band is very popular in Hungarian communities in the Pittsburgh area (Hazelwood, Duquesne, McKeesport, McKeesrock, etc.). Schwartz is a second-generation Hungarian. He is a good entertainer and singer, playing the saxophone, trumpet, and clarinet. The band's violinist in the early 1980s was Árpád Nagy, who was born in Hungary in 1904, and brought by his parents two years later to Pittsburgh. The band is unusual in that it has had a female member, who played accordion.

At this ball, the band played a wide variety of social dances. Besides the csárdás, the band played **tangoes**, **waltzes**, one-steps, **polkas**, and other American social dances. They also played the *gólya tánc* ("stork dance"), a number popular in Hungary in the 1920s and perhaps earlier. The music for the dance, however, is not Hungarian but the well-known "Battle Hymn of the Republic."

Another Hungarian community with a unique dance band tradition is in Lake Ronkonkoma, Long Island, New York. The Hungarian community there (sometimes referred to by Hungarians as the "Hungarian Balaton") goes back to 1921, when a group of Hungarians formed the Hungarian Literary Social Club. Since then, this small group of not more than 130 families, while maintaining fairly close contact with the Yorkville Hungarian community in New York City, has developed quite a unique tradition. The movers and shakers of this community are successful business owners and entrepreneurs, many of them from the "fifty-six" generation.

The so-called May Picnic is an annual event designed to raise money for the club. The group sponsors at least five other major annual gatherings, although almost every weekend there is something going on in the club house. In the early 1980s, two musicians played regularly for club meetings: the famous gypsy *primás* Bélas Babay and the accordionist Francis Saas, both local citizens.

Babay came to the United States in 1938 and became an overnight success. He played at popular establishments and made dozens of records. Due to a heart condition, he retired early but continues to play locally. Saas is a self-taught accordion player who had previously worked as an electrical engineer. The two began playing together in the mid-1970s.

The music that they play has several unique characteristics that are not present in other Hungarian American bands. First, they use a rhythm machine in place of a double bass. The rhythm machine (some people refer to it as the "dummy machine") is operated by Saas. Second, Babay is a virtuosic violinistic, possessing greater skill than the typical band musician. His method of playing is closer to the former gypsy style, exemplified by famous players of an earlier generation. The duo also possesses a unique ability to play together and anticipate changes in dynamics and tempo.

The most popular band of the early 1980s in the New York area was Gypsy Joe and his orchestra. Some organizers claimed that "without Gypsy Joe, there is no profit"; others stated, "If there is no Gypsy Joe, we might break even, if we're lucky. You need him; he brings people." His great reputation was well deserved. His orchestra was exceptionally well organized and its repertoire extensive, including songs of diverse styles and from different eras. They presented their material with good humor and a fine sense of entertainment.

The band was composed of five instruments: accordion, saxophone/clarinet, violin, drums, and electric piano. Gypsy Joe played the accordion and was the vocalist, and his son was at the drums. The other "gypsy" in the band was the violin player. Both of them are members of the "fifty-six" generation.

The band specialized in playing a long set known as the "gypsy czardas," or "the gypsy dance set." This is an important dance style that was unknown in Hungarian American communities until the fifty-sixers introduced it. These types of melodies feature a different beat, referred to as *esztam*, con-

sisting of the pattern eighth rest, eighth note/eighth rest, eighth note, a totally new and unknown beat to both the old-timers and the second-generation musicians. The relation of these "gypsy songs" to authentic gypsy folk music (in other words, Romany-speaking tribal gypsy music) is still being debated by **ethnomusicologists**.

The band would end their sets by playing the Hungarian national song, the "Rákóczi March," in a short, uniquely orchestrated version. This piece is typically played at the end of an evening to signal that the merriment is over.

BIBLIOGRAPHY

Dégh, L. (1980). "Grape-Harvest Festival of Strawberry Farmers: Folklore or Fake?" *Ethnologica Europaca* 10:114–131.

Erdély, S. (1964). "Folksinging of the American Hungarians in Cleveland." *Ethnomusicology* 8:14–27.

Erdély, S. (1979). "Ethnic Music in the United States: An Overview." *Yearbook of the IFMC* (1979):114–137.

Kodály, Z, (1971). *Folk Music of Hungary,* trans. C. Jolly and L. Picken. New York: Praeger.

Kürti, László. (1999). "Symbolism and Meaning in Dance." *East European Meetings in Ethnomusicology* 6:97–112.

Makár, J. (1969). *The Story of an Immigrant Group in Franklin, N.J.,* trans. A. Molnar. New Brunswick, NJ: AHP.

Porter, J. (1979). "Introduction: The Traditional Music of Europeans in America." *Selected Reports in Ethnomusicology* 3:1–23.

Unblocked: Music of Eastern Europe. 1997. Three-CD set. Notes by László Kürti. Ellipsis Arts CD3571, 3572, 3573.

YIDDISH MUSIC IN THE UNITED STATES

Henry Sapoznik

Henry Sapoznik is a Grammy-nominated producer/performer in the fields of Yiddish and Amercian traditional music. A pioneer in the renewal of klezmer music, he is the author of Klezmer! Jewish Music from Old World to Our World *(Schirmer Books, 1999). He has also produced several anthologies of klezmer music from 78s, including the 1981 Folkways set* Klezmer Music 1910–1942 *(Folkways 34021), which was reissued on CD in 1999. The following essay originally appeared in* Jewish-American History and Culture: An Encyclopedia, *edited by Jack Fischel and Sanford Pinsker (Garland Publishing, 1992).*

Yiddish music can be described as the informally accumulated history of the Jews of Eastern Europe and America. Within its numerous forms, from folk songs to **fiddle** tunes, a clear picture emerges of the Jewish people through their music.

The Yiddish language and its culture sprang from the Western European Jewish communities that had settled and grown during the Middle Ages along the Rhine River in what is modern-day Germany (Ashkenaz). It was the success of Moses Mendelssohn's Haskalah (Enlightenment) movement in the late eighteenth century that gradually ended Yiddish and its attendant culture in Germany. However, it continued to grow and thrive in Eastern Europe.

The most influential form of musical expression within the Jewish community was the singing of the *khazn* (cantor). No aspect of Jewish music remained unaffected by the performance and content of this principal form. After the destruction of the Second Temple in Jerusalem (70 C.E.), the rabbinate, in mourning, banned instrumental music. Now, the only officially sanctioned music was unaccompanied liturgy. The cantor, though not seen by the community as ritually indispensable as was the rabbi, was still required to maintain an "above-average" character.

Even with the cantor's commitment to the content of the prayers, there are examples of rabbinical reprimands against cantors because of their beautiful voices, which, as it was claimed, distracted the worshippers from the piety of the prayers. In addition to his role as a leader in the dynamic of community prayer, the khazn was responsible for training the future generations of *khazonim*. The apprentices (*meshoyr'rim*) would learn the rudiments of the special prayer modes to accompany the cantor; some of them might later become cantors themselves. By the end of the nineteenth century trained meshoyr'rim would also go on to

help create the Yiddish musical theater in both Europe and the United States as both composers and performers. In smaller towns that had no khazonim prayers were led in the synagogue by talented "amateurs" such as the *ba'al tfile* and the *ba'al k'riah* or had their services led by one of many traveling khazonim. Religious music also thrived in the *kheyder* and yeshiva (primary and secondary schools), where the whole of Jewish law and traditions were taught to students with the help of specific mnemonic melodies.

Also influential were the myriad forms of unaccompanied folk songs that reflected the broad diversity of Eastern European Jewish life. These included songs of love and marriage, lullabies and children's songs, **work songs**, and **ballads** detailing natural and national disasters. Sung in a plain style, they would, by the beginning of the twentieth century, form a rich source for music of the Yiddish theater. Most of these songs were learned via the "**oral tradition**," that is, from family and friends and later by attending theater performances or hearing records or radio.

It was the Hasidim, and their charismatic interpretation of piety, who encouraged song and dance as a valid approach to prayer. Their fervor accorded a great value to compositions called *nigunim* (wordless songs). These melodies bypassed the "burden" of words in the quest of a oneness with God. The tunes, meant to be sung on holidays and celebrations, would build in intensity as they progressed, accompanied by clapping, stamping, and enthusiastic dancing. Because of the religious mandate of separation of men and women, there was no mixed dancing. This created specific men's and women's dance traditions.

The influence of vocal stylings and inflections could also be heard in the music of the klezmer. The term "klezmer" is a Yiddishized contraction of two Hebrew words, *klei* and *zemer,* meaning "vessel of **melody**." Though looked down upon by the rabbinate for promoting "frivolousness," instrumental music was an important part of both sacred and secular events in Jewish life. Using in-

struments popular in their particular region, *klezmorim* played such **instruments** as the **fiddle**, flute, **bass**, *baraban* (drum), *tsimbl* (**hammered dulcimer**), and *tats* (**cymbals**). By the nineteenth century other instruments—clarinet, trumpet, tuba—were added. Music was heard at weddings, balls, and other celebrations, on market days, and in village inns. More than any other social situation in the Jewish world, Jews and non-Jews could share their art and their economics through the forum of klezmer music.

In addition to playing dance music, the musicians would accompany the improvisatory rhymes and songs of the *badkhn*. The badkhn combined the talents of a poet, satirist, Talmudist, and social critic. His pithy and sly insights into the nature of life and religious responsibilities made him an integral part of any Jewish wedding. The vocal style used by the badkhn was also derived from the religious chanting heard in the synagogue, while the klezmorim, in accompanying him, adapted a Romanian musical **form** called *doina,* favored by star soloists as a showcase for their virtuosity.

Until the mid–nineteenth century, the only way that Jewish musicians could obtain a place in conservatories or orchestras was through conversion. This period saw the eventual erosion of the many socially restrictive measures against Jews and the rise of a new generation of Jewish prodigies. These included Mischa Elman (1873–1967), Jascha Heifitz (1901–1988), and others, who for the first time were able to make the transition from klezmer band to concert hall without the humiliating necessity of conversion.

During the 1870s a new development was taking place in the burgeoning Yiddish world. From the wine cellars of Jassy, Romania, came the Yiddish theater of Abraham Goldfaden (1840–1908). Until Goldfaden's time, the rabbinate discouraged any kind of theater as antithetical to proper Jewish behavior and only tolerated amateur plays, which were presented on certain holidays (Purim, for example, when *purimshpilers*—schoolboy actors—presented the story of the foiling of a plot against the Jewish community of Persia through song, dance, and skit).

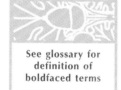

See glossary for definition of boldfaced terms

Alter Goyzman
(Chudnover), fiddler and
orchestral leader
(extreme left); nephew
Louis Grupp on fiddle
(seated far right);
Chudnov, Vollhyn, c.
1905.

By borrowing from all the sources available to him in the late nineteenth century from grand opera to biblical anecdote, Goldfaden crafted a musical theater whose future influence was little imagined in its humble birthplace.

Within a few years of the theater's inception, a number of traveling companies had sprung up, bringing Yiddish variants of everything from the works of William Shakespeare to contemporary plays based on the pages of daily newspapers, as well as episodes from the annals of Jewish history. Singers, comics, composers, artists, and musicians joined the growing numbers of these traveling theater troupes. Like their fellow performers the *klezmorim*, acting companies too suffered at the hands of belligerent local and national governments that instituted restrictive measures against their performances.

Motivated by social, political, and economic upheavals in Eastern Europe, some three million Jews emigrated between 1880 and 1924. The ultimate destination for many of these Jews was to be the United States, and among them were numerous musicians, composers, singers, actors, and dancers. They and their children would soon provide the creators, performers, and audiences for the Yiddish American cultural experience.

The America to which the Jewish musicians immigrated was one of great possibilities and diversity. Popular entertainment was in its awkward growing stages and afforded many opportunities for those who had the skills to take advantage of it. By the mid-1840s, the United States had already tentatively embarked on the establishment of a native popular theater with the rise of the **minstrel show**. These grotesque, stereotyped depictions of "Negro" life in America were the foundation of the soon to emerge variety shows, vaudeville, and burlesque, which continued the older black depictions but added a new cache of ethnic and national peoples: the "depictable types" who were at that moment streaming off the boats at New York's Castle Garden and, by 1892, Ellis Island.

It is ironic that Jewish musicians seeking employment in vaudeville theater orchestras could find themselves accompanying singers who were parodying them with such songs as "Sheenies in the Sand" and "Yiddle on Your Fiddle Play Some Ragtime." More ironic was the fact that Jewish composers themselves, as well as other minorities who were eager to succeed in the highly competitive world of Tin Pan Alley, wrote racist novelty songs about their own people. Add to these musical outlets the myriad number of hotel and cafe orchestras, roof

garden restaurants, circuses, Wild West shows, parties, picnics, political rallies, records, and silent movie houses, and one gets the picture of an emerging leisure class finding numerous outlets for its free time.

Nowhere was this newfound entertainment more evident in the immigrant Jewish community than in the rise of the Yiddish theater. The theater, along with the lyceum lecture hall, now joined the synagogue as a meeting place where the powerful beliefs, devotions, and loyalties of the Jewish community were publicly expressed. It was not uncommon for Jews who religiously attended *shul* Saturday mornings to attend the Yiddish theater on Saturday afternoons. From the rough and energetic offerings of Joseph Lateiner (1853–1935) and "Professor" Moishe Hurwitz (1844–1910) of the late 1890s to the more sophisticated and influential presentations of Jacob P. Adler (1855–1926), Boris Thomashefsky (1868?–1939), and Maurice Schwartz (1888–1960) of the 1920s, the Yiddish theater offered theatergoers (both Jewish and non–Jewish) a colorful and occasionally innovative experience. Rising together with the young actors was the new generation of composers. Many, like Joseph Rumshinsky (1881–1956), Herman Wohl (1877–1936), and Sholem Secunda (1894–1974), received their musical training as meshoyr'rim back in Europe and, once in New York, augmented it with studies in both classical and popular composition.

While Yiddish theater presented a wide variety of popular entertainments, this so-called *shund* (trash) was looked down upon by a growing Yiddish intelligentsia. Championing the rise of Yiddish art music, the *kunst* tradition emphasized a more literary and sophisticated content and performance style. Among the great figures in this tradition were the composers Leo Low (1878–1962) and Lazar Weiner (1897–1982), singers Sidor Belarsky (1900–1975) and Isa Kremer (1885–1956), and musicologists Abraham Zvi Idelsohn (1882–1938), Eric Werner (1901–1986), and Albert Weisser (1918–1982).

Parallel to the rise of political and labor movements were their attendant cultural

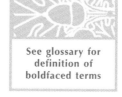

See glossary for definition of boldfaced terms

groups, manifested in both worker's **choruses** and **mandolin** orchestras. From Zionists to communists, the choruses sang the anthems (and the praises) of their particular political perspective. Among the most active political people's choruses were those of the militant pro-Soviet Freiheit Gezangs Ferain, the more moderate Arbeiter Ring chorus, and the labor Zionist Paole Zion Singing Society. Though they all might be singing the glories of a workers' state, the Paole Zionists would be doing it in Hebrew while the others would be singing in Yiddish and other languages, including English. Groups like the Arbeiter Ring benefited from its national network of affiliated chapters in its ability to disseminate these songs to a far-flung constituency.

Many of these political and labor groups also fostered the involvement of their non-singing members by supporting mandolin orchestras. Based on the popular turn-of-the-century trend of college, community, and vaudeville mandolin orchestras, the Yiddish labor and political groups adapted the widely available instrumentation to fit the needs of their cultural/political mandate. The instrumental **repertoire** reflected the same political perspective as that of the choruses (with the groups sometimes performing together) while also featuring traditional folk melodies and classical music.

Within a short time, the marketing of Yiddish music was in full swing. Downtown New York Yiddish publishers expanded beyond their usual fare of sacred and secular books and began giving over part of their press time to printing Yiddish sheet music. Via early journeyman publishers, such as Katzenellenbogen, S. Schenker, A. Teres, and Joseph Katz, to the larger Hebrew Publishing Company and, later, Metro Music, thousands of songs found their way onto the pianos of Lower East Side music devotees. Beginning in the 1880s, Yiddish music publishing peaked in the era around World War I and declined rapidly after World War II. Many of the published pieces tended to be simplified piano arrangements of Yiddish theater, liturgical, socialist, and Zionist songs with a smattering of klezmer music. In 1924

the publishers Jack and Joseph Kammen printed a collection of Yiddish dance tunes, the *Kammen International Dance Folio,* which is still used by many Jewish wedding bands.

Many of the musical comedy stars who popularized the music of Rumshinsky, Wohl, and Secunda were not only performing it on the stages of the numerous Yiddish theaters but also in recording studios. Talents like Aaron Lebedeff (1873–1960), Molly Picon (1898–1992), Ludwig Satz (1891?–1944), Morris Goldstein (1889–1938), Gus Goldstein (1884–1944), and Jenny Goldstein (1896–1960), among many others, were hard at work in the fledgling recording studios, producing three- and four-minute versions of their popular songs.

Cantors as well as theater stars were sought out by the competing recording companies. Yosele Rosenblatt (1880– 1933) (called by some "The Jewish Caruso"), Berele Chagy (1892–1952), and Mordechay Hershman (1888–1940) were among the most popular. The cantors, many of whom were brought to America by synagogues eager to add to their prestige of having a European cantor, were very well suited to the limited recording abilities of the primitive equipment, by dint of their powerful voices. Klezmorim were also recorded: Abe Schwartz (1880?–1950), Naftule Brandwein (1884–1963), Dave Tarras (1897–1989; ironically called by some "The Jewish Benny Goodman"), and Harry Kandel (1890–1940). They preserved a repertoire that was gradually changing Jewish American life. Even the great Yiddish novelist Sholem Aleichem (1859–1916; promoted as "The Jewish Mark Twain") made his way into a studio in 1915 to record excerpts of some of his short stories.

Begun at almost the same moment as the arrival of the Eastern European immigrants, the new recording technology soon grew into a full industry. Record companies vied for the opportunity to sell the music of the immigrants back to them. In doing so, they took on the work of documentors by preserving the traditional music of a culture in transition years before professional ethnomusicologists did. Maintaining separate cat-

alogs of classical, popular, and ethnic music, the companies thought little of issuing records that accurately portrayed the minority communities in one series while badly maligning them in another. There were some 50,000 Jewish discs made in the United States between 1894 and 1942, the vast majority of them before 1925. An interesting side note to the recording of ethnic music by outsiders is the founding of perhaps the first ethnic-owned, operated, and marketed record company. The United Hebrew Disc & Cylinder Record Company (UHD&C) was founded in 1905 by two partners, H. W. Perlman and S. Rosansky. Perlman had already established a piano factory on the Lower East Side, making him one of the first Jewish piano builders in New York, when he

Cover of a catalog for "Hebrew-Jewish Records" issued by Columbia Records in the teens and 1920s. Courting the Jewish ethnic market, the company issued many recordings aimed at new arrivals to the US.

entered into business with Rosansky a few blocks from his piano factory. Perhaps because of the competition of the larger uptown record manufacturers or because of UHD&C's inferior quality, the company did not see out its 1906 season.

Radio was the medium that successfully competed with the recording business. By the mid-1920s, this new technology afforded the listener a truer fidelity than the 78-rpm records, and once the playing apparatus was purchased, the music was free. In addition, the radio offered news, advice, drama, and sports. In fact, with just a twist of the dial, the radio emerged as a preeminent entrée to the understanding of the world surrounding the Yiddish-speaking population and helped as much as night school to bring English into a Yiddish speaker's world.

Though there were several stations that had some Jewish programming (New York's WHN, WBBC, WMCA, Philadelphia's WHAT, Cincinnati's WLW, among those), perhaps the best known of the radio stations that pioneered Yiddish language broadcasts was WEVD. Founded in 1928 and owned by the socialist Yiddish newspaper *The Forward,* this station (whose call letters memorialized twice unsuccessful Socialist presidential candidate Eugene Victor Debs) emerged in response to the needs of both Jewish and Gentile immigrant populations. Because of its diversity of programming, musicians, singers, composers, and arrangers were kept busy meeting the needs of an enthusiastic constituency.

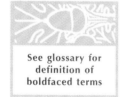

See glossary for definition of boldfaced terms

Another outlet for the creative talents of Jewish performers began quietly outside of New York City. Immigrant workers seeking a temporary respite from the oppression of the urban slums began to vacation in the Catskill region of upstate New York. Small farms taking in "roomers" gradually developed into larger and more sophisticated hotels catering to the cultural and culinary needs of the vacationing community. There were numerous hotels, such as the Majestic, the Normandy, the Concord, and the Gradus, but the best known, opened in 1914 by Zelig and Malke Grossinger, was Grossingers. At hotels like these, performers in Yiddish the-

ater, radio, and recording could vacation and perform during the months when the regular venues in the city were closed.

With the passage of restrictive emigration laws in 1924, the flow of potential new Eastern European Yiddish writers, musicians, and actors, as well as audiences, was halted. This, coupled with the more assimilated children of the American-born Jewish population, saw the appreciative population for Jewish music shrink. Attempts were made by enterprising impresarios to capitalize on the shift of American-born Jews toward American-born music. One of these was the premiere in 1938 on radio station WHN of "Yiddish Melodies in Swing," featuring the Barry (née Bagelman) Sisters, Jan Bart, and the **swing** arrangements of Sam Medoff with the "Yiddish Swingtette" featuring Dave Tarras. The show, sponsored by the B. Manishewitz Company, proved popular for a number of years and was syndicated throughout the United States.

Though Tarras was featured in this more popular venue, the younger Jewish population preferred the clarinet playing of Benny Goodman (1909–1986) to him. Goodman, never at home with the klezmer style, would defer to his star trumpeter Harry (Ziggy Elman) Finkelman (1914–1968) when he needed something played that sounded "Jewish."

Based on the success of Elman's 1938 Bluebird recording of "Frailach in Swing," an arrangement of the traditional tune "Der Shtiler Bulgar," Goodman had Johnny Mercer write words to the modern version and recorded it the next year as "And the Angels Sing," featuring Martha Tilton as vocalist. In 1942, Goodman tried to repeat the formula of a Jewish crossover hit by reworking the 1917 Abe Schwartz hit "Di Grine Kuzine" into "My Little Cousin," this time with vocalist Peggy Lee.

A major contribution to the mix of klezmer and **jazz** was made by clarinetist/saxophonist Sammy Musiker (1922–1963). Musiker had vast experience in the two musical worlds as a reed player in the orchestras of both Gene Krupa and Dave Tarras. In the late 1940s, Musiker arranged for the Savoy

jazz label to record Tarras and his band. Though the discs were musically outstanding, the resulting sales were bitterly disappointing. Musiker's fusion attempt came at a time when Jewish audience interest in both Yiddish music and **big band** was in decline. His innovative instrumentations also failed to develop into a real stylistic trend among mainstream Jewish or jazz players. A more popular mixed **genre** form was pursued by clarinetist/comedian/bandleader Mickey Katz (1909–1985). Fresh from his success with the Spike Jones orchestra, Katz used his experience with Jones to concoct "Yinglish" parodies of Top 40 songs. Employing the finest recording musicians in Los Angeles (including Ziggy Elman and Manny Klein) Katz's records and subsequent tours clearly demonstrated his ability to move seamlessly from *freylekhs* to pop.

What assimilation had begun, the ravages of the subsequent Holocaust seemed to complete. At once, the vital birthplace of Yiddish was destroyed, and New York became the major world center of this culture. This situation was reinforced by New York being the destination of the remnants of the Eastern European Jewish population. Except for the Hasidic communities and the remaining secular Yiddish organizations, Yiddish and its attendant culture were not uppermost in the minds of the post-Holocaust American Jewish community. The creation of the state of Israel in 1948 came with a linguistic, political, and cultural agenda, none of which sought to look back to the Old World. Hebrew replaced Yiddish; Israel replaced Eastern Europe as a Jewish center.

However, almost as gradually as the postwar interest in Yiddish culture faded, a renewed interest in it began in the 1970s. This was stimulated in part by the success of Alex Haley's book and television miniseries *Roots* and by a younger Jewish post-Holocaust generation eager to find a context for its family and group history. Perhaps nothing represents this search better than the revitalization of klezmer music. From the mid-1970s, the klezmer renewal has inspired both young and old Jewish and non-Jewish musicians to begin learning this repertoire.

However, the interest has not focused merely on the melodies. The language, history, and **folklore** of the rich Eastern European experience have all been recalled in an attempt to reinvest the community with its nearly discarded culture. Musicians trained in Appalachian country music, jazz, classical, rock, and Eastern European folk music forms were drawn into playing a music thought to have become passé even by those musicians and the audiences who loved it most. The revival that began with three klezmer bands in the United States in 1979 grew in less than a decade to more than eighty groups across North America. Noteworthy, too, is the reemergence of older, experienced klezmer stylists who have been sought out by younger players eager for musical role models.

For the first time in years record companies are producing albums of traditional Yiddish music as more and more radio stations have begun playing them. In 1990 the recording of *Partisans of Vilna: Songs of World War II Jewish Resistance* was nominated for a Grammy Award, the first time a Yiddish recording was thus honored. Klezmer bands are now performing in concert series, which, until recently, comprised primarily classical and jazz and folk revival groups. Even Hollywood, in its attempt to infuse its films with more "authentic atmosphere," sought out the services of klezmer bands in the production of films such as *The Chosen, Over the Brooklyn Bridge* (Kapelye), *Brighton Beach Memoirs* (New York Klezmer Ensemble), and the third remake of *The Jazz Singer* (The Klezmora).

In 1982, the New York–based YIVO Institute for Jewish Research opened its Max and Frieda Weinstein Archives of Recorded Sound. This open-access sound archives, the largest of its kind in the world, has enabled numerous musicians, scholars, researchers, and composers the chance to study and listen to thousands of rare 78-rpm discs, classic Yiddish radio shows, and unique field recordings of Yiddish music.

In 1985, YIVO sponsored the first Yiddish Folk Arts Institute. Dubbed "KlezKamp," this five-day event brought together 120 teachers and students of Yiddish language, lit-

erature, folklore, song, klezmer music, dance, and the visual arts. By 1990, its sixth year, some 2,000 people from North America, Europe, and Israel attended "KlezKamp" to study these vital Jewish genres.

It is possible that Yiddish culture will never again achieve the popularity it enjoyed at the turn of the twentieth century. However, this current revitalization demonstrates that reports of its demise are, to paraphrase Mark Twain's famous quip, highly exaggerated.

BIBLIOGRAPHY

Mlotek. Eleanor Gordon. (1972). *Mir Trogn A Gezang.* New York: Workmen's Circle.

Mlotek, Eleanor Gordon, and Gottlieb, Malke. (1983). *We Are Here: Songs of the Holocaust.* New York: Workmen's Circle.

Rubin, Ruth. (1979). *Voices of the People.* New York: McGraw-Hill.

Sapoznik, Henry. (1987). *The Compleat Klezmer.* Cedarhurst, NY: Tara.

———. (1999). *Klezmer! Jewish Music from Old World to Our World.* New York: Schirmer Books.

———, ed. (1988). "A Resource Guide to Yiddish Music." In *The Book Peddler.* Amherst, MA: National Yiddish Book Center.

Sapoznik, Henry, and Mlotek, Zalmen. *Pearls of Yiddish Song.* 1990. New York: Workmen's Circle.

Slobin, Mark. (1982). *Old Jewish Folk Music: The Collections of Moshe Beregeuski.* Philadelphia: University of Pennsylvania Press.

———. (1982). *Tenement Songs: The Popular Music of the Jewish Immigrants.* Chicago: University of Illinois Press.

———. (1989). *Chosen Voices: The Story of the American Cantorate.* Chicago: University of Illinois Press.

Spottswood, Richard. (1989). *A Discography of Ethnic Recordings Produced in the United States, 1895–1942.* Chicago: University of Illinois Press.

RECORDINGS

Art of Cantor Joseph Rosenblatt: Masterpieces of the Synagogue, Two volumes. RCA TDK 1003, 1004.

Folksongs in the East European Jewish Tradition from the Repertoire of Mariam Niremberg. 1986. Ed. Barbara Kirshenblatt-Gimblerr. Global Village GVM 117. CD.

Golden Voices of Israel: Gerson Sirota, Zavel Kwartin, Yosell Rosenblatt, Pierre Pinchik, Ben Zion Kapov-Kagan, Samuel Vigoda, Leyb Glantz. 1971. Eastronics K 530248. LP.

Jakie, Jazz'em Up: Old Time Klezmer Music 1912–1926. 1993. Ed. Henry Sapoznik. Global Village CD 101. CD.

Jewish Life: The "Old Country" Ethnic Recordings. 1963. Ed. Ruth Rubin. Folkways FG-3801.

Kapelye's Chicken. 1989. Shanachie 21007. CD.

Klezmer Music (1910–1927): Early Yiddish Instrumental Music. 1983. Ed. Martin Schwartz. Folklyric FL 9034.

Klezmer Music 1910–1942: Recordings from the YIVO Archives. 1999. Henry Sapoznik. Smithsonian Folkways FSS-34021. CD.

Musical Settings of Yiddish Poetry. Lazar Weiner. Tambour 597.

Partisans of Vilna: The Songs of World War II Jewish Resistance. 1989. Henry Sapoznik, with Josh Waletzky. Flying Fish FF 70450. CD.

Songs by M. Gebertig. Sidor Belarsky. Tara B115.

Songs of the Holocaust. 1985. Sidor Belarsky. Tara SB 1001. Audiocassette.

A Touch of Klez! 1985. Klezmer Conservatory Band. Vanguard VMD-79455. CD.

FROM SWEDEN TO AMERICA

Ulf Beijbom, Uno Myggan Ericson, Märta Ramsten
(translated by Robert Carroll)

This essay was adapted from liner notes written in 1981 for a documentary recording of Swedish American music made by a group of ethnomusicologists who traveled to the United States from the Swedish Center for Folk Song and Folk Music Research. Ulf Beijbom contributed the section on Swedish emigration to the United States, Märta Ramsten described the Swedish American folk-song repertoire (with emphasis on its themes and melodies), and Uno Myggan Ericson wrote of visiting Swedish Americans in Minnesota and Illinois. Their recordings are available on the LP From Sweden to America: Emigrant and Immigrant Songs *(Caprice Records 2011), an expanded version of which was issued on CD in 1996 as* From Sweden to America: Swedish Emigrant Songs—Amerikavisor *(Caprice CAP 21552).*

From the mid-1840s until 1930, about 1.3 million Swedes emigrated to North America. Of all European countries, only Ireland and Norway had higher emigration figures than Sweden. At the turn of the twentieth century, about one out of every six Swedish-born persons lived in the United States, and Chicago was the world's second largest "Swedish city."

This great stream of people to the West did not flow steadily. Clearly the migration was influenced as much by Sweden as by the United States. The reason for the first emigration peak in the early 1850s may have been the hard times in Sweden and the stimulus of the California gold rush on the American economy. During the second half of the 1860s, however, there was a great demand for workers and farmers in America, while Swedish agriculture suffered a serious crop failure. This was the cause of the mass migration from Sweden beginning in 1869. Subsequently, the enormous influx of people was dictated by the agricultural situation

and a growing industrialization in Sweden and the demands of the job market in the West. Between 1879 and 1893, almost a half million Swedes emigrated. The emigration movement peaked in 1882 and 1888, with 45,000 registered emigrants per year.

It is hard to point directly to other than economic factors as the cause of the migration from Sweden. From an international perspective, the political development was uneventful. Religious oppressions cannot be overlooked, however; no less than 10 percent of the earliest immigration wave seems to have had a religious background.

The first emigrants often remained farmers, but they improved their conditions through emigration and lived in Swedish colonies where their native language was spoken. Swedish churches, schools, and newspapers preserved the Swedish culture in thousands of settlements in the Midwest. Even cities like Chicago had their "Swede Towns," where Swedes could live their whole lives surrounded by compatriots.

Despite the fact that most pioneers were farmers, a growing number of Swedes were drawn to the industries and cities of the United States. Thus, when Swedish America reached its greatest size in 1910—numbering 1.3 million emigrants and their children—over 60 percent lived in urban areas. The industrial and construction workers, the craftsmen and maids, were, at the turn of the twentieth century, more typically Swedish American than the farmers in Minnesota, Illinois, Iowa, or Kansas.

Around the turn of the century many people were convinced that the Swedish language and culture would live on forever in the Swedish settlements in America. Generally, a Swedish settlement did not consist exclusively of people from the same home province. In the center of a Swedish settlement there would be a church, a school, perhaps a lodge or a newspaper office. In these circles the language, the traditions, and the songs lived on.

The United States, however, had a negative attitude toward the immigrants retaining their ethnic individuality. To do so was considered un-American. Especially during World War I and the 1920s, there was great pressure on Swedish Americans to become Americanized. During that period more and more immigrants changed over to speaking exclusively English. The churches changed the language of the service to English, and the great newspaper decline started.

But since the American bicentennial in 1976 a remarkable change has taken place in the United States. People have begun to recognize that the different immigrant groups have enriched America in numerous spheres. It has become fashionable to have ancestral roots in another country.

See glossary for definition of boldfaced terms

MUSIC AND ENTERTAINMENT

The great waves of emigration from Sweden to the United States had an impact on the folk-song **repertoire**. A large number of emigrant songs—or "America songs," as people preferred to call them—were written and sung. Many have retained their popularity and are still sung today. Others, however, can only be found in written sources, including *skillgtryck* (**broadsheets**) and songbooks.

Homesickness can often be seen in the emotional texts that describe a heartrending farewell from family and home, a difficult crossing, and perhaps failures in the new country. But not all the songs are sorrowful. There are also songs that with a twinkle in the eye depict the great land in the West and its tremendous resources. As regards the melodies of the songs, in general, text was written to an already well-known and popular **melody**.

Over the past few decades, new interest has grown in the music of Swedish Americans. The primary inspiration for this new interest was the material being collected by the Olle i Skratthult Project in Minneapolis, a group of **folklore** enthusiasts headed by the musician and folklorist Maury Bernstein. The project inventoried songs, music, and artists of the hitherto almost completely undocumented world of Swedish American entertainment. Anne-Charlotte Harvey, a Swedish American singer, was active in Bernstein's group.

The project was named for the *bondkomiker* (rural comedian) Olle i Skratthult, whose name was actually Hjalmar Peterson. He was born in Munkfors, Värmland, in 1886 and emigrated to Minnesota with three brothers in 1906. He soon began to perform as a singer and rural comedian, forming his own troupe of performers. His career reached its peak during the years around World War I. At times he had his own troupe of over twenty performers, traveling to Swedish enclaves in the United States as far west as California. His performances often consisted of singing and music, a play, and dancing. Later in life, after the popularity of vaudeville shows had diminished, he settled in Minneapolis, where he joined the Swedish section of the Salvation Army and often assisted at meetings with religious songs.

The culmination of the Olle i Skratthult Project's work—which received almost no support from the Swedish authorities and

was looked upon by many Swedish Americans as only ridiculing and degrading their ancestors—was the Snoose Boulevard Festival, a three-day festival in the Swedish area around Cedar Avenue in Minneapolis, called "Snusboulevarden" because of the many Scandinavians who frequented the Dania Hall meeting place and the countless bars located there. It is true that Snoose Boulevard has since become a college-student neighborhood, but when the festival began in 1972, there were still enough memories to preserve to make the effort worthwhile.

I [Uno Myggan Ericson] came to the Snoose Boulevard Festival in 1976 and was there for three days of singing, storytelling, fiddling fun, Swedish dancing, and smorgasbord. I discovered Swedish American songs, which should not be confused with emigrant songs in Sweden, but which were rather in the popular performer Ernst Rolf's style—somewhat to the surprise of serious researchers in the subject. Later—through recordings, record catalogs, and books—I was able to establish the fact that the songs, often integrated into theatrical productions, were part of the Swedish entertainment tradition, especially during the early twentieth century, and that in many respects it followed American vaudeville's demise in terms of competition with film, radio, and television.

When Märta Ramsten and I traveled to Minneapolis in February 1980 to document Swedish songs among the new generation of Swedish Americans, I thought that we would have an easy job. Actually, it was a little more difficult than we had expected. Based on the Snoose Festival, we thought there would be many performers, but it turned out that they were rather scarce.

We made recordings of Olle i Skratthult's wife, Olga Lindgren, on two occasions. Olga came to the United States at the age of seventeen and traveled with Olle i Skratthult's theater group as a singer and actress. She often sang dressed in folk costume and performed Swedish folk dances on the stage. She married Skratthult but was later divorced and remarried.

Olga sang for us one of the most popular Swedish American songs, "Barndomshemmet" ("My Childhood Home"). It is actually totally American, written by the popular music composer Paul Dresser (1860–1906), who was a brother of the novelist Theodore Dreiser. The original tune was entitled "On the Banks of the Wabash" and was written in 1899. It has since become the unofficial state song of Indiana. The song came to Sweden by way of a German edition—an arrangement of the original—but had already gone by way of Denmark, where it was sung around 1910 under the title "Skamlingsbanken." In Sweden, Ernst Rolf popularized it from 1914 on, with the text written by Karl Ewert on the theme of a homesick Swedish American. It may have come to the United States through Lydia Hedberg or Gustav Fonandern [see below]. Swedish Americans who sing it today think it's a Swedish song and are unaware of its American roots.

A Swedish performer who had a great impact in America was Lydia Hedberg. She was unusual in that she was a female rural comedian, even though she preferred to call herself a **ballad** singer. A trained physiotherapist, from 1908 on she appeared as a singer of ballads and a storyteller in Sweden. She lived for a long time in Sundsvall, and was also a hostess at Furvik, a zoo outside Gävle. Hedberg made extended tours of Swedish communities in the United States between 1921 and 1925. On her longest tour, she gave fifty performances in eighty-one days. She met with entertainers such as Olle i Skratthult and taught them new material. She also made a number of recordings in the United States during this period.

Among other Swedes who had an impact in America was the recording artist Gustav Fonandern. He was by profession an architect but was active as a singer of ballads and revue songs for almost sixty years. He traveled to the United States many times and toured the Swedish American settlements. He was briefly a guest artist in Skratthult's troupe. Fonandern introduced to the Swedish American repertoire songs from the popular Swedish singer Ernst Rolf. He made

many recordings in the United States and toured extensively.

Another member of Skratthult's troupe was Leona Carlson. She was born in the United States. Her parents came from Gunnarskog in Värmland, and only Swedish was spoken in the home—Leona did not know any English when she started school. Today, she sings and plays the **accordion**, often performing with her husband, Ted, another Swedish American.

Another popular entertainer was J(ohannes) A(lfred) Hultman (1861–1942), who began his career as a revivalist preacher and was known as *Solskenssångren* ("The Sunshine Singer"). At the age of eighteen, he began traveling around to Swedish enclaves in the United States, preaching the gospel and accompanying himself on a portable organ (which is now housed at the Swedish American Museum in Andersonville, a traditionally Swedish neighborhood on the north side of Chicago). Hultman issued his "Sunshine Songs" in various periodicals between 1910 and 1939, and also made many recordings and several tours of Sweden, making him perhaps the best known of all Swedish religious singers. During the Prohibition era, he was even suspected of smuggling whiskey (moonshine) in his organ. On being asked if he carried moonshine, he answered that he only smuggled sunshine.

We next met Arthur Erickson (b. 1908), who lives in Grand Haven, Michigan. He emigrated to the United States in 1923 and has worked mainly in the construction business. At one time, he lived in Chicago, but retired to Grand Haven, a predominantly Swedish community. Erickson composes many of the songs that he sings. Like many emigration songs, they are nostalgic evocations of his earlier life, reflecting his longing for his homeland.

We traveled on toward Chicago. We met Selma Jakobsson, a collector of traditional Swedish American objects. She had saved all leftover copies of books from the cellar of a onetime Swedish printing office that was closed in the late 1960s. Among the books

See glossary for definition of boldfaced terms

she saved were copies of the Dalkullan songbooks, which were published between 1903 and 1931, providing Swedish entertainers and amateur musicians with a wealth of popular songs.

In Rockford, Illinois, we met Carl Bruce, an amateur entertainer who was then ninety-three years old (he died several months after our visit). Bruce was born in Gothenburg and emigrated to the United States in 1902. From about 1908 on he resided in Rockford, where he made a living as a factory worker. As a hobby, he sang and appeared on stage frequently. He became one of the leading figures in the Swedish theater group that was usually engaged at the Svea Hall. He appeared often as a rural comedian under the name of Sven på; Lappen ("Sven on the Patch").

Bruce sang for us "I Been a Swede from North Dakota," a popular song from the early twentieth century. It pokes fun at the Swedish American dialect and refers to some well-known locations in Minneapolis, such as Seven Corners on Cedar Avenue, which still exists today. It was possibly new when Bruce first learned it in 1904.

Meeting Carl Bruce at the end of his life was especially fortunate for us. He represented a century's memories of Swedish popular performing styles in America. Bruce was a link between the popular Swedish singers, such as Ernst Rolf, and the newer American traditions. This was perhaps the most remarkable event of our all too short tour.

BIBLIOGRAPHY

Anderson, P. J., and Blanck, D., eds. (1992). *Swedish-American Life in Chicago*. Urbana and Chicago: University of Illinois Press.

Barton, H. A. (1994). *A Folk Divided: Homeland Swedes and Swedish Americans, 1840–1940*. Carbondale: Southern Illinois University Press.

Beijbom, Ulf. (1971). *Swedes in Chicago: A Demographic and Social Study of the 1846–1880 Immigration*. Stockholm: Läromedelsförlagen.

———, ed. (1993). *Swedes in America: New Perspectives*. Växjö: Swedish Emigrant Institute.

Blanck, D., and Runblom, H., eds. (1991). *Swedish Life in American Cities*. Uppsala: Centre for Multiethnic Research, Uppsala University.

Carlsson, S. (1988). *Swedes in North America, 1638–1988*. Stockholm: Streiffert.

Kastrup, A. (1975). *The Swedish Heritage in America*. St. Paul, MN: Swedish Council of America.

NORWEGIAN TRADITIONAL MUSIC IN MINNESOTA

Philip Nusbaum

Please see Chapter 11 in this volume for biographical information on Philip Nusbaum.

The first Norwegian people to immigrate to the United States arrived in New York State in the 1820s. Around the mid–nineteenth century, the first wave of Norwegians came to Minnesota, first settling the southeastern portion of the state. Until about 1880, the majority of those who emigrated were rural people who were motivated by a combination of limited economic opportunities in Norway and the availability of farmland in the United States.

At first, they tended to settle in places populated by others from their original home districts in Norway. However, beginning in the 1880s, reflecting urbanization in Norway, a greater percentage of Norwegian immigrants to the United States were commercially oriented, urban people who settled in cities such as Minneapolis without regard to the home district of their fellow countrymen. In recent decades, emigration has declined greatly, but a trickle of newcomers still enters the state from Norway.

Most estimates conclude that, at the end of the twentieth century, European Americans made up over 90 percent of Minnesota's population. Minnesotans of German heritage are the most numerous, and the population of all the Scandinavian groups combined about equals the German population. However, the Norwegian presence is arguably the strongest in the state, perhaps because many Minnesota Norwegians have an elevated awareness of their shared heritage.

Some observers theorize that this awareness derives from earlier periods when Sweden and Denmark dominated Norway. According to the theory, fear of losing their culture because of foreign domination caused Norwegians to assert their identity and cultural inheritance. Whatever the reason, they continue to assert their culture, many Minnesota Norwegians socialize within the confines of ethnic organizations such as the Sons of Norway, which has numerous chapters in the state, and the *lags,*

social organizations whose members represent specific Norwegian home districts. In addition, in Minnesota, references to Norwegian-based culture are plentiful in mass media. "Norwegian" joke telling, particularly the "Ole and Lena" cycle, or references to folk foods such as *lutefisk* (dried codfish preserved by lye) are standard subject matter in conversations statewide, regardless of the ethnic background of the conversationalists. In addition, there is great in-community interest in Norwegian folk art forms such as *rosemaling* (related styles of decorative painting), woodworking, and wood carving. Through Norwegian food, joke telling, and interest in Norwegian-based material culture, Minnesota Norwegians express their heritage. Such is also the case for Minnesota Norwegians who play and appreciate Norwegian-based folk music.

NORWEGIAN FOLK MUSIC AND DANCE IN MINNESOTA

Not all of the folk music styles brought by Norwegians took root in Minnesota. The first casualty was music with Norwegian language content. Even though many early Norwegian immigrants tended to settle in communities with others speaking the same regional dialect, the fact that English was America's public language and the language taught in public schools reduced both the number of Norwegian speakers and interest in Norwegian-language songs. In addition, particularly with the onset of World War I, suspicion of foreigners caused many European Americans to emphasize their "American-ness" and opt for communicating in English. While a few individuals and musical groups have sought to preserve Norwegian-language singing styles such as *kveding* (which is practiced among rural women), there is limited interest in such material because so few people understand spoken Norwegian.

From the early period of immigration, Norwegian Americans favored social dancing as a form of recreation. The enduring setting of the social dance, as well as in-community interest in Norwegian-based

culture, has shaped Minnesota Norwegian folk music traditions. The most archaic tradition is the **repertoire** associated with the hardanger violin. The hardanger represents one of several medieval European experiments to increase the volume played by one violin, frequently the only **instrument** available to play for dancing. The hardanger has a set of four or five strings strung underneath the fingerboard. Never bowed, they resonate sympathetically when the player bows the strings strung over the fingerboard. The result is that the hardanger has greater sound-level capabilities than the conventional violin. Hardanger pieces are composed in two to five repeated sections, the sections frequently blend with preceding and following ones, and sections of tunes can be lengthened to suit the mood of the performer.

Frequently, the tradition with which the hardanger is associated is called the *bygdedans* tradition. *Bygt* means "built-up place," and there were many small, "built-up places" in Norway, each with its own dance and music dialects. The term *bygdedans* refers to the extremely local character of the Norwegian dance traditions. For example, the *springar* is a major bygdedans form. It is an asymmetrical three-beat dance; in other words, the beats are not of equal emphasis or duration. In the Telemark district of Norway, the beats are rendered (capital letters for emphasis) LONG LONG short, while in the Valdres district, it is short LONG medium. Most Minnesota hardanger players strive to play the codified regional bygdedans styles, while the playing of others represents a compromise between hardanger and conventional violin playing styles and repertoires.

However, by the mid–nineteenth century in Norway, the dance steps connected to hardanger violin playing were fading from popularity. Like other Europeans, Norwegians were falling under the spell of the **waltz**, the **polka**, and the **schottische**. Hardanger music became, to a greater degree than previously, a repertoire performed for listening audiences, not dancing ones, frequently at occasions whose purpose was to celebrate the Norwegian heritage.

113

Harry Johnson, Dance Fiddler

The following essay originally appeared in a Washington State Arts Council publication.

Harry Johnson grew up in the North Dakota agricultural area of Abercrombe. In the close-knit community of 225 mostly Swedish and Norwegian immigrants, the entertainment was social dances, with music provided by "dance fiddlers." It was there that young Harry Johnson learned to play the old-time tunes he loves, first on the guitar and then on the fiddle, by listening to the playing of his father and cousin Helmer. Inspiration also came from listening to the famous Oscar Stensgard Band from Fargo, North Dakota. Johnson moved to Washington state in 1947. He stopped playing for a while, but was drawn back to the old waltzes, hambos, and schottisches that his family played.

Johnson is active in community events, contests, and concerts, twice winning a National Seniors Division championship. He also represented Washington at the Smithsonian Institute's Bicentennial Festival in 1976 and was included in the Washington Traditional Fiddlers Project sponsored by the Washington State Arts Council and the National Endowment for the Arts. At age seventy-three, Johnson, deeply concerned that this Scandinavian immigrant music tradition is not being passed on to younger people, used a 1994 Washington State Arts Council Apprenticeship Program Award to work with Carla Wulfsberg. Wulfsberg, whose own family immigrated to North Dakota from Norway in the 1920s, has been fiddling at Scandinavian old-time dances and festivals for the past eighteen years.

The dances that supplanted bygdedans traditions are called, collectively, *gammeldans,* loosely translated as "old-time dance." Listening to the Norwegian waltzes and polkas, one is aware of their relationships to other European cultures' waltzes and polkas, and also of their Norwegian character. Band performance for dancing is much more common than solo playing. Various types of **accordions** and the conventional violin, and not the hardanger violin, are used for lead playing in old-time music, with accompaniments commonly set on the **guitar**, tenor **banjo**, **bass**, and piano.

Early twentieth-century technical development of the accordion, particularly the number of bass keys available, led to the instrument's rise in popularity. The more bass notes available, the greater the range of musical keys that are within the grasp of the instrumentalist. The modern accordion allows a skilled player to play the melody, a chordal accompaniment, and a bass line simultaneously. Violin players, on the other hand, were limited to playing the **melody** or a parallel **harmony**. A solo accordion could produce what twentieth-century listeners would consider a full sound, yet could be acclimated to a band situation.

Many of the bygdedans steps were three-beat dances. Perhaps the historical preference for three-beat dance steps is the reason why waltzes make up the largest portion of the gammeldans repertoire. The second largest category is the schottische, followed in popularity by the polka. At old-time dances, bands are also requested to play "new time" steps. "New time" includes ballroom dance steps such as the **two-step**, the **fox-trot**, and the **tango**. Bands also adapt other forms for the old-time format. For example, the country song "Waltz Across Texas" is sometimes played stylistically like a Norwegian old-time waltz, and the Anglo-American **fiddle** tune "Flop Eared Mule" is frequently played as a schottische.

HISTORY

The most important event in the history of Norwegian American folk music was emigration. The change from bygdedans to gammeldans was in progress even during the early stages of emigration, and this aesthetic preference has become more marked with each succeeding generation. While bygdedans music persists, its survival owes to the players and dancers committed to preserving it. Movements to preserve the oldest layers of Norwegian folk music date from

about 1920, when certain lags sponsored fiddling groups. Today, the Hardanger Fiddle Association of America and various folk-dance organizations dedicated to cultural preservation play large roles in the survival of bygdedans traditions.

That old-time music and dancing lack the local idiosyncrasies of bygdedans tradition indicates not just a shift in aesthetic preference, but also a change in worldview. While bygdedans tradition is marked by great regional stylistic variations, gammeldans is not. The preference for gammeldans was an indication that, to Minnesota Norwegians, their shared Norwegian heritage was more important than the heritage of their ancestral home districts.

In addition, while discerning ears can tell the difference between Minnesota Norwegian and Minnesota German, Czech, Polish, and Slovenian social dance forms, the differences between them would not prevent members of the different groups from dancing to each other's music. On the other hand, bygdedans steps were specifically Norwegian, and some varied markedly from district to district in Norway. In Minnesota, widespread use of the English language made members of the different groups socially available to each other. Increasingly, from the days of the nineteenth-century frontier onward, Minnesota Norwegians saw themselves with reference to the other ethnic groups sharing the region.

During the days of the frontier, dancing was a major form of entertainment. Gammeldans music for these house parties was provided by family and local friends. Later, local and regional musicians played for social dancing in many Minnesota towns and cities, and more polished bands or small orchestras toured the territory. In the late twentieth century, social clubs such as the Eagles sometimes present evenings of old-time dancing. However, as the generation favoring old-time music has declined, the social role of old-time dancing has also diminished. In the early twenty-first century, nursing homes have become common settings for Norwegian old-time music, and the number of performances having a profes-

sional luster has declined. Old-time music also holds its own during special occasions when the Norwegian ethnicity is presented, such as meetings of Norwegian organizations. At special times such as *Syttende Mai* (Norwegian Independence Day), some cities and towns honor the Norwegian heritage by holding public performances of Norwegian traditional music. These are occasions when the Norwegian heritage is self-consciously presented.

While the era of greatest popularity of social dancing and Norwegian dance has passed, the Norwegian tradition lives on in the efforts of a few professional bands and many other skilled players who play avocationally. Avocational playing makes the tradition similar to the way it was introduced to Minnesota: as a frontier tradition having a place in family- and friendship-based socializing.

DOCUMENTARY RECORDINGS

Philip Nusbaum's *Norwegian-American Music from Minnesota: Old Time and Traditional Favorites* (1989) documents contemporary Minnesota Norwegian musicians or groups, primarily gammeldans players. Phil Martin's *Across the Fields: Traditional Norwegian-American Music from Wisconsin* (1982) documents contemporary Wisconsin Norwegian American musicians and groups, also primarily gammeldans players. *Early Scandinavian Bands and Entertainers* (1983) contains recordings by the dance bands that toured through the Midwest during the first half of the twentieth century.

Little bygdedans music by Minnesota players has been recorded. However, *Old Time Dance Tunes from Norway by Roheim's Trio* documents a hardanger fiddler who lived for a time in Minnesota.

BIBLIOGRAPHY

Larson, Leroy W. (1975). "Scandinavian-American Folk Dance Music of the Norwegians in Minnesota." Ph.D. diss., University of Minnesota.

Qualey, Carleton C., and Gjerde, Jon A. (1981). "The Nor-
wegians." In *They Chose Minnesota: A Survey of the
State's Ethnic Groups,* ed. June D. Holmquist. St. Paul:
Minnesota Historical Society.

RECORDINGS

*Across the Fields: Traditional Norwegian-American Music
from Wisconsin.* 1982. Folklore Village Farm FVF
002.

*Early Scandinavian Bands and Entertainers: Historic Reissue
of Rare Original 78 RPM Recordings.* 1983. Banjar
Records BR 1840.

*Norwegian-American Music from Minnesota: Old Time and
Traditional Favorites.* 1989. Minnesota Historical Society. C002-A (LP) or C002 (audiocassette).

Old-Time Dance Tunes from Norway. c. 1983. Roheim's
Trio. Valtron V-2750. Audiocassette. Available from
the Hardanger Fiddle Association of America, P.O.
Box 23046, Richfield, MN 55423.

FINNISH MUSIC IN SUPERIORLAND

James P. Leary

Please see Chapter 13 in this volume for biographical information on James P. Leary.

More than 300,000 Finns emigrated to the United States between 1880 and the onset of World War I. Variously fleeing evictions from peasant homelands, a population surplus, unemployment, class strictures, a domineering state church, and the political oppression of Swedes to the west and Russians to the east, roughly half settled in the Lake Superior region, known as Superiorland, where life was only a little better.

They toiled as miners in the "copper country" of Michigan's Upper Peninsula, in the Gogebic iron range on the Michigan/Wisconsin border, and in the Vermillion and Mesabi iron mines of northern Minnesota. There "Finn Towns" bloomed amid immigrant Italian and Slavic enclaves in Calumet, Houghton, Hancock, Ironwood, Hurley, Hibbing, and Virginia. Finns likewise labored in the sawmills, fisheries, factories, and ports of Ashland, Superior, Duluth, Two Harbors, and Thunder Bay. They also worked in lumber camps and scratched out small farms from Mass City, Bruce Crossing, and Amasa, Michigan, to Highbridge, Washburn, Oulu, and Herbster, Wisconsin, to Finland, Palo, and Cromwell, Minnesota.

Finnish immigrants and their descendants, like other newcomers to America, continued their old-country musical traditions. **Hymns** and sentimental songs, sometimes accompanied by a pump organ or a plucked *kantele* (a string **instrument** played flat like a zither) echoed from homes. **Polkas**, **waltzes**, and **schottisches**—performed on **fiddle**, **harmonica**, and **button accordion**—dominated house parties and lumber-camp **frolics**.

Institutions fostering music were soon thriving as well. Suomi Synod Lutheran churches, aligned with Finland's state church, established sedate choirs with standard part-singing, and members of the charismatic, democratic Finnish Apostolic Lutheran church composed new hymns and adapted American **gospel music** to be rendered in exuberant full-throated **unison**. Temperance societies

and socialists built halls, formed **brass bands**, put on musical plays, and sponsored social dances. Cooperative stores sold musical instruments and, eventually, both phonographs and Finnish American recordings. Meanwhile, ethnic newspapers such as Superior's *Tyomies* ("Workers") advertised and reported on musical events. Beginning in the 1920s, Finnish American dance musicians and singers such as Viola Turpeinen and Hiski Salomaa took advantage of this institutional infrastructure. Their legacy is evident in the music of performers today.

Viola Irene Turpeinen was born in 1909 in Champion, Michigan, west of Ishpeming, the eldest of four daughters of Walter and Signe Wiitala Turpeinen. Walter was a miner who followed his occupation to Iron River, Michigan, shortly after Viola's birth. Both parents played the *kaks rivinen,* or two-row button accordion, but by her teens Viola had graduated to the more expensive, versatile, and prestigious **piano accordion**. At sixteen,

Finnish Music in Superiorland

while playing in the local Finnish and Italian halls, she attracted the attention of John Rosendahl, an immigrant musician and concert promoter. The two were soon traveling a Finnish American circuit that extended from such eastern outposts as Fitchburg, Massachusetts, and New York City to western mining settlements and the fishing and logging communities of the Pacific Northwest. The tour's core, however, was the Lake Superior region, the Finnish American heartland.

In January 1928, Turpeinen and Rosendahl began making recordings for the Victor label. Their first release included "Kauhavan Polkka," perhaps the duo's most memorable collaboration: a searing, typically fast-paced Finnish polka, with accordion and violin interweaving relentlessly as if to push one another to the border between deft articulation and abandon. Viola Turpeinen continued to tour and make recordings with a succession of regional musicians until her death in 1958. Her playing and presence in-

Finns in Herbster, Wisconsin, along the south shore of Lake Superior, gather around an accordionist, 1920s. *Photo courtesy of the late accordionist Bill Hendrickson (seated, in the white shirt), author's collection*

spired scores of emulators who sustain her **repertoire** and memory, among them accordionist Al Reko of Minneapolis, who also sings Antti Syrjaniemi's 1928 celebration of a Turpeinen dance.

In translation, its lyrics proclaim:

Seldom have people danced the polka at such speed;
Seldom have people stepped more rapidly.
When grandmas asked grandpas for a break,
They say they were already wet with sweat.
And the girl played like a heavenly bell,
Hittan tila tila hittantaa.
And the farmers danced like mowers making hay in the fields.
Hittan tila tila hittantaa.

Antti Syrjaniemi's gift for plain yet witty and evocative poetry was matched by many singing chroniclers of Finnish American life. Hiski Salomaa was among the most prominent. Born in Kangasniemi, Finland, in 1891, Salomaa was raised in humble circumstances by his unmarried mother, from whom he learned a tailor's trade. Emigrating to the United States in 1909, he lived in Minnesota and Michigan mining towns before

settling in New York, where he died in 1957. Hiski Salomaa left behind dozens of songs, sixteen of which he recorded for Columbia. Collectively they sketch the immigrant experience with poignancy and exuberance.

Like Salomaa's own birthplace, the home of the boy in "Taattoni maja" ("My Father's Cabin") "was not greater than the doghouse in the landlord's yard." An immigrant from Savo recalls the ocean journey in "Savon poijan Amerikkaan tulo" ("The Boy from Savo's Arrival in America"):

Some of us started to be already seasick,
Even I when the wind started to blow,
But I took a drink from my bottle
And after that I ate salted fish.
—Salomaa translations by Juha Niemela

The young man soon finds hard work in the ore mines and lumber camps, just as the kitchen maid toils in "Tiskarin Polkka" ("Dishwasher's Polka"):

The hags are yelling and eating
And I am just washing the dishes.
The coffee is nearly running out from the coffeepot
Because I don't have time to fly after everything.

Drudgery notwithstanding, there is occasional joy in dances and parties. Hiski Salomaa's description of eating herring, dancing the waltz, and drinking enough to get a hangover may well have been his experience at a name-day party for his South Range, Michigan, neighbor, Mrs. Dahlmann ("Dahlmanniin paartit"). (A name-day party is much like a birthday party but is celebrated on the feast day of the saint after which a person is named.) Certainly this was the case in "Ryöstö polka" ("Robber's Polka"), with its evocation of dances in Finnish halls on maids' nights off. The musicians are Salomaa's bandmates Antti Kosola from Iron Belt, Wisconsin, and William Syrjälä, of Cloquet, Minnesota.

> *Thursday is the best of days when the girls get out early.*
> *You spend your day in the sauna awaiting the dances at night.*
> *Kosola dries sweat from his shirt, Syrjälä takes the horn from his lips,*
> *So the dancers can pause while earth and sky rock with the polka.*

Nowadays, Superiorland's Finnish Americans still "rock," some "with the polka": the Oulu Hotshots, the Northern Stars, Thimbleberry, RFD North, the Wiita Brothers, and many more less formal **combos**. In the greater Minneapolis area, the folk song revival, romantic nationalism, and ethnic organizations have fostered the kantele ensemble Koivun Kaiku ("Echo of the Birch"), the Finnish brass band Ameriikan Poijat ("American Boys"), and such bilingual singer-songwriters as Diane Jarvi and Eric Peltoniemi.

Conga Se Menne of Michigan's Marquette/Negaunee area, meanwhile, adds a "Finnish **reggae**" beat to hail Heikki Lunta (Hank Snow, the comic and recently invented Finnish "snow god" of the Lake Superior area) in their song "Guess Who's Coming to Sauna? (Heikki Lunta)," a take on Black Uhuru's reggae tune "Guess Who's Coming to Dinner? (Natty Dreadlocks)."

Annual summer events such as Finn Fest, a national gathering of Finnish Americans, and Festival Finlandia, held at northern Minnesota's Ironworld Discovery Center, feature the full range of Finnish American music. The region's ethnic newspapers—*Finnish American Reporter* and *New World Finn*—include regular articles on past and present musicians as well as advertisements for recordings of their music.

Finnish musicians jam in Copper Harbor, Michigan, in 1986: Ed Lauluma (standing), fiddle; George Nousiainen, fiddle; Roy Lindgren, guitar; Vi Wiitala, piano accordion; Ray Wiitala, bass guitar.
Photo by James P. Leary

BIBLIOGRAPHY

Gronow, Pekka. (1977). *Studies in Scandinavian-American Discography*, Vols. 1 and 2. Helsinki: Suomen Aanitearkisto.

Hakala, Joyce E. (1997). *Memento of Finland: A Musical Legacy*. St. Paul: Pikebone Press.

Leary, James P. (1990). "The Legacy of Viola Turpeinen." *Finnish Americana* 8(6):6–11.

Niemela, Juha. (1998). "Finnish American Songs." Turku: Finnish Migration Institute. Available at www.utu.fi/erill/instmigr/articles.htm.

Westerholm, Simo. (1983). *Reisaavaisen Laulu Ameriikkaan Siirtolaislauluja (American Immigrant Songs)*. Kaustinen, Finland: Kansanmusiikki-Instituutin.

RECORDINGS

A Finn Fest Potpourri. 1996. Finn Fest CD FF96.

Finnish-American Recordings, 1907–1938. 1992. Folk Music Institute CD KICD 25.

Finnish Reggae and Other Sauna Beats. 1994. Conga Se Menne. Conga Records CD CR94.

Hiski Salomaa, 1927–1931. 1991. Love Records CD SIBCD 4.

Viola Turpeinen: The Early Days (Finnish American Dance Music, 1928–1938). 1989. Thimbleberry Recordings THC 1006. Audiocassette.

RECENT BIBLIOGRAPHY/
DISCOGRAPHY/VIDEOGRAPHY

Compiled by Jennifer C. Post

BOOKS AND ARTICLES

Ahlborn, Richard E. (1993). *The Mission San Antonio Prayer and Song Board.* Santa Barbara, CA: Santa Barbara Mission Archive–Library.

Ancelet, Barry Jean. (1989). *Cajun Music: Its Origins and Development.* Louisiana Life Series, No. 2. Lafayette: Center for Louisiana Studies, University of Southwestern Louisiana.

———. (1999). *Cajun and Creole Music Makers—Musiciens cadiens et créoles.* Jackson: University Press of Mississippi.

Ancelet, Barry Jean, et al. (1991). *Cajun Country.* Folklife in the South Series. Jackson: University Press of Mississippi.

Ashton, John. (1994). "'The Badger Drive': Song, Historiography, and Occupational Stereotyping." *Western Folklore* 55(3):211–228.

Averill, Gage. (1999). "Bell Tones and Ringing Chords: Sense and Sensation in Barbershop Harmony." *World of Music* 41(1):37–51.

Bane, Michael. (1992). *White Boy Singin' the Blues.* Reprint, New York: Da Capo Press.

Bernard, Shane K. (1996). *Swamp Pop: Cajun and Creole Rhythm and Blues.* Jackson: University of Mississippi.

———. (1996). "Twistin' at the Fais Do-do: South Louisiana's Swamp Pop Music." *Southern Cultures* 2(3–4):315–328.

Bernard, Shane K., and Girouard, Julia. (1992). "'Colinda': Mysterious Origins of a Cajun Folksong." *Journal of Folklore Research* 29(1):37–52.

Burger, Simone. (1997). "'Keeping the Tradition Up-to-Date': Die Lieder der heutigen Pennsylvaniadeutschen als Spiegel ihrer ethnischen Identitat." *Jahrbuch fur Volksliedforschung* 42:78–88.

Cantwell, Robert. (1996). *When We Were Good: The Folk Revival.* Cambridge, MA: Harvard University Press.

Chinn, Jennie A., ed. (1992). *"Don't Ask Me My History, Just Listen to My Music": An Exploration of Kansas Folklife.* Topeka: Kansas State Historical Society.

Dole, Gerard. (1995). *Histoire musicale des Acadiens, de la Nouvelle-France à la Louisiane: 1604–1804.* Paris: L'Harmattan.

Edström, Olle. (1996). "'Cookin' on the West Coast': A Contribution from the Swedish West Coast to Con-

temporary Composition Practice." *Popular Music* 15(1):83–104.

Emoff, Ron. (1998). "A Cajun Poetics of Loss and Longing." *Ethnomusicology* 42(2):283–301.

Födermayr, Franz. (1994). "Zur jodeltechnik von Jimmie Rodgers: Die Blue Yodel." In *For Gerhard Kubik: Festschrift on the Occasion of his 60th Birthday,* ed. A. Schmidhofer and D. Schüller. Frankfurt am Main: Peter Lang.

Francaviglia, Damien. (1995). "Branson, Missouri: Regional Identity and the Emergence of a Popular Culture Community." *Journal of American Culture* 18(2):57–73.

Fusilier, Freida Marie, and Adams, Jolene M. (1994). *The Historical Committee of the West Coast Cajun and Zydeco Music and Dance Association Presents Hé, là-bas!: A History of Louisiana Cajun and Zydeco Music in California.* California: The Historical Committee of the West Coast Cajun and Zydeco Music and Dance Association.

Gould, Philip. (1992). *Cajun Music and Zydeco.* Baton Rouge: Louisiana State University Press.

Greene, Victor. (1992). *A Passion for Polka: Old-Time Ethnic Music in America.* Berkeley: University of California Press.

Grimes, Robert R. (1996). *How Shall We Sing in a Foreign Land?: Music of Irish-Catholic Immigrants in the Antebellum United States.* Notre Dame, IN: University of Notre Dame Press.

Harris, Trudier. (1997). "'The Yellow Rose of Texas': A Different Cultural View." *Callaloo* 20(1):8–19.

Hoven, Margaret, and Earle, David. (1996). "From the Church to the Union Hall: The Songs of Working People." *Sojourners* 25(5):48–51.

Kuhiken, Robert, and Sexton, Rocky. (1991). "The Geography of Zydeco Music." *Journal of Cultural Geography* 12(1):27–38.

Leary, James P. (1991). *Yodeling in Dairyland: A History of Swiss Music in Wisconsin.* Mount Horeb: Wisconsin Folk Museum.

———. (1997). "Czech American Polka Music in Wisconsin." In *Musics of Multicultural America: A Study of Twelve Musical Communities,* ed. Kip Lornell and A. K. Rasmussen. New York: Schirmer Books.

———. (1998). "Polka Music in a Polka State (1991)." In *Wisconsin Folklore,* ed. James P. Leary. Madison: University of Wisconsin.

Lilly, John. (1999). *Mountains of Music: West Virginia Traditional Music from Goldenseal.* Music in American Life Series. Urbana: University of Illinois Press.

Mahabir, Cynthia. (1996). "Wit and Popular Music: The Calypso and the Blues." *Popular Music* 15(1):55–82.

Martin, Philip. (1998). "Hoppwaltzes and Homebrew: Traditional Norwegian American Music from Wisconsin (1985)." In *Wisconsin Folklore,* ed. James P. Leary. Madison: University of Wisconsin.

Mattern, Mark. (1998). "Cajun Music, Cultural Revival: Theorizing Political Action in Popular Music." *Popular Music and Society* 22(1):31–48.

Metyl, R. Carl. (1996). "The Influence of Interethnic Conflicts and Alliances on the Patronage and Performance of Repertoire of the Rusyn American Folk Ensemble 'Slavjane' of McKees Rocks, Pennsylvania." In *Echo der Vielfalt—Echoes of Diversity,* ed. U. Hemetek. Viennna: Böhlau.

Minton, John. (1995). "Creole Community and 'Mass' Communication: Houston Zydeco as a Mediated Tradition." *Journal of Folklore Research* 32(1):1–19.

———. (1996). "Houston Creoles and Zydeco: The Emergence of an African American Popular Style." *American Music* 14(4):480–526.

Nyhan, Patricia; Rollins, Brian; and Babb, David. (1997). *Let the Good Times Roll!: A Guide to Cajun and Zydeco Music.* Portland, ME: Upbeat Books.

Perdue, Charles L. (1995). "'What Made Little Sister Die?': The Core Aesthetic and Personal Culture of a Traditional Singer." *Western Folklore* 54(2):141–163.

Reily, Suzel Ana. (1996). "Tom Jobim and the Bossa Nova Era." *Popular Music* 15(1):1–16.

Sacré, Robert. (1990). *Musique cajun et musiques noires en Louisiane francophone.* Liège, Belgium: Editions CREATAI.

———. (1995). *Musiques cajun, créole et zydeco.* Paris: Presses Universitaires de France.

Sapoznik, Henry. (1997). "Klezmer Music: The First One Thousand Years." In *Musics of Multicultural America: A Study of Twelve Musical Communities,* ed. Kip Lornell and A. K. Rasmussen. New York: Schirmer Books.

Savaglio, Paula. (1996). "Polka Bands and Choral Groups: The Musical Self-Representation of Polish-Americans in Detroit." *Ethnomusicology* 40(1):35–47.

Signell, Karl. (1997). "Mediterranean Musicians in America." *EOL* 3. Available at: http://www.research.umbc.edu/efhm/3/signell/index.html.

Thompson, Carol L. (1996). "Yodeling of the Indiana Swiss Amish." *Anthropological Linguistics* 38(3):495–520.

RECORDINGS

Blues 'n' Boogie Zydeco. 1991. Ryko RCD 10198.

Deep Polka: Dance Music from the Midwest. 1998. Smithsonian Folkways SF CD 40088.

*Cajun and Creole Music, 1934–1937: The Classic Louisiana Recordings.*1987. Rounder CD 1842.

Cajun and Creole Music II, 1934–1937: The Classic Louisiana Recordings. 1999. Rounder CD 1843.

Cajun Music and Zydeco. 1992. Rounder CD 11572.

Cajun String Bands: The 1930s—"Cajun Breakdown." 1997. Arhoolie Folklyric CD-7014.

Cajun Spice Dance Music from South Louisiana. 1989. Rounder CD 11550.

The Early Days: Finnish American Dance Music, 1928–1938. 1989. Thimbleberry THC 1006. Audiocassette.

Early American Cajun Music: Classic Recordings from the 1920s. 1999. Yazoo 2042. CD.

Folksongs of the Louisiana Acadians. 1994. Arhoolie CD 359.

Fragile Traditions: The Art of Pericles Halkias, an Epirot Greek Musician in America. 1989. New York: Ethnic Folk Arts Centre EFAC A8901. Audiocassette.

From Sweden to America: Swedish Emigrant Songs—Amerikavisor. 1996. Caprice CAP 21552. CD.

I'm Never Comin' Back. Amédé Ardoin. 1994. Arhoolie Folklyric CD 7007.

J'ai été au bal/I Went to the Dance: The Cajun and Zydeco Music of Louisiana. 1990. 2 vols. Arhoolie CD 331, 332.

Kings of Freylekh Land: A Century of Yiddish-American Music. 1995. The Epstein Brothers Orchestra. Wergo SM 1611-2. CD.

Klezmer Music: A Marriage of Heaven and Earth. 1996. Ellipsis Arts 4090. CD.

Klezmer Pioneers: European and American Recordings, 1905–1952. 1993. Rounder CD 1089.

King of the Klezmer Clarinet. Nartule Brandwein. 1997. Rounder 1127. CD.

*Let's Go Zydeco.*1994. Arhoolie CD 543.

Louisiana Hot Sauce, Creole Style. 1992. Arhoolie CD 381.

Mademoiselle, voulez-vous danser?: Franco-American Music in New England. 1999. Smithsonian Folkways 40116.

The Mississippi, River of Song: A Musical Journey Down the Mississippi. 1998. 2 vols. Smithsonian Folkways SFW CD 40086.

More Cajun Music and Zydeco. 1995. Rounder CD 11573.

Music of Eastern Europe: Albanian, Greek, and South Slavic Traditions in the United States. 1989. 3 vols. Sounds of the World Series. Music Educators National Conference 3038. Audiocassettes.

Play Me a Polka: Tex-Czech Polkas. 1994. Rounder CD 6029.

The Texas-Czech, Bohemian, and Moravian Bands: Historic Recordings, 1929–1959. 1993. Arhoolie/Folklyric CD 7026.

*Vintage Beausoleil.*Beausoleil. 1995. Music of the World CDC-213.

The Wheels of the World: Early Irish-American Music—Classic Recordings from the 1920s and 1930s. 1997. 2 vols. Yazoo 7008, 7009. CD.

Women's Singing Traditions of New England. 1994. Folklorists in New England and the Folk Arts Network. New London, NH: Cedarhouse Studio. Audiocassette.

Yiddish-American Klezmer Music, 1925–1956. 1992. Dave Tarras. Yazoo 7001. CD.

Zydeco, Vol. 1: The Early Years, 1961–1962. 1989. Arhoolie CD 307.

Zydeco sont pas sale: King of the Real Creole French Zydeco. Clifton Chenier. 1997. Arhoolie CD-9001.

VIDEOS

American Patchwork: Songs and Stories about America. 1990. Alan Lomax. 5 vols. 60 min. each. Beverly Hills, CA: PBS Home Video. Pt. 1: *Jazz Parades*; Pt. 2: *Cajun Country*; Pt. 3: *The Land Where the Blues Began*; Pt. 4: *Appalachian Journey*; Pt. 5: *Dreams and Songs of the Noble Old.*

Cajun Country: Lache pas la patate!—Don't Drop the Potato! 1990. Alan Lomax. 60 min. Cambridge, MA: Vestapol Productions.

Cajun Visits: Les blues de Balfa. 1994. 60 mins. Cambridge, MA: Vestapol.

Clifton Chenier, the King of Zydeco. 1987. Chris Strachwitz. 55 mins. El Cerrito, CA: Arhoolie Productions.

Did Your Mother Come from Ireland? 1989. Roy Esmonde. Conrad Fischer, and Mick Moloney. 50 min. New York: Ethnic Folk Arts Center.

Dry wood. 1990. Les Blank. 37 min. El Cerrito, CA: Flower Films. French-speaking blacks in southwestern Louisiana.

Every Island Has Its Own Songs. 1988. Linda Bassett and Ken Cherry. 41 min. White Springs, FL: Bureau of Florida Folklife Programs. Greek music in Tarpon Springs, Florida.

From Shore to Shore: Irish Traditional Music in New York City. 1993. Patrick Mullins and Rebecca Miller. 57 min. Truckee, CA: Cherry Lane Productions.

A History of Irish Music and Dance. 1994. Ed McGrath. 113 min. Plymouth, MN: Simitar.

Hot Pepper: A Film. 1979. Les Blank. 54 min. El Cerrito, CA: Flower Films. Louisiana zydeco.

The Irish in America: Long Journey Home. 1997. 320 min. (4 vols.). Burbank, CA: Buena Vista Home Entertainment.

A Jumpin' Night in the Garden of Eden. 1987. Michal Goldman. 75 min. New York: First Run Features. Kapelye and Klezmer Conservatory Band.

My Town: Mio paese. 1988. Katherine Gulla. 26 min. Berkeley: University of California, Extension Media Center. Italian immigrants from a small Calabrian town on their life in the United States.

In Heaven There Is No Beer? 1984. Les Blank. 51 min. El Cerrito, CA: Flower Films. Shows Polish American polka musicians and dancers.

J'ai été au bal (I Went to the Dance): The Cajun and Zydeco Music of Louisiana. 1989. Les Blank, Chris Strachwitz, and Maureen Gosling. 84 min. El Cerrito, CA: Flower Films.

Marc and Ann. 1991. Les Blank. 27 min. El Cerrito, CA: Flower Films. A portrait of Marc and Ann Savoy, the Cajun musical couple.

The Mississippi, River of Song: The Grassroots of American Music. 1999 Elijah Wald. 240 min. (4 vols.).Bethesda, MD: AcornMedia.

The Spirit Travels: Immigrant Music in America. 1991. Howard Weiss. 55 min. New York: Cinema Guild.

Zarico. 1985. André Gladu. 58 min. Ottawa: National Film Board of Canada. Music of black Creole culture of southwestern Louisiana.

Ziveli!: Medicine for the Heart. 1987. Les Blank. 51 min. El Cerrito, CA: Flower Films. Serbian American communities of Chicago and California.

Zydeco: Creole Music and Culture in Rural Louisiana. 1984. 57 min. El Cerrito, CA: Flower Films.

GLOSSARY

A

a cappella Unaccompanied vocal music; singing without instrumental accompaniment.

Accordion A free-reed, bellows-driven instrument developed in the early nineteenth century. There are various forms of accordions; most common are the button accordion (with a keyboard made up of one or more rows of buttons) and the piano accordion (with a piano-style keyboard). *See also* Diatonic accordion.

Alabado A free-form lament of Arab-Spanish origin that is heard in Texas-Mexican communities of the southwestern United States.

Angular leap An abrupt jump between two intervals in a melody.

Antiphony See Call-and-response.

Ascending contour or **melody** A melody that generally rises in pitch over its duration.

Autoharp A musical instrument invented by C. F. Zimmerman in the late nineteenth century. It is tuned chromatically, covering about three and a half octaves. The strings are stopped by the player pressing down on "chord bars;" these bars automatically block all the notes except those found in a specific chord. Sold through mail-order catalogs and by traveling salesmen/teachers in the early twentieth century, the autoharp became a popular instrument for accompanying songs and ballads.

B

Bagpipe A common musical instrument found throughout Europe. There are many varieties made in different sizes with different features. The basic bagpipe consists of a large bag (sometimes made of the body of a goat or another animal) that is pumped to provide the air supply for one or more pipes. In the top of each pipe is a single reed that produces the sounds. The chanter is a long pipe with holes in it that produces melody notes; the drone pipes are shorter and play only a single, continuous note. *See also* Uillean (bag)pipes.

Bajo sexto A large-bodied, guitar-like instrument popularized in Mexico. It has a much deeper body than a standard guitar.

Ballad A song that tells a story. Ballads are usually long, and their main subjects are love and death.

Banjo (five-string) An African American–derived instrument featuring a skin or plastic head stretched across a wooden or metal hoop, with four long strings and one short "drone" string. The banjo was originally used in African American dance music and in minstrel music and is now commonly played in old-time and bluegrass music. *See also* Tenor banjo.

Barbershop harmony Traditional four-part harmonies developed by so-called barbershop quartets during the late nineteenth and early twentieth centuries. Barbershop quartets often featured an independent, and active, bass part. This style of singing was carried forward by gospel quartets and other popular harmony groups.

Barrel drum A drum with a long body that is slightly flared at its center, like the shape of a barrel. These drums can have either one or two heads and may vary in size from small to very large. The Japanese *taiko* and Puerto Rican *barile* are examples of barrel drums.

Bass An acoustic or electric four-string instrument used to play the bass harmony accompaniment to a melody.

Bass drum A large cylindrical drum of indefinite pitch with heads on both sides.

Batá drums Sacred drums (imported from Africa) that are played as part of Afro-Caribbean religious ceremonies. They have an hourglass shape with a head stretched across each end of the body. The drums are held vertically across the player's body, and each end is struck with one hand. Batá rhythms have been carried over into secular/popular musical styles from this region.

Bebop A style of jazz involving new harmonic concepts, rapid tempos, and small ensembles. It was developed in the 1940s and is especially associated with saxophone player Charlie Parker.

Big band The primary ensemble of the swing era of American jazz and popular music of the 1930s and 1940s. Big band music is scored for multiple trumpets, trombones, clarinets, and saxophones (melody group), while small groups usually employ, at most, one of each instrument. Usually the sections of the band perform alternately, in call-and-response style. In both big and small bands, the rhythm section is piano and/or guitar, drum kit, and double bass.

Big circle dance An Appalachian dance performed in a large circle. Couples pair off in sets of two to perform figures similar to those in square dances, then fall back into a big circle to perform larger group figures.

Blue note A note that is slightly flattened to give it a "bluesy" effect; often the third or seventh degree of the scale.

Bluegrass A style of music invented by mandolinist Bill Monroe based on old-time string band music, blues, and Western swing. Monroe put together a band that included the rhythms of popular music, the bluesy inflected vocals of African American music, and the tight harmonies of gospel and old-time church singing. The typical bluegrass band is modeled on Monroe's original group that featured mandolin, guitar, banjo, fiddle, and bass.

Blues A traditional African American musical genre. It is in 4/4 time, with a melody characterized by lowered third and seventh (blue notes), and has developed into a stereotyped, twelve-measure harmonic pattern. The term has also been used to describe any song that expresses "blue" or sad feelings.

Bodhrán *See* Frame drum.

Bolero Medium-tempoed dance in triple time, with intricate steps, popular in Spain, Latin America, and the Caribbean.

Bongo drums/Bongos Two small, shallow, single-headed drums that are played with the palms and fingers of the hands. Popular in Latin-Caribbean musical cultures.

Bottleneck A style of playing the guitar in which the guitarist places a glass bottleneck around a finger on the noting hand and slides it over the strings of the instrument, creating a sliding or whining sound. This is a common technique among blues guitarists, who use either a glass bottleneck or a metal bar (called a slide).

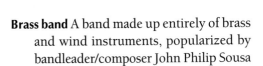

Brass band A band made up entirely of brass and wind instruments, popularized by bandleader/composer John Philip Sousa at the turn of the twentieth century.

Break dancing/Breaking A solo, urban dance style featuring elaborate athletic moves, including spinning, moon-walking, flipping, and popping (isolating certain parts of the body to mimic robot-like movement).

Broadsheet/Broadside ballad A single sheet of paper on which the text (and sometimes music) of a song was printed. Beginning in the seventeenth century, broadsides were popular as a means of spreading new and traditional songs.

Buck dancing *See* Clogging.

Button accordion *See* Accordion.

C

Cajun music A style of music that originated among natives of southeastern Louisiana of French descent. It often consists of dance music or lyrical songs sung in the local dialect (which is itself a mixture of English and French dialects). Typical Cajun bands feature fiddle, accordion, triangle, and guitar.

Call-and-response A vocal or instrumental style in which a short melodic line (the "call") is sung (often by a song leader) and then a second, "responding" phrase follows it (often sung by a group). In European and American classical music, the style is called "antiphony."

Caller A dance leader who "prompts" the dancers by calling out the figures before they are to be performed. Common today among square, contra, and big circle dances.

Calypso A Caribbean song form popularized in the United States during the 1930s featuring improvised songs of topical or humorous content with a syncopated beat.

Camp-meeting song A religious song associated with large nineteenth-century camp meetings, the purpose of which was to convert people to Christianity. Hundreds of congregants converged on a single spot to spend several days praying, sermonizing, witnessing, and exchanging and learning simple songs that were easy to sing by ear.

Canción A traditional love song of the Latino communities of the southwestern United States, Mexico, and Latin America.

Ceili Gaelic for "dance." Thus, any gathering where Irish dancing is performed.

Ceili or **Ceilidh band** An Irish dance band that combines traditional Irish melody instruments—fiddle, flute, bagpipe, and accordion—with a regular, heavy rhythmic accompaniment provided by piano, bass, and military-style drumming.

Celtic music Music of the Celts, the original inhabitants of Ireland and Wales; often used to describe Irish traditional music in general.

Chanson A short lyric song in the French language.

Chanter (1) A song leader. In the Native American tradition, the chanter (usually male) may also serve as the drummer who accompanies dancers. (2) The melody pipe of the bagpipe.

Chantey *See* Shanty.

Chanteymen Sailors who sing traditional shantys; also used to describe any sailors who work on a boat.

Chicago blues A style of urban blues that emerged on the South Side of Chicago after World War II, centering around performers such as Muddy Waters and Howlin' Wolf. Generally, Chicago blues is performed by a combo featuring electric guitar, piano, harmonica, and drums.

Chicken scratch music A common name (regarded by some as disparaging) for a type of dance music played by Native American and Tex-Mex bands that is derived from European styles such as quadrilles, waltzes, and polkas.

Chinese opera An elaborately staged and costumed musical theater tradition of China. Different Chinese regions have their own operatic styles, which are referred to as Peking opera, Cantonese opera, and so on.

Chorus (1) *See* Refrain. (2) A large vocal group made up of voices of different vocal ranges.

Chromatic scale All twelve divisions of the octave (not just the eight of the do-re-mi scale.) On a piano, for instance, the chromatic scale includes all of the white and black keys within the span of an octave.

Cittern A Renaissance-era string instrument similar to a guitar.

Clave rhythm The defining rhythm of much Latin-Caribbean music. It is a repeated two-bar pattern around which all other rhythmic patterns are organized. It goes "123-123-12 34-12-12-34," keeping an even pulse and stressing "1."

Claves Two sticks that are beat rhythmically together in Latin-Caribbean musical styles. *See also* Rhythm sticks.

Clog (1) *See* Clogging. (2) A dance tune to accompany clogging or step dancing, usually in 2/4 or 4/4 time.

Clogging Complicated step dances often performed by a solo dancer, with movement restricted to the lower legs and feet, while the remainder of the body is held straight. Similar to Irish step dancing and perhaps derived from it. Styles that involve keeping the feet close to the ground are known as "flat-foot clogging" or "flatfooting." Also called "buck dancing."

Coda An ending passage of a musical composition.

Combo A small instrumental ensemble.

Concertina A name loosely given to a wide variety of free-reed, bellows-driven instruments. The concertina played by German, Polish, and other immigrants in the American Midwest is really a form of button accordion. The Irish concertina is much smaller and plays a different note on the push and pull.

Conga drums *See* Tumbadoras.

Conjunto (1) A small ensemble, usually led by an accordion, popular in the southwestern United States and Mexico. (2) The type of music played by such an ensemble. *See also* Norteño music/*La música norteña*.

Contour Literally, "shape." The shape of a melody—whether it moves up or down gradually or in leaps—is called its contour.

Contra dance A New England form of couple dance, danced in two facing lines. The figures are performed by two couples and are similar to those found in square dancing. Chorus figures are performed by the entire line. Couples progress up or down the line as they become "active" (initiators of a figure) or "inactive."

Contradanza *See* Contra dance.

Contredanse *See* Contra dance.

Corrido A narrative folk song or ballad (often tragic and with elements of social protest) found among both Native American and Tex-Mex traditions in the southwestern United States and Mexico, its country of origin.

Cotillion A French ballroom dance of the late eighteenth and early nineteenth centuries that was popular in the American colonies as well as in England. It involved couples in square formations performing repeated figures and was a predecessor of the quadrille and square dance.

Cotillo *See* Cotillion.

Countermelody A contrasting second melody played simultaneously with the principal melody.

Counterrhythm A second rhythmic line played in contrast with the principal rhythmic line.

Couplet Two lines of a song's lyric that form a complete thought.

Cowbell A small, hollow metal bell—similar to those placed around the necks of cows—that is struck with a metal stick.

Csárdás A stylized Hungarian folk dance in 2/4 time that became popular in the first half of the nineteenth century. The melodies are noted for their minor keys and dramatic changes in tempo.

Cuatro A Puerto Rican guitar-like instrument, but with a smaller body and five pairs of strings.

Cubop A blend of Cuban rhythms and drums with bebop-style music. Pioneered by Dizzy Gillespie's bands of the 1950s.

Cycle (1) A group of songs or instrumental compositions that are usually performed together. (2) In square dancing, a group of four couples who form a single square. Also called set.

Cymbals Paired percussion instruments consisting of two brass discs that are struck together. They can be very small (for example, finger cymbals) or quite large.

D

Deejay *See* Disc jockey.

Descending contour or **melody** A melody that generally falls in pitch over its duration.

Diatonic accordion An accordion with buttons that play different notes when the bellows are opened (pulled) or closed (pushed). Sometimes called "push-pull accordions" for this reason.

Diatonic scale The eight-tone scale from octave to octave; the do-re-mi scale without chromatic tones.

Diddley bow Traditional African American one-stringed instrument. The string is made of hay baling wire stretched over two cans or jars and fastened horizontally to a wall or a board at each end.

It is plucked with the fingers of one hand. Different tones are produced by stopping the string with a small bottle or other slide.

Disc jockey An announcer who selects, introduces, and plays records, either "live" or on the radio. Commonly called a "deejay" or "DJ."

Disco Dance music of the 1970s noted for its loud, regular beat.

Dissonance In Western classical music, any harmony part that is based on seconds, sevenths, augmented, or diminished intervals. More generally, a harmony part that sounds unpleasant to the ear. "Consonance" is the term used to describe simultaneously played tones that are pleasant to the ear.

DJ *See* Disc jockey.

Dominant The fifth degree in the Western major or minor scale. Also, the chord built on this note.

Dorian mode A sequence of tones from one octave to the next, neither major nor minor, which can be sounded by the eight white keys of the piano starting and ending on "D."

Drone A continuous, unchanging tone that sounds throughout a musical composition or a portion of it.

Drop-thumb/double-thumbing (banjo) *See* Frailing.

Drum-rattle A skin-headed drum that features small rattles, either mounted on the outside of the instrument or along the rim of the drumhead itself, so that it can create both percussive and rattling sounds.

Dulcimer (Appalachian dulcimer or **lap dulcimer)** A three- or four-stringed instrument held on the lap. The strings run the length of the instrument over a fretted fingerboard, and the player frets the notes either with a small stick or the fingers while strumming the strings with a feather quill or pick. Not related to the hammer/hammered dulcimer.

Duple time/beat A rhythm that is divisible by two or with two primary accents.

E

Electric guitar An amplified guitar; the guitar's sound is enhanced through pickups that translate the sound into electrical energy that is amplified and broadcast over speakers. Amplification further allows changing the guitar's timbre.

Ethnography The systematic description of human culture.

Ethnology The scientific comparison of human cultures.

Ethnomusicology The study of people making music, all over the globe.

F

Fa-sol-la singers *See* Shape-note.

Falsetto An artificially high voice; often a male singer singing well above his normal range.

Feis An Irish competition/festival in which musicians and dancers compete for prizes.

Fiddle A bowed lute with four strings, ordinarily tuned GDAE like the European violin. Although fiddles and violins are now structurally more or less identical, fiddle players use different techniques and sometimes modify their instruments (flattening the arc of the bridge, for example) and play in nonstandard tunings.

Field holler An a cappella, African American work song.

Fiesta A religious celebration popular in Latino communities and among some Native Americans.

Fife A short, open-holed, transverse flute with six to eight holes.

Fifth The fifth scale degree; the related interval between the tonic and the fifth scale degree.

Fill An embellishing musical phrase, often improvised by an ensemble musician not responsible for carrying the main melody.

Finger cymbals Tiny paired cymbals that are attached to the fingers with small leather straps.

Finger pick To play a banjo or guitar with the tips of the finger or finger picks (metal or plastic extensions attached to the thumb or fingers to enable the player to produce a louder sound) rather than strumming across the strings with a flat pick held between the thumb and first finger.

Fipple flute A flute with a mouthpiece that has a plug with a notch at one end, such as that found on the recorder.

Flageolet A simple flute, often made from a reed or bone, that is blown from one end. It features four fingering holes and two thumb holes to vary the tones produced.

Flatfooting *See* Clogging.

Floating stanza or **verse** A common set of lyrics that moves from one song to another.

Folklife Study of the day-to-day lives of ordinary people in close-knit communities, with special attention to traditional ways of thinking and doing.

Folklore The oral and customary traditions of a group of people, including their stories, songs, recipes, clothing, holidays, architecture and use of space, and so on.

Foodways The traditional eating habits and cooking practices of a specific cultural group.

Form Musical structure; the way the musical design coheres as a whole.

Fox-trot Popular dance form of the 1920s and 1930s in duple time that has survived as one of the standard couple dances.

Frailing (banjo) The old-time style of playing the banjo that involves brushing

the back of the nail of the second or third finger across the strings while "catching" the thumb on the short drone string in a rhythmic pattern. Also called clawhammer, rapping, banging, thumping, or drop-thumb (a more melodic variation of frailing, where the thumb is used to pick notes as well as to hit the drone string). *See also* three-finger style (banjo) and two-finger (up-picking) style (banjo).

Frame drum A round drum with a shallow body. The rim of the drum is often made from a single bent piece of wood. Examples of frame drums are the bodhrán, which is used in Irish traditional music, and the tambourine.

Free reed A small, single reed—made of metal, bamboo, or some other material—that is held firmly at one end, usually in a frame. A Jew's harp is a simple free-reed instrument. Accordions, concertinas, the Japanese shō, and harmonicas are also free-reed instruments.

Freedom song Song performed during the civil rights movement of the 1950s and 1960s expressing the message of the movement.

Frolic An older term for a dance, often held at a private home, that might last all night long.

Funk (1) An African American popular music that developed in the 1960s from African polyrhythms and call-and-response textures. Funk music often uses a single chord or a few alternating, sometimes complex harmonies, through which clipped, syncopated lines emerge in the electric guitar and bass parts, drums and percussion, keyboards, winds (saxophones, trumpets), and vocal parts. Interjections by different instruments and voices, often repeated, is another typical element. Funk has been able to blend into successive styles, exerting influence on reggae, disco, hip-hop, and rap. (2) A roots movement in jazz during the

1950s that drew on blues, rhythm and blues, and gospel music in a reaction against increasingly abstract bebop and cool jazz styles.

G

Gaelic The family of traditional languages of Ireland and Scotland.

Genre A named type of musical composition and performance, such as jazz, blues, bluegrass, zydeco, and so on.

***Gesangverein* ("Singing society")** A private, German American social club dedicated to choral singing, often of patriotic and sentimental songs, traditionally sung in German.

Gigue Originally a popular Baroque dance in a rapid tempo that was performed by men. In the Franco-American tradition, the gigue has evolved into a virtuosic solo step dance performed by both men and women. *See also* Jig.

Glide A smooth, rapid movement from one note to another, slurring over the intermediate pitches. In classical music, called "portamento" or "glissando."

Glissando *See* Glide.

Glottal stop An abrupt interruption of the breath by rapidly closing the glottis (the elongated open space between the vocal cords).

Gong A large, round, metal plate that is often suspended in a frame. It plays a single note when it is struck with a metal stick or mallet.

Gospel music Modern Protestant religious music that is more personal and informal than the traditional Christian hymn.

Gospel quartet A small ensemble of four or more singers who sing religious-themed songs in four-part harmony.

Gourd rattle A dried gourd that has been hollowed out and filled with seeds or small pebbles. When shaken, it makes a rattling sound.

Grace note An ornamenting or embellishing note, usually performed before the primary tone.

Griot An African storyteller; specifically applied to the master harpists of the Gambia who accompany themselves on a harp known as the kora while relating their political and cultural history.

Guitar A six-stringed instrument of seventeenth-century Spanish origin, successor to the lute. It was popularized among folk and amateur musicians in the United States in the late nineteenth century as an accompaniment for songs.

H

Habanera A traditional Latin-Caribbean dance form with a 3+3+2 rhythmic structure.

Half-tone or **half-step** The smallest interval in the Western scale; also called a semitone. For example, the interval C-C# is a half-step.

Hammer/hammered dulcimer A traditional instrument found in many regions of the world. It consists of a square or trapezoidal-shaped body with strings running across the length of the box. The strings are usually paired (i.e., each note is produced by two strings). The player strikes the strings with two small "hammers" made of wood (sometimes covered with felt). Unrelated to the Appalachian lap dulcimer, despite the shared name.

Hammond organ An electronic organ developed in the late 1940s that was far less expensive and much smaller and lighter than a conventional pipe organ and therefore appealed to smaller churches and home organists. Besides organ sounds, this instrument was also capable of producing some "special effects" electronically.

Harmonica A small, free-reed instrument. A series of reeds are mounted in small air chambers that are open at one end. The player either sucks or blows into these openings to make the reeds sound. By cupping their hands over the harmonica and opening or closing them while playing and by playing in keys other than what the harmonica is meant for, blues musicians have created many different timbres and effects. Also called a "mouth harp," "harp," or "mouth organ."

Harmonium A small reed organ. The reeds are set in motion by air from a bellows pumped by the player's feet.

Harmony Musical tones sounded at the same time. *See also* Melody.

Heterophony Two or more slightly different vocal or instrumental parts played simultaneously. Slight intentional variations in ornamentation and attack may account for some of the differences.

Hexatonic A six-note scale.

Highland fling The Irish name for traditional Scottish tunes played briskly in 4/4 time.

Hillbilly music The recording industry's pejorative, in-house name for early country music (c. 1923–1930).

Hip-hop African American popular dance music of the last two decades of the twentieth century that became the underlying musical basis for rap. While inheriting the strong beat of disco, hip-hop re-emphasized the backbeat of 1960s popular music and also drew upon house music of the late 1970s. It developed as sampling technology evolved, allowing musicians and producers to "sample" or record small excerpts from earlier popular songs. These small pieces were then electronically treated, looped (or repeated), and put one on top of another to form a dense musical texture.

Hoedown A community dancing party, originally in the rural American South and West, featuring square dances with calling and old-time music.

Honky-tonk A small bar or club featuring country music. Marked by the sound of electric guitars and pedal steel guitars, honky-tonk music emerged as a popular style in the late 1940s and early 1950s.

Hornpipe Since the sixteenth century, a dance and tune in 4/4 or 2/4 time. Originally played slowly to accompany step dancing, hornpipes are now often played as quickly as reels.

Hula Originally a form of religious dance from Hawaii; subsequently popularized as a show dance style.

Hurdy-gurdy A stringed instrument most commonly found in Eastern Europe and France (Brittany). The fret board is covered with an elaborate mechanism that allows the player to fret the strings by pushing down on a key (like the keyboard of a piano). The notes are sounded by turning a crank that activates a rosin-covered wheel that rubs up against the strings from underneath.

Hymn A religious song praising God.

I

Idiophones Musical instruments whose sounds are produced by striking or shaking a metallic, wooden, or other surface directly. Thus, idiophones produce their sound by the substance of the instrument itself. Cymbals, rattles, rhythm sticks, and triangles are examples of idiophones.

Improvisation The creation of new melody, lyrics, or harmony parts in the midst of performance.

Instrument A device that produces musical sounds.

Interval The distance in pitch between two notes. Intervals are usually measured from the lower tone to the higher. In the C major scale, the interval C-E is a major third.

J

Jam/jamming A dance competition held on the street; "jamming" is to compete with other dancers. *See also* Street dancing; break dancing/breaking.

Jam session An informal gathering of musicians to play tunes.

Jazz A number of popular musical styles invented by African Americans beginning around the turn of the twentieth century based on improvised melodies and syncopated rhythms.

Jew's harp A small musical instrument consisting of a metal tongue (or reed) mounted in a frame. The player holds it up against his or her open teeth, and, while vigorously plucking the instrument's tongue, breathes in and out to create a whirring sound. Also called "jaw harp."

Jig An Irish dance tune in triple time; also the rapid movement of the feet in a "jig" step.

Jubilee An African American religious song that has had different meanings over time and that may refer to (1) songs sung during the emancipation celebrations of 1862 and that refer to a liberation, (2) songs that are uptempo and rhythmic (such as "When the Saints Go Marching In"), and (3) the Fisk Jubilee Singers and their strong influence on a new singing style and songs written during Reconstruction. The Fisk singers and these new songs were important in the development of gospel quartets. Written in the context of freedom, not slavery, this music exhibited a different attitude and style.

Jug band An informal jazz group, often featuring homemade or inexpensive musical instruments, including the kazoo, washboard, washtub bass, and a large, empty jug. The jug player either blows or sings into its opening in a rhythmic fashion to create a bass harmony part.

Junkanoo music A style of vibrant, Bahamian percussion music performed

by costumed marchers (Junkanooers) at special parades and festivals that were originally held during the Christmas season but now occur at other times of the year as well.

K

Kazoo A small wind instrument featuring a thin membrane that is set into vibration when the player hums or speaks into one end of the instrument. A simple version can be made by placing a piece of tissue paper over a comb and humming through it.

Kitchen racket or **kitchen junket** An informal dance held in the home; the term was most commonly used in New York and New England for informal contra dances.

Klezmer A Yiddish term literally meaning "vessel of melody," it was the name given to Jewish American dance bands of the 1920s and 1930s who played a mixture of traditional and jazz-influenced music. Klezmer music has enjoyed a strong revival since the mid-1970s.

Konpas Haitian small-band music that incorporates elements of rock, jazz, disco, soul, and funk.

L

Ländler A couple dance in 3/4 time that originated in alpine central Europe in the early nineteenth century.

Leader *See* Song leader.

Lining out A term used to describe a style of hymn singing in which a group leader first sings a line of music and the leader and congregation then repeat the words to a different but related melody. The hymn continues in this way line by line.

Long bow style A fiddle technique in which several notes are played on a single bowstroke; smoother than playing "short bow" style, in which the direc-

tion of the bow is changed with the majority of notes.

Longways Dances performed in two long lines. *See also* Contra dance.

Lulus *See* Vocables.

Lute A generic name for a variety of plucked string instruments, most popular from the sixteenth through the eighteenth centuries. The body of the lute is shaped like half of a pear, with its neck turned back at a right angle. It usually has five sets of double strings, plus a single string for the highest sound, and they are plucked with the fingers. The mandolin is of the lute family, as are the Chinese pipa and the Japanese biwa. *See also* Guitar.

Lyric song A song that primarily expresses an emotion (e.g., love, loneliness, or anger). Lyric songs are shorter than narrative ballads. Usually in a verse-refrain format, a common structure in which one melodic part (a verse whose lyrics often change) is alternated with a repeated chorus or refrain.

M

Major The primary Western classical scale since the eighteenth century. A major chord consists of a first, major third, and fifth intervals.

Mambo A ballroom dance derived from the rumba. It appeared in Cuba during the 1940s and by the 1950s had spread to non–Hispanic audiences in the United States. The mambo uses forward and backward steps (beginning on the upbeat) to percussive polyrhythmic accompaniment.

Mandolin An eight-string, guitar-like instrument. The mandolin's strings are paired in four and tuned like those of a violin. Mandolin orchestras were popular in the early twentieth century. Today they have largely disappeared, but the instrument is featured in bluegrass music.

Maracas Popular Latin-Caribbean gourd rattles.

Mariachi A modern musical ensemble—often heard along the border between Texas and Mexico—consisting of vocalists accompanied by various stringed instruments, including guitars and violins and usually brass (trumpets) as well.

Marimba A wooden-keyed instrument with small resonators placed below the bars. It is played with a stick or a pair of sticks. A type of xylophone.

Matachina and ***Matachines*** Matachina are dances of conquest, originally Spanish in origin but later adapted by the Pueblo Indians; *matachines* are the male dancers who perform them. The matachines dance in two lines facing each other, often wearing elaborate crowns featuring long ribbons and carrying rattles. They may also perform circular dances around a maypole.

Mazurka A Polish dance style in triple time brought to the United States by immigrants beginning in the mid–nineteenth century.

Mele Chanted poetic texts that express the relationship of Hawaiians to everything around them (the land, the ocean, their gods, and all living things) and also serve as orally transmitted records of the legends and lore of the Hawaiian people, including family histories, plant names, place names, and medical practices.

Melisma Characterized by singing three or more tones per syllable of text.

Melody A succession of musical tones. *See also* Harmony.

Membranophones Musical instruments that produce a sound through a vibrating membrane, or skin head. Drums are the most common membranophones.

Merengue or **meringue** Characteristic Afro-Cubanesque song dance of Venezuela, Haiti, and the Dominican Republic. It uses four-line stanzas and refrain verse forms. Responsorial singing, polyrhythms, and 5/8 effects are layered over the basic 2/4 beat.

Metallophone Similar to a xylophone, but with metal keys instead of wooden ones.

Microtone Any interval smaller than the half-tone; often used to describe tiny divisions of a tone (such as 1/4 of a tone).

Minor The second most common Western classical scale, also known as the Aeolian mode.

Minstrel show A nineteenth-century American amusement in which actors and musicians mimicked African American dialect, music, and dance.

Mixolydian One of the Greek modes, rarely heard today in classical music, although still common in some folk traditions. Neither major nor minor, it is a sequence of tones that can be achieved by playing the eight white keys of the piano starting and ending on G.

Monochord A single-stringed instrument, such as the diddley bow.

Montuno The call-and-response section of Cuban son. It features a short, simple harmonic ostinato that forms the basis for call-and-response passages and solo instrumental improvisation.

Motown A type of African American popular music (created specifically to appeal to teenagers of all races) that was produced by the Detroit-based record label of the same name during the 1960s.

Music notation Any system of symbols for writing down music.

N

Narrative song A song that tells a story or relates history; a ballad.

Norteño* music/*La música norteña Contemporary accordion-based folk music of Tex-Mex origin characterized by stylistic simplicity and working-class themes. The style is known inside Texas as conjunto.

Note value The length of time or duration that a specific note is sounded. Also called "time value."

O

Octave The eighth or final scale step; the interval whose distance is eight diatonic tones, as from middle C to C above middle C on the piano.

Off-beat A beat that is normally not stressed or accented.

Old-time (1) The traditional songs and fiddle tunes of the southeastern United States. (2) Songs and tunes that were popular in the past but now are remembered by only a small group of musicians. (3) A term used by many European American cultures of the Midwest to describe the ethnic-based styles of social dancing and social dance music centered around waltzes, polkas, and often the schottische. Ballroom dances (such as the fox-trot) that have developed in more recent years are considered part of the "new-time" tradition.

Oral history (1) History that is passed from generation to generation by the telling of stories rather than through written texts. (2) A method of collecting history by means of interviews.

Oral tradition Songs, stories, and other customs that are passed down from generation to generation by imitation and by word-of-mouth rather than by being written down.

Ornament Formulaic decoration or embellishment of a musical tone.

Ostinato A melodic phrase that is persistently repeated (usually in the same voice part and at the same pitch) throughout a composition.

P

Panpipes A collection of reeds of different lengths that are tied together. The player blows across the top of the reeds to play different notes. Panpipes are found in many Pacific and Latin American musical traditions.

Parallel thirds A type of harmonic accompaniment in which the melody line is doubled by another part, two scale tones above it, in parallel movement.

"Pendulum-like" melody A melody that predominantly alternates between two notes.

Pennywhistle *See* Tin whistle.

Pentatonic scale A five-note scale, common in folk and traditional styles. On the piano, it can be obtained by playing the black keys only.

Phrase A short musical or lyrical thought; a portion of a melody.

Piano accordion *See* Accordion.

Pipa A short-necked, Chinese wooden lute.

Pitch The acoustical highness or lowness of a musical tone resulting from its frequency of vibration.

Play-party song A short, often nonsensical song sung primarily by children at informal parties to accompany a dance or a game involving physical activity (musical chairs, for instance).

Plena A Puerto Rican ballad similar to the calypso songs of Trinidad.

Polka A vigorous Eastern European couple dance in 2/4 time, introduced by immigrants to the United States in the mid–nineteenth century.

Polyphony More than one vocal or instrumental melodies sung or played at the same time.

Polyrhythm Two or more conflicting rhythmic parts played simultaneously.

Powwow A modern, intertribal gathering of Native Americans to perform traditional dance and song forms.

Pulsation A slight interruption in breath; a continuous revoicing of a note in rapid succession.

Q

Qeej A bamboo-reed mouth organ of the Hmong people of Cambodia. Similar to the Japanese shō.

Quadrille A precursor of the square dance, the quadrille originated in the ballrooms of France and attained its greatest popularity in the early nineteenth century throughout Europe, Russia, and the United States. It is performed by either four or eight couples and features five main figures (patterns of movement).

Quills See Panpipes.

R

R&B *See* Rhythm and blues.

Race records A term used by record companies to describe the special line of recordings marketed primarily from the 1920s through the 1940s to the African American audience.

Ragtime Originally a piano style with a regular, repeated bass line and a syncopated melody; later, any syncopated composition. Ragtime was developed by African Americans in the late nineteenth century.

Range In describing a melody, the overall intervallic distance covered between lowest and highest notes.

Rap A style of urban African American popular music characterized by (often) improvised, sung-spoken rhymes performed to a rhythmic accompaniment. Rap is frequently performed a cappella, with sexual, socially relevant, or political lyrics. The music itself became known as hip-hop.

Rasp/Rasping sticks A rasp is a small, notched piece of wood that is rubbed with a stick or scraper to make a grating sound. Rasping sticks are also notched in such a way that when they are rubbed together, they produce a similar effect.

Rattle A gourd, shell, or can filled with pebbles that makes a rattling sound when it is vigorously shaken.

Reel A fast Anglo-American dance tune, often played on the fiddle, in 4/4 or cut (2/2) time.

Refrain The repeated chorus of a song that alternates with the verse. Unlike the verse, the words to the refrain usually do not change. Sometimes a refrain is shorter than a chorus.

Reggae A popular Jamaican musical style that melds Western rock instrumentation with a loping, syncopated beat and often topical lyrics.

Repertoire The songs, dance tunes, or other musical pieces that are characteristically performed by an individual or a group of people.

Resonator An empty vessel—often a gourd—placed under a musical instrument to increase the sound produced.

Rhythm and blues (R&B) A generic term used to describe African American popular song styles in the late 1940s and early 1950s. Imitation soon led to rock and roll, the white equivalent of rhythm and blues.

Rhythm sticks Two sticks that are rubbed together to create a percussive rhythm.

Rhythmic pattern The patterns of beats that occur throughout a piece of music.

Rhythmic pulse The underlying beat.

Riff A short, memorable melodic phrase that is repeated throughout sections of an instrumental composition or accompaniment. *See also* Ostinato.

Ring shout Historically, a circular African American dance song expressing religious feeling. The song is half-sung, half-shouted as the dancers move slowly in a ring formation. Also called simply a "shout."

Rock and roll A popular white American style of the 1950s that was copied from

black rhythm and blues and featured a percussively heavy reinforcement of the meter (beat) played by combos consisting, minimally, of piano, bass, drums, and guitars, often with a single saxophonist or small wind section. Blues harmonic structures were common, but without the corresponding mood. By the mid-1960s, rock and roll had run out of steam, only to be revitalized and transformed into rock by the so-called "British Invasion" of musical groups that emphasized electric guitars and nonblues harmonic patterns. *See also* Rhythm and blues.

Rockabilly A musical style of the late 1950s and early 1960s that blended country music with rock and roll's sensibility, instrumentation, and heavily accented beat. The term was coined from a combination of "rock" and "hillbilly."

Round dance Any traditional dance that is performed in a circular figure. *See also* Big circle dance.

Rumba A syncopated Latin American dance form, originally from Cuba, that was popularized in the United States in the 1930s.

S

Sacred Harp, The The name of a religious songbook first published in the early nineteenth century; now applied to any song from this book or others in the shape-note tradition.

Salsa A vigorous Latin American dance form combining Latin rhythms with big band instrumentation. Based on the traditional Cuban son style.

Samba A Brazilian American dance style featuring a medium tempo and pronounced rhythms.

Scale A sequence of tones, arranged in ascending or descending order, and used in a characteristic way in a musical performance or composition.

Schottische An Eastern European dance that is a variant of the polka. It is performed by couples in a circle, in 2/2 time, at a slower pace than the polka.

Scraper A small stick used to rub against another object to make a sound.

Scratching A technique used by disc jockeys in which records are spun back and forth while being played so that a percussive, scratching sound is created.

Sean-nós singing A traditional Irish singing style. Highly ornamented, it is particularly suited to singing songs in Gaelic but is also used for English-language songs.

Secular music Music without religious content; music performed for entertainment, not to express religious feelings.

Seísun Literally, "session." An informal gathering of Irish musicians.

Set A generic term for any square dance. The group of four couples who perform the dance are often described as a "set." Also called cycle.

Shanty A short lyric song sung by sailors to aid in their work or pass the time.

Shape-note A system of musical notation in which different scale notes are represented by notes of different shapes, including diamonds, circles, squares, and triangles. Singers can therefore learn their parts without "reading" conventional music by associating the shape with its scale tone (sung as "fa-sol-la," etc.). This method was used to promote music literacy and teach hymn singing to people both in the northern and southeastern United States. *See also* Sacred Harp, The.

Shellshaker In the Native American tradition, a turtle shell filled with small pebbles that is usually attached to the leggings or boots of a female dancer. The name "shellshaker" may be applied to the turtle shell or to the dancer herself.

Shō A Japanese musical instrument consisting of a group of thin bamboo pipes (each containing at its base a small reed) clustered around a small wind

chamber. The player blows into the chamber to sound the reeds. Small fingering holes at the base of each pipe are used to regulate which reed sounds. Variants of this instrument are found throughout Southeast Asia.

Shout *See* Ring shout.

Shuffle (step) (1) A walking step in which the feet are dragged slightly. (2) A syncopated beat.

Slide (1) Moving from one tone to another without a break; similar to a glide but usually covering a smaller range. (2) In reference to the guitar, the use of a bottleneck or metal bar to stop the strings; this technique is known as slide guitar. (3) In Irish music, a jig in 12/8 time, often in three or more parts.

Snare drum A small, two-headed drum of wood or metal, across the lower head of which are stretched several gut strings or strands of metal wire (snares), whose rattling against the head reinforces and alters the tone. The upper head is struck alternately or simultaneously with two drumsticks.

Soca Caribbean music that combines traditional calypso with disco rhythms and soul vocal styles.

Son (1) Generic name of indigenous songs of Cuba and neighboring islands, reflecting the influence of African rhythms and set usually in a strongly accented 2/4 time. *Son* was the principal form of Cuban popular music in the twentieth century and remains an important form of expression in New York's Cuban and Puerto Rican community. It is characterized by a two-part structure in which two or three verses (usually sung by a lead soloist but sometimes by a chorus) are followed by a call-and-response section known as the montuno. *See also* Salsa. (2) A traditional dance piece performed by Mexican mariachi musicians. It varies in style from region to region in Mexico, but is often fast-tempoed with raucous and sometimes improvised lyrics containing social commentary.

Song leader (1) In call-and-response form, the person who sings the melody first, unaccompanied ("the call"), to whom the chorus then answers or "responds." (2) Anyone who leads a large group in song, whether in a religious or secular setting (as, for example, during the rallies of the civil rights movement).

Soul music A term used to describe the gospel-flavored performances of popular African American singers such as Ray Charles and Aretha Franklin.

Spiritual A genre of popular religious songs, chiefly from the nineteenth century. Spirituals composed by African Americans during the slavery period are the best-known examples.

Square dance A traditional American dance form, usually performed by four couples in a square formation. Specific "figures" (dance patterns) are performed by the couples in succession, as prompted by a caller.

Squeezebox or **squeeze-box** A common name for any bellows-driven instrument, such as an accordion or a concertina.

Stanza *See* Verse.

Steel band A large ensemble of steel drum players.

Steel drum/steel pan A Caribbean musical instrument made out of the shell of an oil drum. Small indentations are made in the face of the drum. By striking in different areas with a metal or wooden stick, the player can sound different scale notes.

Steel guitar An electric guitar that is held, face up, on the player's lap (and is therefore sometimes called a "lap steel"). The instrument is tuned to an open chord and played with a metal bar that is moved across the fret board. Also called a "fry pan," because early models were small and thin; the small

body attached to a long neck resembled the common piece of cookware.

Step dancing A dance style of European origin that features rapid movement of the lower legs and feet while the remainder of the body is held rigidly. Similar to clogging.

Stomp dance In the Native American tradition, the term used for a variety of both secular and sacred dances in which the movement of the dancers' feet provides the rhythmic accompaniment. The percussive sound is often provided by rattles tied in bunches around the calves of the dancers.

Strathspey A Scottish dance tune named for the valley of the River Spey. It is characterized by its "Scotch snap" rhythm: a sixteenth note followed briskly by a dotted eighth note. In traditional Scottish fiddling, the sixteenth note is played with a slight upbow, followed by a sharp downwards stroke for the dotted eighth, giving the characteristic "snapping" sound. Played in 4/4 time, but slower than a reel.

Strawbeater In some traditions of the southeastern United States, a strawbeater would hold two small pieces of reed or straw and beat them rhythmically on the strings of the fiddle while the fiddler was playing. This would add a rhythmic texture to the fiddle's sound.

Street dancing A highly virtuosic, exhibition dance style, often performed on urban street corners. *See also* Break dancing/Breaking.

String band A group of musicians who accompany dances, usually consisting of stringed instruments such as banjos, fiddles, guitars, and mandolins. Nonstringed instruments—such as harmonicas—can also be heard in a string band.

Strophic Made up of stanzas or strophes; songs based on a repeated melody line that is used to accompany a series of stanzas.

Swing A style of big band jazz that was a major type of social dance music from the 1920s through the mid-1940s. Small swing groups featured improvisation, while the larger groups presented lavish arrangements of songs with interpretations that accented smoothness.

Symmetrical rhythm A balanced, or repeating, rhythmic pattern used consistently throughout a musical composition.

Sympathetic strings Strings that run under the neck (or in the body) of a musical instrument and thus are inaccessible to the player for either fretting or strumming. Instead, these strings vibrate "in sympathy" when the instrument is played; that is, they may vibrate when either the body of the instrument or the other strings vibrate. The Scandinavian hardanger fiddle is an instrument that features sympathetic strings.

Syncopation Accenting the off-beat; placing an accent on a beat that is usually unaccented.

T

Taiko A Japanese double-headed barrel drum, usually of great size.

Tambourine A small, shallow hand drum featuring a single head with small metal "jingles" placed in the frame.

Tamburitza An Eastern European folk lute.

Tango An Argentine dance form first popularized in the 1920s and 1930s that is marked by dramatic, strongly syncopated melodies.

Tap dancing A popular dance form of the 1920s and 1930s that has been revived over the past few decades. It is an elaborate form of step dancing in which the performer wears metal taps on the bottom of his or her shoes in order to emphasize the percussive sounds. Most of the movement occurs as the dancer alternates between tapping the front of the shoe and the heel; arm movements and other gestures are added for emphasis.

Tarantella A popular and energetic folk dance of Italian origin.

Tempo The rate of speed of a musical performance.

Tenor banjo A four-string instrument based on the original banjo but developed at the turn of the twentieth century specifically for playing accompaniment work in ragtime and early jazz. Tenor banjos were adopted by Irish musicians for playing melody as well.

Tex-Mex music *See Norteño* music/*La música norteña.*

Texture The interrelationship of the musical lines in a composition or performance.

Third The third scale degree; the related interval between the tonic and the third scale step.

Three-finger style (banjo) A more modern method of playing the banjo in which patterns are picked by the thumb and two fingers. This is also called bluegrass style because it was popularized by Earl Scruggs and other bluegrass banjo players.

Timbales Paired tom-tom drums mounted on a stand, popular in Latin-Caribbean dance music.

Timbre The characteristic sound quality of an individual voice or musical instrument; why a flute sounds different from a violin when they play the same note.

Tin whistle A small, six-holed, end-blown flute, popular in Irish music. Originally made of tin with a wooden mouthpiece, it is now more commonly made of brass with a plastic mouthpiece. Also called a "pennywhistle."

Tom-tom Generic term for African, Asian, or Latin American indigenous drums, of high but (usually) indefinite pitch. They may be played with the hands or sticks.

Tonic The first note of a scale and the pitch to which others in a composition gravitate.

Transcription A written version or notation of a musical composition.

Triangle A triangular piece of metal that makes a clanging sound when struck with a short metal stick.

Triple time/beat A rhythm with an accent every three beats.

***Tumbadoras*/Conga drums** Tall, cylindrical, single-headed drums based on African models but popularized in Cuban dance music. They are played with fingers and palms of the hands and come in three sizes: The larger drum is called the *tumba*; the *secundo* is medium-sized; and the smallest is called the *quinto.* Usually, the tumba and secundo play one rhythmic pattern, while the quinto plays a counterrhythm.

Two-finger (up-picking) style (banjo) A style in which the banjo player picks upwards with the index finger, alternating or coinciding with a rhythmic downward pick of the thumb.

Two-step A popular and simple couple dance, found throughout the United States. It can be performed to any duple-time melody.

U

Uilleann (bag)pipes Irish bagpipes; unlike the Scottish version, they are driven by a small bellows that is held under the elbow and pumped. In addition to drone and melody ("chanter") pipes, they feature so-called regulator pipes that play chords.

Undulating (contour) Melody lines that seem to meander or wander without any definite goal.

Unison Two or more vocalists (or instrumentalists) singing (or playing) the same melodic part at the same time.

V

Variation Slight changes in the melody line, often occurring on its second statement or repetition.

Veillée A house party; the Franco American equivalent of a kitchen racket.

Verse The changing text of a song that alternates with the chorus or refrain. Usually, the verse is sung to one melody and the refrain to another one.

Vibrato A trembling, "vibrating" pitch; a slight variation in intensity in pitch creating a sense of vibration or fluttering.

Vocables Untranslatable but not necessarily meaningless syllables (such as "fa-la-la") that are sung to a melodic line in place or instead of words.

W

Waila A type of social dance music with European roots that has been incorporated into Native American traditions.

Waltz A European couple dance in 3/4 time, introduced by immigrants to the United States in the mid–nineteenth century.

Washboard A metal board used to launder clothes, which, when adapted as a musical instrument, is vigorously "rubbed" by the player, who wears thimbles or other small pieces of metal on his or her fingers. Also called a "rubboard."

Water drum A small, skin-headed drum made of a crock or vessel that is filled with water to alter its tone.

Well-tempered (or **equal-tempered**) **scale** The modern Western scale with twelve equal steps. The piano is tuned to this scale.

Western swing A musical style that developed in the Texas-Oklahoma region during the 1930s, led by fiddler Bob Wills. A marriage of old-time string band music with big band jazz, Western swing bands performed popular songs and blues in jazzy, up-tempo arrangements. Typical bands included fiddle, guitar, electric steel guitar, piano, drums, and often a small brass section.

Whistle A short, single-note flute, often made of a short piece of hollowed-out cane. The player blows into one end of the instrument to create a sound.

Woodblocks Small, square blocks of wood that are used as percussion instruments; they are usually paired and struck with a small stick.

Work song A rhythmic, repeated song, often in call-and-response form, used to coordinate a group of workers.

X

Xylophone A wooden-keyed instrument played with two small mallets. The keys are of different lengths, mounted on a frame or connected with strings, so that they can freely vibrate.

Z

Zither A stringed instrument with strings that run parallel to the full length of the body of the instrument. The Chinese ch'in (or q'in) and the autoharp are both zithers.

Zydeco A dance music of southeastern Louisiana that combines African American and Cajun styles. Alternately spelled "zodico."

INDEX

**Page references in bold refer to a main essay or sidebar on
that topic. Page references in italics refer to illustrations.**

H